"Claudia Fleming's first book, *The Last Course,* has been both a touchstone and an unending source of inspiration for me throughout my career. Now, with *Delectable,* Claudia moves seamlessly from the restaurant kitchen to the home kitchen with this collection of gorgeous, simple desserts and savory bakes that most any home cook could pull off. Underpinning the recipes are genius techniques clearly honed through years of restaurant work, but Claudia's friendly voice and careful instruction ensure nothing feels intimidating or out of reach. Just as *The Last Course* inspired a generation of pastry chefs, *Delectable* will surely inspire a nation of home bakers."

—Claire Saffitz, *New York Times* bestselling author of *Dessert Person*

"Wave your whisks in celebration and fire up your mixers in joy. Claudia Fleming, who inspired so many of today's great bakers, is back! This new book, which is like a gift, is just as its title declares: 'Delectable.' The collection is signature Claudia—beautifully simple, elegant, and deeply satisfying. *Delectable* is a reason to rejoice!"

—Dorie Greenspan, *New York Times* bestselling author of *Baking with Dorie*

"Whether in a restaurant or a home, Claudia Fleming has the uncanny ability to make craveable desserts no matter the setting. Following the recipes in *Delectable* will help you develop your inner pastry chef and create delicious desserts for your family and friends within the comfort of your own kitchen."

—Tom Colicchio, chef and owner, Crafted Hospitality

"For nearly twenty years, Claudia Fleming's legion of fans have been pleading for a follow-up to her debut cookbook, *The Last Course*—now a treasured classic—and *Delectable* more than rewards us all for the wait. I dare you to thumb through the pages and not get extremely hungry and curious. Not only will you be tempted to eat every single tasteful recipe Claudia lovingly shares and describes, but perhaps, more than any other book on baking I've seen, this one generously teaches you along the way, and gives you the confidence that *you can do it* and that all will turn out well."

—Danny Meyer, *New York Times* bestselling author of *Setting the Table*

"Some heroes wear aprons and create magic with butter. Claudia Fleming is one of the greatest inspirations to my baking, and her joy for creating is just as infectious as her desserts. Her pastry soars in the realm of genius and yet Claudia's recipes are down to earth and accessible. The flavors she creates, from her Rhubarb Scones, Fennel Tea Cake, Pecan Olive Shortbread, Ricotta Tart with Roasted Cherries, to savory Shiitake Sticky Buns, are truly delectable. She may be a rock star pastry chef, but Claudia breaks down all the recipes into easy-to-follow steps and shares her kitchen tricks. This book is a gift to every baker, from the novice to the professional. Claudia Fleming has written another classic!"

—Zoë François, author of *Zoë Bakes Cakes*

Delectable

Delectable

SWEET & SAVORY BAKING

Claudia Fleming

with Catherine Young

PHOTOGRAPHS BY JOHNNY MILLER

RANDOM HOUSE
NEW YORK

Published in the United States by Random House, an
imprint and division of Penguin Random House LLC,
New York.

RANDOM HOUSE and the HOUSE colophon are
registered trademarks of Penguin Random House LLC.

Hardback ISBN 978-0-593-23054-1
Ebook ISBN 978-0-593-23055-8

PRINTED IN CHINA ON ACID-FREE PAPER

randomhousebooks.com

9 8 7 6 5 4 3 2 1

First Edition

Book design by Elizabeth Rendfleisch

I dedicate this book
to my husband, Gerry Hayden,
one of the most talented cooks
I have had the privilege to know.
I miss him every day.

CONTENTS

INTRODUCTION

The Next Chapter

A lot has changed since I wrote my first cookbook, *The Last Course*, more than twenty years ago. One thing that hasn't is my fascination with the world of baking. Breads, cakes, pies, and cookies occupy a special place in the culinary realm, distinguished by the fact that fancy and rustic sit side by side—centuries-old recipes alongside novel creations. As a professional pastry cook, I share a lot with bakers. We use the same ingredients, have a common tool box, and our related branches of the culinary family both benefit from a deft touch. Mastering the proper ratios, managing things just so, and heating to the right temperature are all necessary to avoid disappointment. This is true in cooking generally, but the opportunities for transformation are more extreme and margins thinner when you are playing with flour, sugar, and eggs. That test of skill draws me, but alone it has never been enough. I want to touch people with my cooking, to strike resonant chords. I hope each dish I prepare—elaborate or not—links to something deep inside. I am a pastry cook, a composer of desserts by trade, but baking inspires me.

Because my career has shaped and defined me, it was no real surprise that I felt anxious when it came time to say goodbye to my restaurant after fourteen years. I worried I might be leaving not only the North Fork Table and Inn behind but an important piece of myself as well. The sale was necessary. I wanted a change and needed time—hard to find in a life defined by long workdays. In January of 2020, when the sale was done, I hoped to travel. I did, but not for very long. I yearned for adventure but missed order and soon settled into a routine at home, firing up my anything-but-fancy oven to bake ingredients I bought at my not particularly well-stocked local grocery. I started by "tweaking" old recipes, fiddling until I felt completely pleased with them, then I moved on to cooking things I never had. At some point—I can't say when—I realized my practice of baking at home was just what I needed.

I had been at it for almost two months when the world sputtered to a halt. I was fortunate to be spared the hard decisions my friends in the restaurant business coped with during the unfolding pandemic. I never had to let people go because Covid-19 infection rates made operating a restaurant impossible. I could just keep on doing what I had recently begun, cooking at home by myself, happy to have my time organized by refining recipes, hoping the effort would lead to my next step and turn into a collection I could share. Weeks became months and I kept at it. Along the way, a new relationship to my food developed. I was lightened by what evolved into a freewheeling approach to my craft. I felt renewed, even as I rolled out time-tested doughs and poured favorite batters.

I made chocolate-covered-marshmallow cookies modeled after my dad's favorite snack. I had served them at the North Fork Table and now cooked them for friends. I added salted peanuts to the chocolate caramel tart I developed at Gramercy Tavern and liked it even better. As is my habit, I followed the seasons, baking with rhubarb and strawberries, peaches, then plums, quince, and apple, putting the fruit in pies, piling berries on cakes, and spooning preserves onto cookies. When I wanted a challenge, I would take on things I'd never attempted. I made pretzels and then batches of sticky buns filled with shiitakes. A gift of squash blossoms stirred me to make a tart. It was stimulating to cook this way and very gratifying to be able to head to a neighbor's with focaccia or a crostata during a time when it was easy to feel isolated.

In the summer, I longed for good, homemade ice cream. I don't have a machine, so I started making semifreddos. I experimented with different techniques and lots of flavors. I made some tasty ones, stacked three, and found I had made a dessert that reminded me of spumoni, something I hadn't had since I was a kid.

My mother's parents came to New York from Caltanissetta in Sicily. An excellent cook, my mom passed on her love of the flavors she'd grown up with. I thought of her more and more often as I cooked at home. I made an eggplant caponata tart and then an escarole pie. I baked taralli (a batch of fennel, then pecorino, and then another flavored with pancetta) and made dozens of pizzelles and pignoli cookies. I worked out my own adaptation of a Sicilian cassata and baked a more-or-less traditional pastiera—"grain pie"—a sweet ricotta dessert we ate every Easter. It was as though I'd found a source of inspiration that had just been waiting for the right moment to be tapped, so I delved deeper, comforted by the feeling that I had time, my goals and inspirations shifting over the course of a year.

The sweet and savory treats I made in my kitchen were not nearly so elegant as the food I've served in restaurants, but, like those dishes, each was intentional, and carefully wrought—the product of an effort to make things taste not just as good as you'd imagine but even better. Making stripped-down preparations truly delicious is a challenge I have always embraced. Cooking on my little electric stove imposed new limits, but working one recipe at a time, by myself, at my own pace, afforded unanticipated opportunities to get things precisely how I wanted them. While I'd never claim to have produced the ultimate version of anything, I did get the recipes I worked through to a place that satisfied me, and I was delighted to see them eaten with joy.

My home stay is now behind me (at least for the moment). I am glad to be back at work, but I don't want to forget what I felt, learned, and produced during my time baking solo. So, I've gathered the recipes that resulted from my meanderings, along with thoughts on how to make each one well. The following pages provide maps that will lead to tasty food—a delicious end in itself—but I hope you find, as I did, that the process, too, is worth savoring. For me, it proved both heartwarming and soul-sustaining.

ABOUT THIS BOOK

Weights and Measures

Pastry cooks and professional bakers require exactitude, so we weigh our ingredients. But, you might ask, is it worth the bother to pull out the scale at home? Absolutely. Simply put, weight measuring equals reliable results.

I weigh dry ingredients because it is more accurate (and tidier), but I know some people prefer to measure by volume, in cups and tablespoons. With certain ingredients, white table sugar for example, that is alright. Sugar is processed, so the small grains are a consistent size, and it is dense, so it settles just about the same way all the time. This means you can move between weight (grams or ounces) and volume (cups or milliliters) without a problem. You'll find general agreement that 1 cup of white sugar weighs approximately 200 grams (7 ounces).

On the other hand, many ingredients are subject to processing variation and/or are unevenly shaped or not sufficiently dense to fill a measure in a dependable fashion. For bakers and pastry cooks, foremost among these problematic ingredients is flour. **There is no standard conversion of a cup of flour to grams (or ounces).** Writing up these recipes, I knew I

needed to understand the scope of this issue, so I did some research. Picking two authorities on food measurement that I am generally inclined to rely on, I found that the United States Department of Agriculture (USDA) assigns a cup of all-purpose (AP) flour a weight of 128 grams (4.5 ounces), while *Cook's Illustrated* magazine, after extensive testing, averaged their results as 141.7 grams (5 ounces). The difference is definitely enough to impact outcomes.

There are several possible explanations for the inconsistency. First off, brands of flour differ. Per their respective websites, 1 cup of King Arthur AP flour weighs 120 grams (4.2 ounces), 1 cup of Bob's Red Mill AP flour weighs 136 grams (4.8 ounces), and 1 cup of Pillsbury AP flour weighs 129 grams (4.5 ounces). These disparities are, in part, because the products are not identical. Each manufacturer has its own blend of hard and soft wheat, leading to AP flours with gluten contents ranging from below 8 percent to over 11 percent. The differences also reflect the fact that powdery flour is hard to measure, and experts don't all go about it the same way. Although all agree that a cup of compacted flour weighs more than aerated flour, the professionals do not share a common response. At *Cook's Illustrated*, they scoop flour directly from the container with a cup measure, then sweep away the excess. Testers at *Serious Eats* spoon flour from the container, pour it into a cup, and then swipe extra. (This is also my preferred method.) To complicate things further, how flour settles (compacts) in the container and in a measure is affected by humidity.

Even when the same person works with the same volume measure and product on the same day, the results vary if you are not *extremely* careful. I measured cups of King Arthur's AP—the type of flour I used to test many of the recipes in this book—then weighed my results. I found 1 cup quite consistently weighed *about* 140 grams (4.9 ounces). Note that my results are different from the manufacturer's. Why? They indicate on their website that they measure using a method they call "fluff, sprinkle, and scrape." I don't fluff—or stir flour up before it's measured. I've found that step adds an unpredictable amount of air, so the volume changes inconsistently.

Experts all agree that weighing flour (and other ingredients) is the best way to avoid the problematic variability of volume measurement. Beyond that, weight is a better way to precisely convey an amount. Finicky-seeming measurements like 1 cup plus 1 tablespoon plus 2¾ teaspoons of flour are generally adjusted down to 1 cup or up to 1 cup plus 2 tablespoons. Bakers compensate by directing: if the dough is dry, add a bit more water; if it's tacky, work in more flour. That's fine sometimes, but not ideal if you don't know what you're aiming for.

My solution to the measurement conundrum is to urge everyone to buy a kitchen scale and use it. That is the only way to be sure you add the same amount of flour to your cake that I did to mine. That said, I know old habits sometimes die hard, so after a good deal of thought, I have determined to adopt a hybrid approach to communicating ingredient amounts as follows:

- Bulk dried ingredients—flours, sugars, oats, and so forth—are measured in grams. I use grams rather than ounces because confusion can arise between weight ounces and fluid ounces (a measurement of volume), but I will provide an equivalence in ounces and an approximation in cups and tablespoons.

- Specialty ingredients—nuts, chocolate, and fruit—are measured in grams with an equivalence in ounces and, when appropriate, an approximation in cups.

- Butter is measured in grams with an equivalence in ounces.

- Small amounts of dried ingredients other than salt—baking powder, baking soda, gelatin, etc.—are measured in teaspoons and/or tablespoons.

- Salt (I use Diamond Crystal kosher) is measured in grams and indicated in teaspoons and/or tablespoons. **Brands of kosher salt are not interchangeable by volume.** The other widely available kosher salt, Morton, is ground smaller than Diamond Crystal, so a teaspoon of Morton contains almost twice as much salt as a teaspoon of Diamond Crystal. By weight, the two are interchangeable but working in volume, expect you'll need about half as much Morton salt as I call for.

- Eggs are indicated by number and size classification—I rely on USDA standards and use large eggs. Size varies a little but not enough to cause problems; for more on this, see page 226.

- Liquid measures are given by volume in cups, tablespoons, and teaspoons. I use familiar U.S. liquid volume measurements, because they are much less variable than dry volume measurements—in other words, they work just fine.

Equipment and Ingredients

There are things a Maserati can do that a Subaru can't, but I don't think you need a fancy car to get where you're going. I feel the same about cooking. I appreciate a spare-no-expense kind of meal, but I don't need luxury ingredients or top-of-the-line equipment to make tasty food. My home kitchen has an electric stove. I keep one burner on high and another on low so I can make quick heat adjustments and I hang a thermometer in the oven and use that to accurately manage the temperature. I make it work.

Speaking of thermometers, I recommend investing in a good digital candy thermometer. It makes all the difference when you are cooking jam, custard, or Italian meringue. Also in the equipment investment department, I rely heav-

ily on both my stand mixer and food processor. I could have made the recipes that follow without either but, if I'm honest, probably wouldn't have. Beyond that, I need a scale, bench scraper, rolling pin, flexible spatulas, several whisks, large and small offset spatulas, and pans and bowls in a range of sizes. That's all I require, although I also should say I like to use parchment paper to line pans and to ease rolling out particularly tricky doughs.

I am fussy about ingredients. My mother learned to touch and smell at the market from her parents. I picked up the habit, then started in restaurants at a time when cooks were emphasizing regional produce in a new way. In 1984, Jonathan Waxman and Melvyn Master opened Jams, the restaurant credited with bringing "California cuisine" to New York. There, on Seventy-ninth Street, I saw what it meant to mindfully handle exquisite ingredients. My job—as a server—was my introduction to the restaurant world and to a philosophy that has defined my work.

While I was pastry chef at Gramercy Tavern, I cooked with the best ingredients money could buy. Becoming the owner of a small restaurant, I had to simplify my cooking in order to meet our margins, and so I focused on spotlighting North Fork produce. Cooking at home, my approach had to change some more. There were times when my pantry choices were limited to what was in stock—the brand of butter the grocery had. Nevertheless, I made food that was every bit as delicious in my kitchen as I did in Gramercy's. My trick: knowing when ingredient compromise is okay and when it is not.

Whenever I can, I use fresh, local produce.

That's one area where I don't scrimp. If a farmer has grown something lovely, I celebrate it. I choose carefully at the market, and, when I get home, taste and adjust as needed. If the pretty berries are a bit bland, I concentrate and reinforce their flavor by reducing some into a syrup I then use as a "sauce" (incidentally, frozen berries make a fine reduction). I treat chocolate—ground processed cacao seeds—with the same reverence. I buy the best I can; the type depends on the use. I use extra bitter chocolate a lot. It's worth noting that the terms *semisweet, bittersweet, extra bitter,* and *dark* are used without official distinction to describe chocolate containing at least 35% cacao and a sliding scale of sugar (the more cacao, the less sugar). When I want extra bitter, I make sure mine is 63% or more cacao and typically use E. Guittard or Valrhona at home. I store chocolate in a cool, dry place; it keeps best between 65°F and 70°F, protected from sunlight and moisture. I only resort to the refrigerator, which is a humid environment, in the height of the summer. To keep the chocolate from getting blotchy (developing sugar bloom), I wrap it in dish towels when I take it out of the fridge. This prevents condensation from forming on the surface as it warms.

Though I appreciate the flavor of small-batch butter, at home I typically use Cabot or Land O'Lakes unsalted grade AA butter. I reserve higher-fat imported butter for spreading on toast. Finishing a quick review of baking basics, I use whole milk and most often buy King Arthur brand all-purpose flour. Because I've given amounts in grams, you're free to substitute whatever kind you like. That's not true of salt. As I mentioned earlier, I've given the measures in grams and teaspoons. I use Diamond Crystal kosher salt, a teaspoon of which contains 3 grams of salt, but be aware that a teaspoon of Morton kosher salt contains 4.8 grams, so if you measure by volume, be sure to adjust.

Delectable

CHAPTER 1

Breakfast and Breads

Morning Baking

It had been almost two months since the sale of the North Fork Table closed. The late February sun was weak, and I felt the chill as I sat on my porch, thumbing through a bread book.

Working in fine dining, my experience baking bread was limited. Back when I started cooking, upscale restaurants in New York relied on a regimented French system of organization and specialization: the *rotisseur* cooked the meats, the *poissonier* handled the fish, and the pastry chef developed and executed sweets. At Gramercy Tavern, my team made multi-element plates and small tastes all intended to be eaten at the end of a meal. Bread was not our department, although it once would have been. In the 1990s, it was the fashion to buy bread from artisan bakers, and that's what we did.

When my husband, Gerry, and I opened the North Fork Table and Inn, we were on a tight budget. We wanted to serve breakfast to overnight guests, so I got up early to make quick breads and pastries. I enjoyed it. Fast-forward to that February morning at home with unaccustomed time, I distractedly leafed past image after image until I came to a picture of an English muffin. I stopped, struck by the fact that I had never made them. Curious, I did some reading and looked up recipes, then, for the first time in a while, I turned on the oven. I learned English muffins were born in New York. They were the creation of Samuel Bath Thomas, a transplanted Brit who started selling "toaster crumpets" at his Manhattan bakery in 1880. He coined the name "English muffin" a decade later. It took some time, but I figured out I wanted my version to taste of rye and caraway, and then more time to nail the technique, but when they were done, my Rye English Muffins (page 38) were properly reminiscent of the now-familiar packaged product, just tastier.

Breakfast baking organized my first months at home. I love scones and wanted to perfect mine, but rhubarb, my favorite ingredient to incorporate, was not yet available. So I decided to start with biscuits, scones' American cousin. Because biscuits are so well loved, they presented a special challenge. Of course, I'd made them before, but I could now go as slowly as I liked. I tried "soft" lower-gluten flour and made batches with butter, lard, and cream in various combinations. I wound up somewhat obsessed, baking not only classic rolled biscuits (North Fork Biscuits, page 8), but Drop Biscuits (page 5), Sweet Potato Biscuits with Bitter Chocolate and Pecans (page 9), and Gruyère and Onion Cocktail Biscuits (page 209), finding satisfaction with each before moving on. By the time I was done, it was late spring, and I could turn to my rhubarb scones.

Generations of bakers have made magic by combining flour, water, and leavening (sometimes yeast and others not). They led me as I baked at home. I made batches of muffins, retested the focaccia we'd served daily at the restaurant (I was the only artisan Gerry and I could afford), and replicated the prosciutto bread my grandmother brought us from the Bronx. I worked through a recipe for Chocolate Babka Buns (page 31) and, in the summer, revisited biscuit craft and tinkered with my Blackberry Shortcake (page 16). Bread is the staff of life—they say. For me, baking loaves, rolls, muffins, and biscuits remains a wonder and challenge.

Drop Biscuits

Makes about 8 biscuits

Sometimes called "cathead biscuits," these are a quick and easy-to-make answer to a yearning for biscuits when there is not enough time to rest and roll a classic batch. This recipe is fun to make with kids; they love dolloping the forgiving dough onto the pan. If I don't have buttermilk, I use yogurt instead. The rise won't be quite as high, but the biscuits will be deliciously tangy. Thin Greek yogurt, with a little milk, but don't use milk alone—the biscuits will taste flabby.

227g	all-purpose flour (8oz / about 1½ cups + 2 T)
4g	sugar (0.1oz / about 1 tsp)
2 tsp	baking powder
¾ tsp	baking soda
3g	Diamond Crystal kosher salt (1 tsp)
85g	unsalted butter (3oz), chopped into ½-inch dice and frozen
¾ cup + 3 T	buttermilk

Preheat the oven to 400°F and line a baking sheet with parchment paper. Combine the flour, sugar, baking powder, baking soda, and salt in a food processor. Pulse to mix. Add the frozen butter and process until the mixture is the texture of coarse meal, about 15 seconds (when it's right, the frozen butter will no longer sound rumbly and the largest bits will be no bigger than a lentil).

Transfer the flour mixture to a bowl. Stir in the buttermilk with a fork, mixing just until the liquid is incorporated. The dough will be clumpy and shaggy. Using a floured ¼-cup measure (or a large spoon), scoop the dough and drop it onto the prepared baking sheet.

Bake until the biscuits are golden, about 17 minutes, turning the pan front to back halfway through. Serve warm.

Biscuit and Scone Notes

A read-up on biscuits reveals that the flaky American favorite traces its roots back not to light European pastry but to the flat flour-and-water cakes known as hardtack, eaten by Roman soldiers and carried on the *Mayflower*. An un-yeasted "flat bread," which today would probably be designated a cracker, early biscuits were valued because they kept better than yeasted bread. By the eighteenth century, cooks on both sides of the Atlantic had taken to enriching biscuits with eggs, milk, and/or butter and sometimes sweetening them. Some cooks experimented with using pearl ash (or potash) to leaven their doughs, but the strong taste limited the appeal. In the southern United States, bakers added tenderness and a little loft to their biscuits by beating them hundreds of times with a mallet, causing the dough to express and trap gas.

The biscuit game changed in the nineteenth century when baking soda became commercially available. Baking soda is a compound that produces carbon dioxide bubbles when combined with an acidic liquid. Baking powder (a combination of baking soda and a liquid-activated, powdered acid—think cream of tartar) was developed shortly thereafter, and bakers' lives were forever changed. Vigorously beaten eggs and slow-to-activate and slightly sour natural yeast were no longer the only leavening options. The door to the world of "quick breads" opened, and tender, layered American biscuits arrived.

Rolled biscuits and scones (their close kin) are not hard to make, but like many simple things, the devil is in the details. Below are a few rules that I always follow:

- Start with cold ingredients. I chop, then freeze my butter before I add it to the flour.
- I like to bag the flour/butter "mix" ahead. I keep the bags in the freezer labeled and ready to go. That way, when morning comes (or the impulse strikes), I can simply add liquid, roll, and bake.
- Don't overwork the dough. I usually add the butter in the processor, then move the mixture to a bowl and stir in liquid with a fork, mixing just enough to moisten the flour. I finish incorporating the wet ingredients into the dry with my hands. (If your hands tend to be hot, run them under icy-cold water before you touch the dough.)
- Build layers to create flakiness. I create separated layers by cutting the dough in quarters and stacking them. I then roll out the layered dough, cut it, and bake it.
- Resting the dough is the cure for activated gluten. Activated gluten makes dough elastic and therefore chewy—not what you want in a biscuit or scone. When my dough springs back as I roll it, I wrap it in plastic and refrigerate it for forty minutes to allow it to rest.
- Biscuits and scones are best fresh; if yours are day-old biscuits, toast them. Unbaked, rolled biscuits and scones can be frozen. I cut then freeze them flat, and bag them. I don't recommend freezing drop biscuits.

North Fork Biscuits

A light hand is key to making great biscuits. That comes with practice. When it comes to ingredients, I've heard that in South Carolina, White Lily flour is sold in small bags, so bakers are assured of freshness. I am limited to ordering large bags of the famous "soft" wheat, lower gluten flour. Perhaps that's why my biscuit tests led me to choose all-purpose rather than White Lily as my go-to for classic rolled biscuits. I was honestly surprised that the batches I made with all-purpose flour were more tender and flaky. My ultimate preferences for butter over lard and a mix of cream and buttermilk also weren't what I would have expected, but that's where I landed. As far as leavening goes, I like to divide the job between baking powder and baking soda. I love biscuits with a traditional buttermilk tang, so I tried just baking soda at first but found a combo yielded the best results.

227g	all-purpose flour (8oz / about 1½ cups + 2 T)
4g	sugar (0.1oz / about 1 tsp)
2 tsp	baking powder
¾ tsp	baking soda
3g	Diamond Crystal kosher salt (1 tsp)
85g	unsalted butter (3oz), chopped into ½-inch dice and frozen
½ cup	buttermilk
¼ cup + 1 T	heavy cream

Preheat the oven to 400°F and line a baking sheet with parchment paper. Combine the flour, sugar, baking powder, baking soda, and salt in a food processor. Pulse to mix. Add the frozen butter and process until the mixture is the texture of coarse meal (when it's right, the frozen butter will no longer sound rumbly and the largest bits will be no bigger than a lentil), about 15 seconds.

Transfer the flour mixture to a bowl. Stir in the buttermilk and cream, mixing with a fork just until the flour is moistened and the dough is clumpy and shaggy. Turn the dough out onto a work surface lightly dusted with flour. Gather the dough together with your hands (with an assist from a bench scraper). Form the dough into a square about 6 × 6 inches. Using a sharp knife or bench scraper cut the square lengthwise, then crosswise into 4 equal parts. Stack the quarters on top of each other and then roll the layered dough into another 6 × 6-inch square. Trim the edges and cut out 9 biscuits (squares are most efficient). Arrange the biscuits on the prepared baking sheet. Bake for 10 minutes, rotate the pan front to back, then bake until the biscuits are golden, about 5 minutes more. Serve warm.

Sweet Potato Biscuits with Bitter Chocolate and Pecans

Makes 12 biscuits

Years before my time at Gramercy, I worked at Bright Food Shop, a Chelsea luncheonette that served delicious Mexican- (and some Chinese-) inspired food. This biscuit—which combines sweet potatoes (*camotes*), pecans (*nueces*), and chocolate, all native ingredients that are prized in Mexico—reminds me of the cooking we did there. For a traditional southern-style sweet potato biscuit, see the variation below.

2	medium to large sweet potatoes (about 454g / 16oz)
43g	pecans (1.5oz / about ⅓ cup)
43g	extra bitter chocolate (1.5oz)
227g	all-purpose flour (8oz / about 1½ cups + 2 T)
14g	light brown sugar (0.5oz / about 1⅛ T)
1 T	baking powder
4.5g	Diamond Crystal kosher salt (1½ tsp)
85g	butter (3oz), cut into ½-inch dice and frozen
About 2 T	milk, for glazing
About 2 T	crystallized sugar, such as turbinado, Demerara, or Sugar In The Raw

Preheat the oven to 300°F and line a baking sheet with parchment paper. Poke holes in the sweet potatoes and bake them until they are soft, about 1½ hours. Allow the potatoes to cool, then peel and mash them in a bowl, cover, and refrigerate.

Meanwhile, roast the pecans in a small ovenproof skillet until they smell toasty, about 15 minutes. Remove the pecans from the oven, cool them, then chop them and set aside.

Using a serrated knife, thinly shave the chocolate and set it aside (reserve it in the refrigerator if it's a hot day).

Combine the flour, brown sugar, baking powder, and salt in a food processor. Pulse to mix. Add the frozen butter and process until the mixture is the texture of coarse meal (when it's right, the frozen butter will no longer sound rumbly and the largest bits will be no bigger than a lentil), about 15 seconds.

Transfer the dough to a bowl. Add the chopped chocolate and pecans, mixing with a fork to distribute them evenly. Using a wooden spoon, mix the sweet potato into the dough, stirring just until the potato is evenly distributed.

Using a floured ¼-cup measure, drop the biscuits onto the prepared baking sheet. Brush them with milk and sprinkle with crystallized sugar.

Bake for 10 minutes, then rotate the pan front to back and continue to bake until the biscuits are golden, about 10 minutes more. Serve warm or at room temperature.

Variation: To make plain Sweet Potato Biscuits, roast the sweet potatoes as described above. Combine the flour, brown sugar, baking powder, and salt in a food processor. Pulse, then add the butter and process as above. Omit the chocolate and nuts. Stir in the mashed sweet potatoes, drop biscuits onto the prepared baking sheet, and bake as directed above.

English-Style Scones

Makes about 10 scones

The scones you'll find in London have a great deal in common with American biscuits. I make the simple but delicious, slightly sweet dough the old-fashioned way, in a bowl, mixing with my fingers. When it's right, expect it to be slightly tacky. As with all scones and biscuits, the dough should not be handled more than necessary and these scones should not be rolled too thinly. If you like currants, feel free to do as the Brits do and add some—about ½ cup.

170g	all-purpose flour (6 oz / about 1¼ cup + 3½ T)
57g	cake flour (2oz / about ½ cup)
2¼ tsp	baking powder
1.5g	Diamond Crystal kosher salt (½ tsp)
25g	sugar (0.9oz / about 2 T)
50g	butter (1.8oz), cut into pieces, room temperature
1	egg
About ⅓ cup	milk, plus extra for brushing

Preheat the oven to 400°F and line a baking sheet with parchment paper. Combine the all-purpose and cake flours, the baking powder, salt, and sugar in a large bowl. Add the butter and rub it into the flour mixture with your fingertips until it looks like fine bread crumbs.

Break the egg into a measuring cup and add enough milk to measure ½ cup total. Stir the egg into the milk, then stir the mixture into the flour to form a sticky dough.

Turn the dough out onto a lightly floured work surface and knead it gently just until it is smooth. Roll the dough out into a square about 1 inch thick. Using a 2-inch biscuit cutter, cut as many rounds as possible.

You should get about 10 (I don't reroll the scraps of this dough; they make for stodgy scones). Place the scones on the prepared baking sheet and brush them with milk.

Bake for 5 minutes, then rotate the pan front to back and continue baking until the scones are nicely risen and pale golden brown, about 5 minutes more. Cool the scones on a wire rack. Serve with jam or clotted cream, if desired.

Note: These scones freeze well after they are baked and cooled. To reheat, defrost them in the refrigerator and heat them in 350°F oven for about 10 minutes.

Cheddar and Stilton Scones

Makes 8 scones

Cheese scones are popular in England, but this recipe is not traditional. It is my mash-up of British flavors and American biscuit-making moxie. I start with a mix of white and whole-wheat flours and add oats because I find they give the finished product savor. I mix Stilton with the traditional cheddar for the same reason.

50 g	rolled oats (1.8oz / about ¼ cup)
120g	all-purpose flour (4.2oz / about ¾ cup + 2 T)
55g	whole-wheat flour (1.9oz / about 5½ T)
2½ tsp	baking powder
1.5g	Diamond Crystal kosher salt (½ tsp)
42g	unsalted butter (1.5oz), cut into ½-inch dice and frozen
¾ cup	milk, plus extra for glazing
95g	extra-sharp aged cheddar cheese (3.35oz / about 1 cup), grated
55g	crumbled Stilton (1.9oz / about 2 T)

Preheat the oven to 375°F and line a baking sheet with parchment paper. Put the oats in a skillet and roast for 5 minutes, toss and continue roasting until they smell toasty, about 5 minutes more. Put the oats in a food processor and allow them to come to room temperature. Increase the oven temperature to 400°F.

Add the all-purpose and whole-wheat flours, baking powder, and salt to the oats and pulse to mix. Add the frozen butter and process until the mixture is the texture of coarse meal (when it's right, the butter will no longer sound rumbly and the largest pieces will be no bigger than a lentil); check after 15 seconds.

Transfer the flour mixture to a bowl. Stir in the milk with a fork, mixing just until the flour has absorbed the milk. Add 85 grams (3 ounces) of the cheddar and all the Stilton, then, using your hands and taking care to handle the dough no more than you need to, mix until the cheeses are distributed.

Turn the dough out onto a lightly floured work surface—it will be shaggy. Form it into a compact square about 1 inch thick. Using a sharp knife or bench scraper cut the dough in half lengthwise, then crosswise, and stack the quarters. Using a rolling pin, gently flatten the stacked dough and roll it out again into a square about 1 inch thick. Cut the dough in half lengthwise, then crosswise, and each quarter on the diagonal, to form triangular scones.

Arrange the scones on the prepared baking sheet. Brush the scones with a little milk and sprinkle them with the remaining 10 grams (0.35 ounces) cheddar.

Bake for 10 minutes, then rotate the pan front to back and continue baking until the scones are nicely browned, about 13 minutes more. Serve warm or at room temperature.

Rhubarb Scones

Makes 8 scones

We served these American-style fruit scones for brunch when we first opened the North Fork Table and every spring for the next fourteen years. They are my favorite. The bad news from my vantage is that rhubarb has a short season; the good news, though, is you can consider this scone recipe as a "master" and substitute other fruit. If I use juicy chopped fruit, like plums, I dry it in the oven (as I do the rhubarb). If I'm adding berries, I freeze them before I mix them into the dough. I use this same dough to make Raisin and Caraway Scones; see Variation, below.

Rhubarb:

114g	rhubarb (4oz), leaves removed and discarded, stalks cut into 1-inch dice
12g	sugar (0.4oz / about 1 T)

Scones:

170g	all-purpose flour (6oz / about 1 cup + 3½ T)
57g	cake flour (2oz / about ½ cup)
25g	sugar (0.9oz / about 2 T)
1½ tsp	baking powder
½ tsp	baking soda
1.5g	Diamond Crystal kosher salt (½ tsp)
½ tsp	orange zest
85g	unsalted butter (3oz), diced and frozen
1	large egg
About ⅓ cup	buttermilk, plus extra for glazing
About 2 T	crystallized sugar, such as turbinado, Demerara, or Sugar In The Raw

To prepare the rhubarb, preheat the oven to 325°F. Arrange the diced rhubarb on a baking sheet. Sprinkle the fruit with 1 tablespoon of the sugar (12 grams) and bake it until the rhubarb releases its juices and dries without browning, about 40 minutes. Remove the rhubarb from the oven and set it aside to cool.

To make the scones, raise the oven temperature to 400°F and line a baking sheet with parchment paper. Combine the all-purpose and cake flours, 25 grams (0.9 ounces) sugar, baking powder, baking soda, and salt in a food processor and pulse to mix. Add the zest and frozen butter and process until the mixture is the texture of coarse meal (when it's right, the frozen butter will no longer sound rumbly and the largest bits will be no bigger than a lentil), about 15 seconds.

Transfer the dough to a bowl. Mix in the rhubarb. Crack the egg into a measuring cup and add enough buttermilk to measure ½ cup. Stir to combine, then mix the liquid into the dough with a fork, stirring just until the dough has absorbed the wet ingredients.

Turn the dough out onto a lightly floured work surface—it will be shaggy. Form it into a compact square about 1 inch thick. Using a sharp knife or bench scraper cut the dough in half lengthwise, then crosswise, and stack the quarters. Using a rolling pin, gently flatten the stacked dough and roll it out again into a square about 1 inch thick. Cut the dough in half lengthwise, then crosswise, and each quarter on the diagonal, to form triangular scones.

Place the scones on the prepared baking sheet. Brush the scones with buttermilk and dust them with the crystallized sugar.

Bake for 10 minutes, then rotate the pan front to back and continue baking until the scones are golden, about 10 minutes more. Serve warm or at room temperature.

Variation: To make Raisin and Caraway Scones, preheat the oven to 400°F and line a baking sheet with parchment. Mix both flours, 25 grams (0.9 ounces) sugar, baking soda, and baking powder together in a food processor as above. Omit the orange zest, but add the butter and process as above. Transfer the mixture to a bowl, add 1 cup golden raisins (instead of the rhubarb) and 1 tablespoon caraway seeds. Mix ⅓ cup buttermilk with an egg, then add it to the dough. Turn the dough out onto a lightly floured surface and roll, cut, stack, reroll, and cut it as described into 8 scones. Glaze them with buttermilk and bake until golden, about 20 minutes.

Blackberry Shortcake

Makes 9 shortcakes

This dough contains hard-boiled egg yolks—an old trick for making a rich and tender biscuit. (See the Note below for my preferred egg-cooking method.) Although I don't generally reroll biscuit dough, I make an exception here so that I wind up with an extra cake, which I often as not keep for myself. By the way, this sweet dough is great not only for shortcake; it is also wonderful for cobblers. You'll need to halve the recipe if you want to substitute this dough for the biscuits in the Peach and Blackberry Cobbler with Ricotta Biscuits (page 139) or use it for the Plum Cobbler (page 151).

Shortcake biscuits:

340g	all-purpose flour (12oz / about 2¼ cups + 3 T)
55g	sugar (2oz / about ¼ cup)
2 T	baking powder
0.7g	Diamond Crystal kosher salt (¼ tsp)
2	hard-boiled egg yolks*
114g	unsalted butter (4oz), chopped into ½-inch dice and frozen
About 1 cup + 1 T	heavy cream
12g	crystallized sugar, such as turbinado, Demerara, or Sugar In The Raw (0.4oz / about 2½ tsp)

Blackberry reduction:

340g	fresh or frozen blackberries (12oz / about 2½ cups)
70g	sugar (2.5oz)
2 tsp	orange zest

Yogurt cream:

1 cup	heavy cream
1 tsp	vanilla paste or pure vanilla extract
2 T	confectioners' sugar
1 cup	Greek-style yogurt (or yogurt drained overnight)
420g	fresh blackberries (15oz / about 3 cups)
	Confectioners' sugar, for dusting

To make the shortcake biscuits, combine the flour, sugar, baking powder, and salt in a food processor. Pulse to mix. Add the yolks, pulse to combine, then add the butter and process until the mixture is the texture of coarse meal (when it's right, the butter will no longer sound rumbly and the largest pieces will be no bigger than a lentil), about 15 seconds.

Transfer the dough to a bowl. Add 1 cup and 1 tablespoon cream and stir with a fork just until the flour is moistened and the dough is clumpy and shaggy (if the dough seems very dry, add up to another tablespoon of cream). Turn the dough onto a lightly floured work surface. Gather the dough together with your hands and form it into a compact square, and, using a rolling pin, roll the dough into a 6-inch square.

---

* To hard-boil eggs, put them in a single layer in a small saucepan with water to cover by about 1 inch. Heat over medium heat until the water starts to steam, then increase the heat to medium-high. When the water reaches a rolling boil, take the pan off the stove, cover it, and set aside for 8 minutes. Drain the eggs, shock them in ice water, and peel them.

Trim the ragged edges and cut out 8 shortcakes with a sharp knife or cutter (squares are most efficient). Roll the trimmed scraps into an additional shortcake.

Line a baking sheet with parchment paper. Arrange the shortcake biscuits on the prepared baking sheet and allow them to rest in the refrigerator for at least 30 minutes.

Preheat the oven to 375°F. Brush each biscuit with cream, sprinkle with crystallized sugar, and bake for 10 minutes. Rotate the pan front to back and continue baking until the biscuits are golden, about 10 minutes more. Set the biscuits aside to cool.

To make the blackberry reduction, combine 340 grams (12 ounces) blackberries, 70 grams (2.5 ounces) sugar, and the zest in a small saucepan. Crush the berries with the back of a wooden spoon. Bring the mixture to a boil over medium-high heat, then lower the heat and simmer until the berries are soft and have released their juices, about 10 minutes. Press the berry compote through a fine sieve. Reserve the reduced syrup and discard the berry pulp.

Shortly before serving, make the yogurt cream. Combine 1 cup cream, the vanilla, and confectioners' sugar in a stand mixer or bowl. Whip until the cream holds soft peaks. Add the yogurt and whisk together until blended.

To assemble the shortcakes, slice each biscuit in half horizontally with a serrated knife. Arrange the bottom halves on serving plates. Put 420 grams (15 ounces) fresh berries in a large bowl and dress them with the berry reduction, stirring gently to coat the berries evenly. Dollop whipped yogurt cream on the bottom biscuit halves, spoon blackberries over the cream, then finish the cakes by topping them with the other biscuit halves. Dust with confectioners' sugar and serve.

Blueberry Muffins

Makes 10 muffins

This is my basic muffin recipe. Substitute another berry or an equivalent amount of chopped fruit for the blueberries (oven-dry the fruit if it's juicy—see Rhubarb Scones on page 14 for details). For a good rise and the best taste, I use both baking soda—activated by the acidic sour cream—and baking powder to leaven this batter. As always, for tender muffins (and other quick breads), I avoid working the gluten in the flour—I just stir the batter enough to get things mixed.

⅓ cup	sour cream	100g	sugar (3.5oz / about ½ cup)
2	large eggs	½ tsp	baking soda
1	large egg yolk	½ tsp	baking powder
2 tsp	vanilla paste or pure vanilla extract	0.7g	Diamond Crystal kosher salt (¼ tsp)
1 T	lemon zest	85g	unsalted butter (3oz), room temperature, plus extra for the pan
140g	all-purpose flour (5oz / about 1 cup), plus extra for the pan	200g	blueberries (7oz / about 1⅓ cups)

Preheat the oven to 375°F. Prepare a muffin tin by buttering and flouring 10 muffin cups or lining them with paper liners. Combine the sour cream, eggs, yolk, vanilla, and zest in a bowl. Mix well and reserve.

Combine the flour, sugar, baking soda, baking powder, and salt in the bowl of a stand mixer. Add the butter and beat with the paddle attachment until the mixture is the texture of coarse crumbs. Add half the sour cream mixture, beat until it is incorporated,

scrape down the bowl with a rubber spatula, then add the remaining sour cream mixture and beat until the batter is fluffy. Fold in the blueberries. Evenly divide the batter among the prepared muffin cups.

Bake the muffins for 10 minutes, then rotate the pan front to back and continue baking until the muffins are nicely browned and springy, about 10 minutes more. Allow the muffins to cool. Remove them from the pan and serve.

Date, Nut, and Coconut Muffins

Makes 12 muffins

When I was growing up, I thought it was a special treat when my mother and I took the train into "the City." After shopping or a trip to the museum, we'd stop to refuel at her favorite coffeeshop, Chock Full o'Nuts. We always ordered the same things: I'd have a whole-wheat doughnut dusted with powdered sugar, and she'd order date nut bread, a choice I remember questioning every time. I just couldn't understand the appeal of that dusky, deeply flavored bread. Now I do. This muffin is my ode to that bittersweet "quick bread" I was too young to appreciate.

230g	pitted dates, chopped (8.1oz / about 1½ cups)
40g	shredded unsweetened coconut (1.4oz / about ½ cup)
57g	unsalted butter (2oz), room temperature, plus extra for the pan
1 tsp	baking soda
2.3g	Diamond Crystal kosher salt (¾ tsp)
120g	coconut sugar (4.2oz / about ¾ cup)
½ cup	brewed coffee
½ cup	freshly squeezed orange juice
1 ½ tsp	orange zest
165g	all-purpose flour (5.9oz / about 1 cup + 3 T), plus extra for the pan
40g	coconut flour (1.4oz / about ⅓ cup)
½ tsp	baking powder
1	large egg
1 tsp	vanilla paste or pure vanilla extract
70g	chopped walnuts (2.5oz / about ⅔ cup)

Preheat the oven to 350°F. Prepare a muffin tin by buttering and flouring 12 muffin cups or lining them with paper liners. Combine the dates, shredded coconut, butter, baking soda, salt, and coconut sugar in the bowl of a stand mixer. Heat the coffee and orange juice in a saucepan set over medium heat. When the liquid simmers, pour it into the mixer bowl and let the mixture steep until the dates soften, about 15 minutes. Stir in the orange zest.

Sift the all-purpose flour, coconut flour, and baking powder into another bowl. Using the paddle attach- ment, mix the softened date-butter mixture until it forms a paste. Mix in the egg and vanilla. With the mixer on low, incorporate the flour mixture, then the walnuts. Evenly divide the batter among the muffin cups.

Bake the muffins for 12 minutes, then rotate the pan front to back and continue baking until the muffins are nicely browned and springy to the touch, about 10 minutes more. Allow the muffins to cool. Remove them from the pan and serve.

Oat and Banana Muffins with Pecans

Makes 12 muffins

Maple sugar goes wonderfully with banana and pecans, so I combine all three in these muffins that are good to keep in mind if you are avoiding wheat. Be aware though, that not all oat flour is fully gluten-free.

	Cooking spray
50g	pecans (1.8oz / about ½ cup)
110g	oat flour (3.9oz / about 1 cup + 3½ T)
2 tsp	baking powder
1 tsp	baking soda
1.5g	Diamond Crystal kosher salt (½ tsp)
⅓ cup	neutral oil, such as canola

2	large eggs, beaten
70g	maple sugar (2.5oz / about 7 T)
½ cup	milk
1 tsp	vanilla paste or pure vanilla extract
1 heaping cup	mashed ripe bananas (about 3 medium bananas)

Preheat the oven to 325°F. Prepare a muffin tin by greasing 12 muffin cups with cooking spray or lining them with paper liners. Put the pecans in a pie plate and roast them until they smell toasty, about 12 minutes. Remove the pecans from the oven and let cool, then finely chop them. Put the chopped nuts in a large bowl. Increase the oven temperature to 400°F.

Add the oat flour, baking powder, baking soda, and salt to the bowl of nuts and mix well. In a separate bowl, whisk together the oil, eggs, sugar, milk, and vanilla, then stir in the bananas. Stir the flour/nut mixture into the wet ingredients and mix until just combined. Evenly divide the batter among the muffin cups.

Bake the muffins for 9 minutes, then rotate the pan front to back and continue baking until the muffins are nicely browned and springy, about 9 minutes more. Allow the muffins to cool. Remove them from the pan and serve.

Mom's Irish Soda Bread

Makes one 8-inch loaf

My mother made this quick bread for my father every St. Patrick's Day, along with a heart-shaped chocolate cake topped with green whipped cream. I am not sure where my Italian mother got the recipe for her loaf. Maybe from her Irish mother-in-law, though I wonder, because casual research suggests that raisins and caraway are American additions. Whatever the source, I remember that, despite the allure of the cake, it was the bread I looked forward to.

2 tsp	caraway seeds
490g	all-purpose flour (17.3oz / about 3½ cups), plus extra for the pan
100g	sugar (3.5oz / about ½ cup)
3g	Diamond Crystal kosher salt (1 tsp)
2 tsp	baking powder
½ tsp	baking soda
2	large eggs
2 cups	sour cream
28g	unsalted butter (1oz), melted and cooled, plus extra as needed
1 cup	golden raisins (about 150g)

Preheat the oven to 325°F. Butter and flour an 8-inch cake pan. Put the caraway seeds in a small ovenproof sauté pan and roast them in the oven until they smell toasty, about 3 minutes. Remove the seeds from the oven and allow them to cool. Raise the oven temperature to 350°F.

In a large bowl, whisk the caraway seeds with the flour, sugar, salt, baking powder, and baking soda. In a small bowl or measuring cup, mix the eggs with the sour cream and melted butter. Using a wooden spoon, stir the wet ingredients into the dry until just combined, then fold in the raisins.

Using a rubber spatula, scrape the dough into the prepared pan. Then, with a sharp knife, make a cross in the top of the bread.

Bake the loaf until it has risen, is golden, and sounds hollow when tapped, about 1 hour. Turn the bread out of the pan onto a wire rack. Brush the bread with more melted butter and let it cool slightly. Serve warm with butter or cool completely, then toast slices.

Chipotle Cornbread

Cornbread is one of my very favorite quick breads. When done right, it has a moist, grainy texture and a subtle earthy flavor that I can push different ways. Here I use smoky chipotle peppers in adobo sauce to steer the taste in a Mexican direction. I cook this in cast iron. If you don't have a skillet the right size, precook the corn and scallions, then use a cake pan to bake the bread.

110g	medium-grind cornmeal (3.9oz / about ¼ cup + 3½ T)
1 cup	buttermilk
166g	unsalted butter (5.8oz)
½	chipotle chile in adobo sauce, finely chopped, plus 1½ tsp adobo sauce
1 cup	fresh corn kernels
¾ cup	sliced scallions (white parts only)
5.3g	Diamond Crystal kosher salt (1¾ tsp)
½ tsp	freshly ground black pepper
2 tsp	chopped fresh marjoram or oregano
2	large eggs
92g	queso fresco or mild cheddar cheese (3.2oz / about ¾ cup), coarsely grated
187g	all-purpose flour (6.6oz / about 1⅓ cups)
37g	sugar (1.3oz / about 3 T)
3¼ tsp	baking powder
½ tsp	baking soda

Preheat the oven to 350°F. Soak the cornmeal in the buttermilk in a large bowl for at least 15 minutes. Melt 140 grams (5 ounces) of the butter in a small skillet over medium-low heat. Remove from the heat and allow the butter to cool slightly. Stir the chopped chipotle and adobe sauce into the butter.

Melt half of the remaining butter (13 grams / 0.5 ounces) in a 10-inch skillet, preferably cast iron, over medium heat. Add the corn and scallions. Season the vegetables with 2.1 grams (¾ teaspoon) of the salt and the black pepper. Increase the heat to medium or medium-high, so the butter sizzles, and continue to cook, stirring frequently, until the corn begins to color, about 5 minutes. Remove the pan from the heat and stir in the marjoram. Set aside to cool.

In a bowl, combine the flour, the remaining 3.2 grams (1 teaspoon) salt, the sugar, baking powder, and baking soda.

Add the eggs and the cooled corn mixture to the buttermilk-soaked cornmeal. Stir in the chipotle butter and then the grated cheese.

Wipe out the skillet. Put it in the oven and allow it to heat up for at least 10 minutes. Remove the skillet from the oven and add the remaining 13 grams butter (0.5 ounces) to the hot skillet. While the butter melts, stir the wet ingredients into the flour mixture using a wooden spoon. Swirl the melted butter around the skillet, then spoon the batter into the pan, spreading it evenly.

Place the cornbread on the middle rack of the oven and bake for 15 minutes. Rotate the pan front to back and continue baking until the cornbread is golden and pulling away from sides, about 10 minutes more. Remove from the oven and allow the cornbread to cool in the pan. Serve at room temperature with Honey Butter (page 289), if desired.

Working with Commercial Yeast

I don't keep a starter at home. Though I love bread, I live alone and don't eat enough of it to justify the investment in time and refrigerator space. I refuse, however, to completely forgo the clear benefits of starting bread with wild yeast: the superior flavor—including a characteristic tanginess I love—and better structure. My solution: Let the dough rise slowly and use pre-ferments.

What is a pre-ferment? According to Francisco Migoya, author of *Modernist Bread*, the term refers to "a portion of the dough that's made in advance of the final dough; it's already ripe (ready to use) when it's mixed into the final dough." Even when made with commercial yeast, a pre-ferment still offers many (though admittedly not all) of the benefits of leavening with a starter.

There are different kinds of pre-ferments, and frankly, the terminology surrounding them is confusing. Rather than attempt to define and distinguish them all, let me just explain how I'm using terms in these pages. I use two kinds of pre-ferment: a poolish and a sponge. I use a poolish in the dough for Rye English Muffins (page 38). A poolish is a "wet pre-ferment" made of flour, a lot of water (100 percent hydration in baker's terms), and a small amount of yeast. Because not much yeast is used, leavening takes a while, in my recipe, 12 hours at room temperature. This slow growth gives the poolish time to develop gradually, which is great for flavor development. When it is mixed into the dough (which always includes additional yeast) you wind up with bread (or in my case, English muffins) with good structure and deep taste. Note that because I use rye flour, it is essential that I give the poolish time to fully ferment. The ripening process produces the acid necessary to stabilize enzyme-rich rye flour, and that prevents my muffins from being gummy.

I use a sponge to start Chocolate Babka Buns (page 31) and Shiitake Sticky Buns (page 193). As is typical, I use a sponge with egg-enriched yeasted dough. A sponge is still considered (by most) a "wet pre-ferment," but it is far less liquid than a poolish. Per the norm, my sponges contain a lot of yeast, all that will go into the final dough, but they contain only a portion of the flour. Because they are full of yeast, the sponges ferment and double quickly, in about an hour at room temperature. While a sponge doesn't produce as much acidity as a poolish, I find that there are times when a little added flavor and strength go a long way.

Another way I manipulate my dough is aimed at exaggerating the soft, airy quality commercial yeast brings by starting with what I refer to as a bread roux. This technique, called *tangzhong* in China and *yudane* in Japan, involves heating a mixture of flour and liquid, which causes the gluten in the flour to gelatinize, making it more absorbent and flexible. From a practical vantage, starting with a bread roux makes for a higher rise and a fluffier bread or, as I've discovered, doughnut. I use this approach to make the Cheese Rolls (page 27), Cider Doughnuts (page 48), and Chocolate Doughnuts with Espresso Glaze (page 51).

Cheese Rolls

Makes 16 rolls

These airy, yeasted rolls are made with a dough that starts with a bread roux (for more on this, see facing page) and finishes like brioche—meaning butter is added at the end. For a light, springy texture, you want to activate the gluten. Once the flour is coated with fat, the gluten no longer develops, so for these rolls, I work the dough and then I add the butter. This is the opposite of how I make shortbread—which I want crumbly, so there I integrate the flour with the butter immediately.

Bread roux:

25g	bread flour (0.9oz / about 2¾ T)
½ cup	milk

Dough:

2 tsp	active dry yeast
350g	bread flour (12.3oz / about 2¼ cups + 3 T)
8g	sugar (0.3oz / about 2 tsp)
6g	Diamond Crystal kosher salt (2 tsp)
1 T	milk powder
1 tsp	smoked paprika

1	large egg
½ cup	milk
125g	sharp cheddar cheese (4.4oz / about 1¾ cups), grated
25g	Parmigiano-Reggiano (0.9oz / about 5 T), grated
	Neutral oil or unsalted butter, for the bowl
30g	unsalted butter (1oz), room temperature, plus 114g unsalted butter (4oz), melted

To make the roux, put 25 grams (0.9 ounces) flour in a saucepan. Whisk in ½ cup milk, then switch to a wooden spoon or heatproof spatula and stir constantly over medium-high heat, cooking the dough until the roux thickens to a paste and a thermometer indicates a temperature of approximately 150°F. Take the roux off the heat and transfer it to a small bowl. Cover the roux directly with plastic, and allow it to cool to room temperature. Chill for at least 4 hours, then remove the roux from the refrigerator and allow it to come to room temperature. (If the roux is cold, it will be impossible to mix into the dough.)

To start the dough, combine the yeast, 350 grams (12.3 ounces) flour, the sugar, salt, milk powder, and paprika in the bowl of a stand mixer. In a measuring cup, mix the egg and milk. Whisk the roux into the egg, then add this mixture to the dry ingredients. Add the cheddar and Parmigiano cheeses. Using the paddle attachment, beat the dough until the liquid ingredients are fully incorporated. Switch to the hook attachment and knead the dough until it comes together, is smooth and elastic, and begins slapping against the side of the bowl. With the mixer running, gradually add 30 grams (1 ounce) room-temperature butter, mixing until it is integrated and the dough is smooth and elastic. To check if the dough is sufficiently kneaded, do the windowpane test: pinch off a piece of dough and see if it can be stretched thinly enough to see through; if it breaks, continue kneading until the dough is stretchy and supple. Grease a bowl and transfer the dough to it. Turn the dough over to coat, cover the bowl tightly with plastic wrap, and set aside in a warm place to rise until doubled in bulk, about 1 hour.

Line a baking sheet with parchment paper. Punch down the dough, folding it in on itself and pressing out the air, then divide it in half. Press the dough into 2 rectangles, each about 10 × 12 inches. Form the rectangles into logs, then cut each into 8 equal pieces. Working a piece at a time, flatten the dough in the palm of your hand and, using your fingertips, pinch the sides into the middle a bit at a time to form a taut ball. Set the dough ball seam-side down on a clean, unfloured work surface. Roll the ball with your lightly floured palm against the work surface, using friction to help you make it neat and tight. Continue with the remaining dough. Arrange the rolls about 1½ inches apart on the prepared baking sheet. Cover them loosely with greased plastic wrap and set aside to proof in a warm place until they have risen visibly (though have not doubled) and a finger pressed in the dough leaves a lingering impression; begin checking after 45 minutes.

Preheat the oven to 350°F. Remove the plastic, brush the rolls with melted butter, and bake 7 minutes, then rotate the pan front to back and bake until they are golden, about 7 minutes more. Serve warm.

Sweet Potato Rolls with Miso

Makes 6 to 8 rolls

Adding miso to these rolls deepens the flavor of the sweet potatoes without emphasizing their starch or sugar. I use mild white miso not only in the yeasted dough (leave time for it to rise twice) but also in the maple glaze. It is a nontraditional combination, but a good one.

Rolls:

1	small sweet potato (about 170g / 6oz), peeled and diced
⅓ cup	milk
30g	unsalted butter (1oz), room temperature, plus extra for greasing
¼ cup + 1 T	white miso
8g	sugar (0.3oz / about 2 tsp)
2 ½ tsp	active dry yeast
1	large egg
324g	bread flour (11. 4oz / about 2¼ cups)

Glaze:

1 T	maple syrup
14g	unsalted butter (0.5oz), melted
½ tsp	white miso

To start the rolls, combine the diced sweet potato and milk in a small saucepan and bring the mixture to a boil. Reduce the heat to low to medium-low, cover the pan, and simmer until the potatoes are soft, about 20 minutes. Add 30 grams (1 ounce) room-temperature butter and ¼ cup plus 1 tablespoon miso to the sweet potatoes and, using a potato masher or fork, mash them until the mixture is smooth. Stir in the sugar, then set the mash aside to cool.

In a small bowl, dissolve the yeast in 2 tablespoons warm water. Set the yeast aside until it activates and becomes creamy, about 10 minutes. In the bowl of a stand mixer, combine the mashed potatoes, yeast, and egg. Using the paddle attachment, mix until combined, then add the flour and mix until the dough comes together. Switch to the dough hook and knead the dough until it is homogeneous, about 8 minutes. Turn the dough out onto a lightly floured surface and knead it until the dough comes together and is smooth and elastic. Put the dough in a greased bowl, turn it over to coat, cover the bowl with plastic wrap, and set aside to rise in a warm place until the dough has doubled, about 1½ hours.

Grease an 8-inch round cake pan. Punch the dough down, folding it in on itself and pressing out all the air, then divide it into 8 equal-size pieces. Working a piece at a time, flatten the dough in the palm of your hand and, with your fingertips, pinch the sides into the middle a bit at a time to form a taut ball. Set the dough ball seam-side down on a clean, unfloured work surface. Roll the ball with your lightly floured palm against the work surface, using friction to help you make it neat and tight. Continue with the remaining dough. Fit the rolls into the prepared cake pan, cover the pan loosely with greased plastic wrap, and set the rolls aside to proof until almost doubled, about 50 minutes.

Preheat the oven to 375°F. Remove the plastic and bake the rolls for 10 minutes, then rotate the pan front to back and continue baking until the rolls are evenly browned, 10 to 15 minutes more.

Meanwhile, make the glaze. Mix the maple syrup with the melted butter and ½ teaspoon miso in a small bowl. Brush the hot rolls with the glaze. Serve the rolls warm or at room temperature.

Chocolate Babka Buns

Makes about 16 buns

These delicious chocolate-and-nut buns are at their very best the day they are made. If you have extra, freeze them after they are formed. Defrost them in the fridge, then bake them in a 350°F oven. For more about starting dough with a sponge, see page 26.

Sponge:

3½ tsp	active dry yeast
44g	all-purpose flour (1.6oz / about 5 T)

Dough:

350g	all-purpose flour (12.3oz / about 2½ cups)
44g	sugar (1.6oz / about 3½ T)
1.5g	Diamond Crystal kosher salt (½ tsp)
1	large egg
1	large egg yolk
52g	unsalted butter (1.8oz), cut into 6 pieces, room temperature, plus extra for greasing

Filling:

⅔ cup	chopped Candied Orange Rinds (page 275)
3	oranges
300g	sugar (10.6oz; about 1½ cups)
1 T	light corn syrup
¾ cup	Chocolate Crumble (page 298)
114g	unsalted butter (4oz)
1 tsp	orange zest

147g	all-purpose flour (5.2oz / about 1 cup + 1 T)
75g	sugar (2.6oz / about 6 T)
75g	light brown sugar (2.6oz / about 5½ T)
0.7g	Diamond Crystal kosher salt (¼ tsp)
½ tsp	ground cinnamon
¼ tsp	baking soda
47g	Dutch-processed cocoa powder (1.7oz / about ½ cup)
60g	shelled hazelnuts (2.1oz)
½ cup	crème fraîche
¼ tsp	ground cinnamon
114g	extra bitter chocolate (4oz), chopped

Glaze:

200g	confectioners' sugar (7oz / about 1⅔ cups)
¼ cup	crème fraîche
1 tsp	orange zest
2 T	orange juice

To make the sponge, dissolve the yeast in 3 tablespoons warm water in a medium bowl. Set the mixture aside until the yeast activates and looks creamy, about 10 minutes. Stir in 44 grams (1.6 ounces) flour. Cover the bowl with plastic wrap and set aside in a warm place until the sponge is bubbly and has doubled, about 1 hour.

To start the dough, put 350 grams (12.3 ounces) flour, 44 grams (1.6 ounces / about 3½ tablespoons) sugar, and 1.5 grams (½ teaspoon) salt in a bowl and whisk to combine. Put the egg and yolk in the bowl of a stand mixer. Add 6 tablespoons water and whisk until frothy. Add the sponge, then, using the paddle attachment, beat until the ingredients are integrated.

(recipe continues)

Add the flour mixture all at once and beat until the dough comes together—it will be quite wet. Switch to the dough hook and knead the dough until it is smooth and elastic and begins to pull from the sides of the bowl, about 5 minutes. Add the butter, one piece at a time, kneading the dough between additions until it is fully incorporated. Continue kneading once all the butter has been added until the dough begins to slap against the sides of the bowl, about 5 minutes more. Put the dough in a greased square or rectangular container (it is easier to roll the dough into a rectangle later if it rises in that shape, but a bowl will also work). Turn the dough over to coat, cover it with plastic wrap, and refrigerate until it doubles, at least 4 hours and up to 12.

To start the filling, make the candied orange rinds according to the instructions on page 275. Chop ⅔ cup, set aside, and reserve the rest for another purpose. Make the chocolate crumble according to the directions on page 298. Preheat the oven to 325°F. Put the hazelnuts in a small ovenproof skillet and roast until they smell toasty, about 12 minutes. Allow to cool, then finely chop them.

To shape the dough, punch it down on a lightly floured surface. Divide it in half, then roll each half out into an 8 × 9-inch rectangle. Working with one half at a time, with a long side of the rectangle facing you, spread the dough with ¼ cup of the crème fraîche, taking care to cover the whole surface. Sprinkle half the cinnamon over the crème fraîche, then half the chocolate crumbs, chopped chocolate, candied rind, and finally half the chopped nuts. Starting at the long end closest to you, use your hands to roll the rectangle into an even cylinder. Seal the seam by pressing it against the work surface. Repeat with the remaining dough and filling ingredients. Line a baking sheet with parchment paper.

Cut each cylinder into 8 equal pieces. Arrange the buns on the prepared baking sheet (including the end pieces), placing them cut-side up about 1½ inches apart. Cover the buns loosely with greased plastic wrap and set aside to proof in a warm place until the buns have risen visibly, tiny bubbles appear, and a pressed finger leaves a lingering impression; begin checking after 45 minutes.

Preheat the oven to 350°F. Remove the plastic and bake the buns for 5 minutes, then rotate the pan front to back and continue baking until they are golden brown, about 10 minutes more.

Meanwhile make the glaze. Whisk the confectioners' sugar with the crème fraîche, zest, and juice. When the buns have cooled just enough so they can be handled, dollop icing on each, spreading it evenly with the back of a spoon. Allow the buns to cool and serve.

Prosciutto Bread

Makes 1 loaf

After lots of experimentation, I decided the best way start this Neapolitan classic was with the same dough I use to make focaccia (see page 41). That said, I treat it very differently. The result is a bread that is packed with flavor. In addition to prosciutto, I include soppressata, a southern Italian salami typically spiced with black pepper and chiles. It adds just the right punch.

60g	piece unsliced prosciutto (2.1oz.), cut into ½-inch dice	333g	bread flour (11.7oz / about 2 cups + 5 T)
1 T	extra-virgin olive oil, plus extra as needed	10g	Diamond Crystal kosher salt (1 T)
60g	soppresatta (2.1oz), cut into ½-inch dice	1½ tsp	coarsely ground black pepper
2 tsp	active dry yeast	25g	Parmigiano-Reggiano (0.9oz / about 5 T), freshly grated
		80g	provolone (2.9oz / about ⅔ cup), diced

Combine the diced prosciutto and olive oil in a skillet and cook gently over medium-low heat until the fat renders and the meat is lightly browned, about 8 minutes. Stir in the soppresatta and take the pan off the heat (the soppresatta is already cooked but will add flavor). Cool to room temperature, then drain the meat, reserving the oil.

In the bowl of a stand mixer, dissolve the yeast in 1 cup plus 2 tablespoons room-temperature water. Set aside until the yeast activates and the mixture looks creamy, about 10 minutes. In a separate bowl, whisk the flour together with the salt, pepper, and Parmigiano. Add the flour mixture to the yeast and mix with the paddle attachment until the ingredients are integrated. Switch to the dough hook and knead the dough for 15 minutes (expect it to be wet). Add the meat and provolone and knead 5 minutes longer.

Grease a large bowl with olive oil. Put the dough in the bowl. To ensure a good structure, lift an edge of the dough and fold it into the center, repeat with the opposite edge and then each of the sides, forming a smaller, tighter ball of dough. Flip the dough over to coat it with oil, cover the bowl with plastic wrap, and set it aside until the dough has doubled, about 2 hours in a warm kitchen or overnight in the refrigerator.

To shape the dough, turn it out onto a lightly floured surface. Pat the dough down, then gently mold it into an 8 × 12-inch rectangle. Arrange the rectangle so the long sides are at the top and bottom. Fold the dough in thirds letter-style, stretching one long side to the middle and the opposite long side over it; repeat, folding the right edge into the middle and then the left edge over it. Using your hands, form the dough into a compact log about 12 inches long. Let the dough rest for 15 minutes. Line a baking sheet with parchment paper.

Finish shaping the dough by stretching and hand-rolling the dough into a rope about 30 inches long, pausing from time to time to let the dough rest if it begins to resist. Wet the ends of the rope and press

them together to form a ring. Place the loaf, seam-side down, on the prepared baking sheet. Cover the bread loosely with greased plastic wrap (I use olive oil but any neutral oil or cooking spray is fine) and set aside until the dough has risen visibly (though has not doubled) and a finger leaves a lingering impression; begin checking after 1 hour.

Preheat the oven to 450°F. Remove the plastic and brush the bread with the reserved prosciutto oil or olive oil. Bake for 10 minutes, then reduce the temperature to 400°F and continue baking until the bread is nicely browned, about 20 minutes more. Place the bread on a wire rack to cool. Serve warm or at room temperature.

Rye English Muffins

I tried shaping this yeasted dough two ways: forming the muffins by hand and cutting them. I found that cutting resulted in waste—which annoys me—but it produced more consistent results, so that's the course I chose. You can shape the scraps into additional muffins and proof them, although I don't. I leave the scraps to rise as they are, then use them to test the skillet temperature before I cook the muffins. For more about starting with a poolish, see page 26.

Poolish:

140g	bread flour (4.9oz / about 1 cup)
¼ tsp	active dry yeast

Dough:

215g	rye flour (7.6oz / about 2 cups + 2 T)
400g	bread flour (14.1oz / about 2¾ cups)

¾ tsp	active dry yeast
6g	Diamond Crystal kosher salt (2 tsp)
1 tsp	caraway seeds
1 T + 1 tsp	extra-virgin olive oil, plus extra for greasing
About ¼ cup	cornmeal, plus extra for dusting

To make the poolish, mix 140 grams (4.9 ounces) bread flour with ¼ teaspoon yeast in a large bowl, then stir in 1 cup cold water using a wooden spoon. Cover the bowl with plastic wrap and set it aside in a cool spot (but not the refrigerator) until doubled and bubbly, about 12 hours.

To make the dough, combine the rye flour with 400 grams (14.1 ounces) bread flour in the bowl of a stand mixer. Add ¾ teaspoon yeast, the salt, caraway, poolish, and 1½ cups cold water and, using the paddle attachment, mix until the liquid is incorporated into the dry ingredients. Allow the dough to rest for 30 minutes in the mixer bowl, then switch to the dough hook and knead the dough until it is smooth though still sticky, about 5 minutes. Drizzle in the olive oil and continue kneading until the dough is supple and elastic, about 5 minutes more. Transfer the dough to a greased bowl. Turn the dough over to coat, cover the bowl with plastic wrap, and refrigerate until the dough has doubled, 8 to 12 hours.

To shape the muffins, turn the dough out onto a lightly floured surface. Using your hands, pat the dough down gently and mold it into a 20-inch square. Line two baking sheets with parchment paper and dust each with cornmeal. Cut the dough into 16 rounds, each 3½ inches across (I use a doughnut cutter). Place the muffins (and scraps—rerolled and shaped or not) on the prepared baking sheets. Dust the dough with a little more cornmeal, cover the dough loosely with a kitchen towel, and set aside to proof until small bubbles appear and a finger pressed in the dough leaves a lingering print; begin checking after 20 minutes.

To cook the muffins, preheat the oven to 350°F. Place a large, heavy skillet (preferably cast iron) on the stovetop over medium heat. Working a few at a time, lightly "toast" the muffins in the skillet until they are golden on the bottom, about 5 minutes, then flip them and cook the second sides until they, too, are lightly browned, about 5 minutes more. Place the toasted muffins on the parchment-lined baking sheets and finish cooking and drying them in the oven, about 7 minutes. The muffins will not look very different but they will feel more "hollow" when done. (I recommend you toast and bake a few scraps first to get the hang of it). Split and eat the muffins warm with butter and/or jam or allow them to cool, then toast before serving. (Note: These freeze beautifully.)

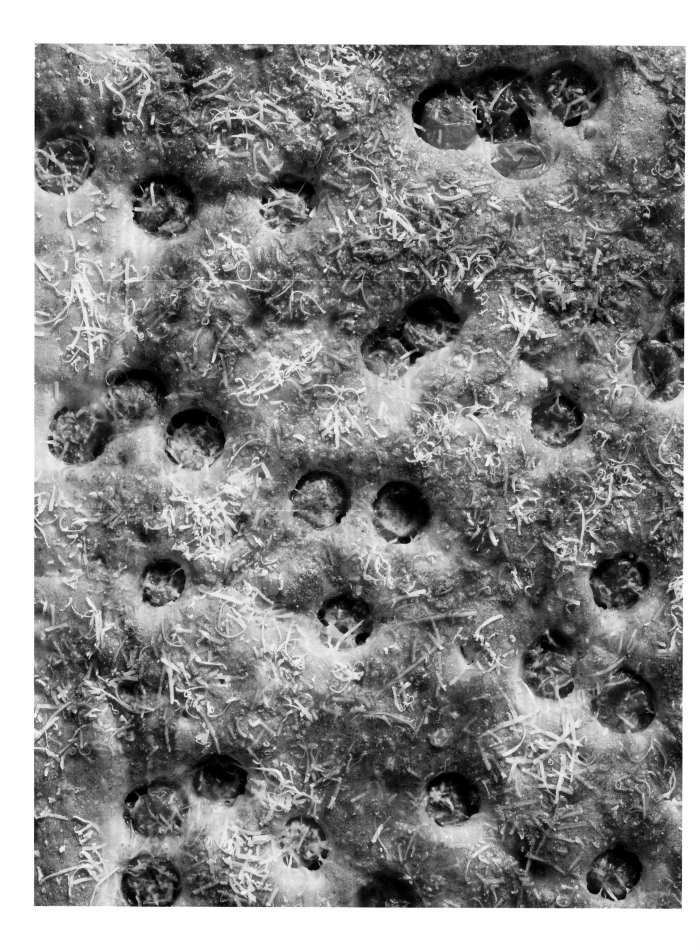

North Fork Focaccia

Makes 1 sheet tray

I baked focaccia at the North Fork Table every day, so I have had plenty of practice with this, one of the first yeasted breads I feel that I mastered. You can make the dough start to finish in about 4 hours, or do the first rise overnight in the refrigerator. Both work equally well—I make the choice based on when I want to pull the hot loaf from the oven—that's how it is best enjoyed. I cut leftovers into serving-size pieces and freeze them to heat and eat on a whim, sometimes topped with halved cherry tomatoes and grated Pecorino and others simply with sea salt and rosemary.

2 tsp	active dry yeast		10g	Diamond Crystal kosher salt (1 T)
667g	bread flour (23.5oz / about 4½ cups + 2 T)		6 T	extra-virgin olive oil, plus extra for greasing

In the bowl of a stand mixer, dissolve the yeast in 2 cups plus 2 tablespoons room-temperature water and set aside until the yeast activates and the mixture looks creamy, about 10 minutes. In a separate bowl, whisk the flour with the salt. Add the flour mixture to the yeast and mix with the paddle attachment until the ingredients are combined. Allow the dough to rest for 30 minutes in the mixer bowl, then use the dough hook and knead it on medium-high speed until the dough is smooth, about 20 minutes.

Grease a large bowl with olive oil and place the dough in it. To ensure a good structure for your focaccia, lift an edge of the dough and fold it into the center; repeat with the opposite edge and then with each of the sides, forming a smaller, tighter ball of dough. Flip the dough over to coat it with oil, cover the bowl with plastic wrap, and set it aside until the dough has doubled, 1 to 2 hours in a warm kitchen or overnight in the refrigerator.

To shape the dough, turn it out onto a lightly floured surface, pat it down into a squarish shape, then stretch it into a rectangle about 16 × 20 inches. Arrange the dough so the long sides are at the top and bottom. Fold the dough into thirds, letter-style, one long side to the middle, then the other long side over it. Fold the short sides the same way, right side to the middle and then the left on top. Square the dough and press out any air. Pour the extra-virgin olive oil onto a 13 × 18-inch baking sheet with an edge (aka a jelly-roll pan or half sheet pan). Put the dough on the pan, turn to coat it with oil, and let it rest 10 minutes. Stretch the dough to fit the pan, letting it rest again if it begins to resist. Dimple the dough all over using your fingers, cover it with plastic wrap, and let it proof in a warm place until it has inflated around the dimples; begin checking after 30 minutes.

Preheat the oven to 500°F. Remove the plastic and top the focaccia as you like, then bake it for 8 minutes. Rotate the pan front to back and bake until it is nicely browned, about 7 minutes more. Slice and serve warm or at room temperature.

Focaccia Rolls

Makes 18 rolls

These are ideal to serve with a roast chicken. I also like them as the starting point for sandwiches. When that's my plan, I make them a little bigger. Like the dough for North Fork Focaccia (page 41), this can be made from start to finish in a day, or it can rise in the refrigerator overnight.

2 tsp	active dry yeast
667g	bread flour (23. 5oz / about 4½ cups + 2 T), plus extra for dusting

10g	Diamond Crystal kosher salt (1 T)
	Extra-virgin olive oil, for greasing

In the bowl of a stand mixer, dissolve the yeast in 2 cups plus 2 tablespoons room-temperature water. Set it aside until the yeast activates and the mixture looks creamy, about 10 minutes. In another bowl, whisk the flour with the salt. Add the flour mixture to the yeast and mix with the paddle attachment until the ingredients are combined. Allow the dough to rest for 30 minutes in the bowl, then use the dough hook to knead the dough on medium-high speed until it is smooth, about 20 minutes.

Grease a large bowl with olive oil and put the dough in the bowl. To ensure your rolls have good structure, lift an edge of the dough and fold it into the center; repeat with the opposite edge and then with each of the sides, forming a smaller, tighter ball of dough. Flip the dough over to coat it with oil, cover the bowl with plastic wrap, and set it aside until the dough has doubled, 1 to 2 hours in a warm kitchen or overnight in the refrigerator.

Punch down the dough, folding it in on itself and pressing out any air. Divide it into 18 equal-size pieces. Working with one piece at a time, flatten the dough in the palm of your hand and, using your fingertips, pinch the sides into the middle a bit at a time to form a taut ball. Continuing to work one at a time, set a dough ball seam-side down on a clean, unfloured work surface. Roll the ball with your lightly floured palm against the work surface, using friction to help you make it neat and tight. Continue with the remaining dough. Place the shaped rolls on a parchment-lined baking sheet. Let the dough rest for 10 minutes. Gently pat down the rolls, cover the dough with greased plastic wrap, and set aside to proof until the rolls have risen visibly and a finger leaves a lingering impression; begin checking after 30 minutes.

Preheat the oven to 450°F. Remove the plastic, brush the rolls with olive oil and bake for 8 minutes. Rotate the pan front to back and bake until they are golden, about 7 minutes more. Remove the rolls from the oven and brush with additional olive oil. Allow the rolls to cool for at least 10 minutes, then serve warm or at room temperature.

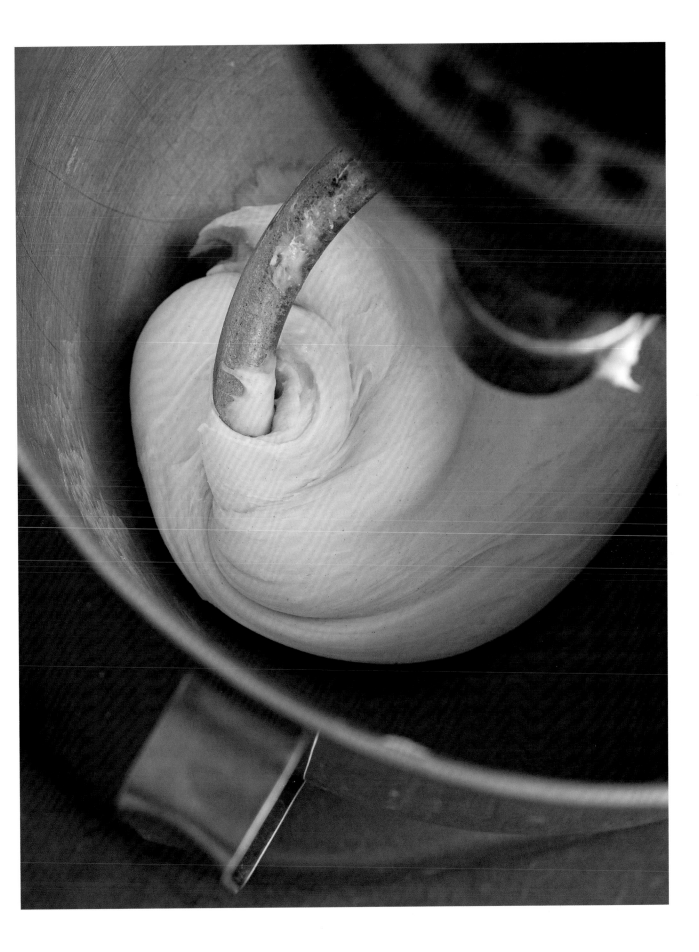

CHAPTER 2

Doughnuts and Cakes

A Cake Problem?

Growing up, cake was never my favorite dessert. It's not that I'd turn down a piece, but I always preferred cookies, pies, and doughnuts. I've had plenty of cause to think about this—doing what I do for a living—and I've realized that my hesitation never extended to all cakes, but was targeted at frosted layer cakes. "What was the problem?" you might ask. The answer, I think, comes down to the fact that American cakes, the kind you get at a birthday or see in a bakery window, often look better than they taste. In my mind, cake, mounded with fluffy frosting, looks to be the ultimate dessert, but then, when I take a forkful, I find soft, sweet, but otherwise mildly flavored (or even flavorless) crumb, coated with very sugary frosting. Over and over I was disappointed by the one-note flavor and uninspired, often dry texture of the cakes I ate.

On the other hand, thinking back, I have always liked coffee cakes and tea cakes, and I confess an ongoing love affair with cake doughnuts (which you might say are quite like cake—and you'd be right). I am particularly fond of them glazed, like the Chocolate Doughnuts with Espresso Glaze (page 51). What I like about those doughnuts may get to the heart of my cake problem: The dough is deeply flavored. The resulting crumb is tender, moist, and yummy. You don't need the glaze to make the doughnuts delicious; rather, the glaze affords an opportunity to add another layer of flavor and make something delectable even more so.

Thinking about this focused my attention on the recipes in this chapter in specific ways. I wanted to make a layer cake that I, myself, love. The Ginger-Stout Layer Cake (page 77), which began as an adaptation of my gingerbread recipe, helped me nail my approach. I needed the cake to be good enough to eat without frosting, and it is. The question then became how to frost it in such a way that the elements joined to create an even better whole. My solution was to use a southern-style milk/roux-based frosting, but substitute buttermilk for whole milk (see Buttermilk "Ermine" Frosting, page 91). The tangy finish plays off the warm and soulful flavor notes in the cake in a slightly unexpected but very satisfying way. Inspired, I went on to put together a roster of layer cakes that I offer here—a chocolate, a coconut, and a white cake. I am truly happy with them all.

I also share recipes in this chapter for cakes that I consider seasonal, including several tea cakes, a cheesecake, and my take on a Sicilian cassata cake (page 59). And, because they do seem to me to be kith and kin to cake, I open this section with doughnut recipes, all of which work in my world for dessert as well as breakfast.

Cider Doughnuts

Makes 16 doughnuts and 16 doughnut holes

These are cake doughnuts, meaning they are leavened with baking powder (and in this case, baking soda), not yeast. I start by making a "bread roux." This extra step helps hydrate the dough, which makes for nicely soft, light-textured doughnuts (see page 26 for more on this). I use cider in the roux to intensify the fermented apple flavor. I typically make both the roux and dough a day ahead, do the first rise in the refrigerator overnight, then proof, cut, and fry the next morning.

Bread roux:

43g	unsalted butter (1.5oz)
¼ cup + 2 T	apple cider
50g	all-purpose flour (1.8oz / about 6 T)

Doughnuts:

3 cups	apple cider
1 cup + 2 T	heavy cream
100g	sugar (3.5oz / about ½ cup)
2	large eggs
4 tsp	vanilla paste or pure vanilla extract
325g	whole-wheat flour (11.5oz / 2 cups + 1⅓ T)

325g	all-purpose flour (11.5oz / 2⅓ cups)
1 tsp	freshly grated nutmeg
4 tsp	baking powder
1 tsp	baking soda
12g	Diamond Crystal kosher salt (4 tsp)
	Canola or other neutral oil, for frying

Cinnamon sugar:

200g	sugar (7oz / about 1 cup)
1 T	ground cinnamon

To make the roux, melt the butter and ¼ cup plus 2 tablespoons cider in a saucepan over medium heat. Whisk 50 grams (1.8 ounces) all-purpose flour into the hot liquid, then switch to a wooden spoon and stir constantly, cooking the roux over medium-high heat, until it thickens to a paste and a thermometer indicates a temperature of about 150°F. Take the roux off the heat and transfer it to a small bowl. Cover the roux directly with plastic wrap, and allow it to cool to room temperature, then refrigerate for at least 4 hours or overnight.

To start the dough, reduce 3 cups cider by two-thirds in a small saucepan over medium-high heat. Allow the reduced cider to cool completely.

Combine the roux and reduced cider in a blender. Add the cream, sugar, eggs, and vanilla and blend until combined. Strain the reduced cider slurry through a fine sieve. In a large bowl, combine the whole-wheat flour with 325 grams (11.5 ounces) all-purpose flour. Mix in the nutmeg, baking powder, baking soda, and salt. Using a wooden spoon, stir the strained slurry into the flour mixture.

Line a baking sheet with plastic wrap. Turn the dough out onto the baking sheet and spread the dough in an even layer. Cover the dough directly with plastic wrap and refrigerate for at least 4 hours and up to 24 hours.

To finish the doughnuts, turn the dough out onto a lightly floured work surface, roll it out about ½ inch thick, then cut out 16 doughnuts using a 3-inch round cutter, dipping it in flour as you go and applying downward pressure without twisting. With a 1-inch cutter, cut doughnut "holes" from the center of each. (Reroll the dough scraps and cut additional 1-inch holes.) Arrange the doughnuts and holes on the plastic-lined baking sheet and allow them to warm to room temperature.

Heat about 3 inches of oil in a large, heavy pot over medium-high heat to 375°F, adjusting the heat as necessary to maintain the temperature. Set a wire rack over a baking sheet near the stove. Working in very small batches to avoid lowering the oil temperature, fry the doughnuts until they are brown at the edges, about 1 minute, then flip them over, brown the second sides for about 1 minute more, and flip them back over and cook a final 30 seconds. (Expect the holes to brown in a total of 2 minutes.) Drain the doughnuts on the wire rack.

In a bowl, mix 200 grams (7 ounces) sugar with the cinnamon. While the doughnuts are still warm, roll them in the cinnamon sugar. Serve immediately or at room temperature.

Chocolate Doughnuts with Espresso Glaze

Makes 12 doughnuts and about 15 doughnut holes

These devil's food cake doughnuts are fancy enough to work as dessert. They are delicious simply rolled in confectioners' sugar but even better finished with this chocolate-and-espresso glaze, which can be served as a sauce on the side, if you prefer. Like the Cider Doughnuts (page 48), I begin my dough by making a "bread roux" (see page 26 for more about this). Also like the Cider Doughnuts, these can be made from start to finish in a day, but I prefer to spread the work over two, keeping in mind that all doughnuts are tastiest shortly after they are made.

Bread roux:

21g	unsalted butter (0.7oz / about 1½ T)
3 T	prepared espresso or strong, dark coffee
25g	all-purpose flour (0.9oz / about 3 T)

Doughnuts:

½ cup	prepared espresso or strong, dark coffee, room temperature
½ cup + 1 T	heavy cream
100g	sugar (3.5oz / about ½ cup)
1	large egg
1	large egg yolk
2 tsp	vanilla paste or pure vanilla extract
400g	all-purpose flour (14.1oz / about 2¾ cups + 2 T)
30g	natural (not Dutch-processed) unsweetened cocoa powder (1oz / about ⅓ cup)
2 tsp	baking powder
½ tsp	baking soda
6g	Diamond Crystal kosher salt (2 tsp)
100g	extra bitter chocolate, chopped (3.5oz)
	Canola or other neutral oil, for frying

Glaze:

110g	extra bitter chocolate, chopped (3.9oz)
¼ cup	prepared espresso or strong, dark coffee
¼ cup	heavy cream

To make the bread roux, melt the butter with 3 tablespoons espresso in a small saucepan over medium heat. Whisk 25 grams (0.9 ounces) flour into the hot liquid, then switch to a wooden spoon and stir constantly, increasing the heat to medium-high and cooking the roux until it thickens to a paste and a thermometer indicates a temperature of about 150°F. Take the roux off the heat and transfer it to a small bowl. Cover the roux directly with plastic wrap, allow it to cool to room temperature, and then refrigerate it for at least 4 hours and up to 12 hours.

To make the doughnuts, combine the roux and ½ cup espresso in a blender. Add ½ cup plus 1 tablespoon cream, the sugar, eggs, yolks, and vanilla and blend until combined. Strain the espresso slurry through a fine sieve into a bowl and set aside. In a large bowl, mix 325 grams (11. 4 ounces) of the flour with the cocoa powder, baking powder, baking soda, and salt.

Melt the chocolate in a heatproof bowl set over a pan of simmering water (take care that the bowl doesn't touch the water), stirring occasionally. When the chocolate is melted, remove it from the heat. Stir the strained espresso slurry into the warm chocolate, then stir this mixture into the dry ingredients.

Line a baking sheet with plastic wrap. Turn the dough out onto the baking sheet and spread the dough in an even layer. Cover the dough directly with plastic wrap and refrigerate for at least 4 hours and up to 24 hours.

To make the glaze, put the chopped chocolate in a bowl. Combine ¼ cup espresso and ¼ cup cream in a saucepan and bring to a boil over medium-high heat. Pour the hot mixture over the chocolate, allow it to sit until the chocolate begins to melt, about 1 minute, and then whisk until smooth. Cover the glaze directly with plastic wrap (to prevent a skin from forming) and set it aside to cool enough so it is the consistency of thickened cream (about 85°F), about 1 hour. (Note: The mixture will remain liquid enough to use as a glaze for at least another hour, but it will eventually solidify. Return it to glaze consistency by reheating it in the microwave in 10-second intervals until it liquefies or by warming it in a bowl over simmering water for about 2 minutes.)

To finish the doughnuts, turn the dough out onto a lightly floured surface and allow it to come to room temperature, then roll it about ½ inch thick. Cut out 12 doughnuts using a 3-inch round cutter, dipping it in flour as you go and applying downward pressure without twisting. Using a 1-inch cutter, cut out doughnut "holes" from the center of each. (Reroll the dough scraps and cut additional 1-inch holes.) Arrange the doughnuts on the plastic-lined baking sheet.

Heat about 3 inches of oil in a large, heavy pot over medium-high heat to 375°F, adjusting the heat to maintain the temperature. Set a wire rack over a baking sheet near the stove. Working in very small batches to avoid lowering the oil temperature, fry the doughnuts until they are brown at the edges, about 1 minute, then flip them, brown the second sides for about 1 minute, then flip them back over and cook a final 30 seconds. (The doughnut holes will brown nicely in a total of 2 minutes). Drain the doughnuts on the wire rack. Allow them to cool completely, then dip one side of each doughnut in the glaze. Return them to the wire rack to allow the glaze to solidify. (If you want extra-chocolaty doughnuts, dip each a second time in the glaze and, once again, let it set.) Serve at room temperature.

Vanilla Cream Doughnuts

Makes 10 to 12 doughnuts

These yeasted doughnuts are cousins of Italian *bombolini*. You can eat them plain, but I like mine filled with pastry cream or with jelly (see Variation 2, below). Either way, they are wonderful in the morning or as an anytime sweet. The pastry cream can be made a day ahead.

Doughnuts:

1¾ tsp	active dry yeast
½ cup	milk
52g	unsalted butter (1.9oz), melted and cooled, plus extra for greasing
1	large egg
370g	all-purpose flour (13oz / about 2½ cups plus 2½ T)
70g	sugar (2.5oz / about ⅓ cup), plus extra for dusting
1.5g	Diamond Crystal kosher salt (½ tsp)
¼ tsp	ground cinnamon
¼ tsp	ground mace
	Canola or other neutral oil, for frying

Pastry cream:

2	large egg yolks
	Pinch of Diamond Crystal kosher salt
1 T	cornstarch
1 cup + 2 T	milk
60g	sugar (2.1oz / 4¾ T)
28g	unsalted butter (1oz)
2-in piece	vanilla bean

To start the doughnuts, put ¼ cup lukewarm water in the bowl of a stand mixer. Stir in the yeast and let it sit until it activates and looks creamy, about 5 minutes. In a measuring cup, mix together ½ cup milk, 52 grams (1.9 ounces) melted butter, and the egg. In a separate bowl, combine the flour, 70 grams (2.5 ounces) sugar, 1.4 grams (½ teaspoon) salt, cinnamon, and mace.

Add the milk mixture to the activated yeast and then add the dry ingredients. Using the paddle attachment, mix the dough until it comes together. Switch to the dough hook and knead until the dough pulls away from the sides of the bowl, 8 to 10 minutes. Grease a medium bowl. Put the dough in the bowl, turn it over, then cover the bowl with plastic wrap. Set the dough aside in a warm place until it doubles, about 2 hours.

To start the pastry cream, set a fine sieve over a bowl. Whisk the egg yolks, a pinch of salt, and the cornstarch in a medium bowl, then whisk in 2 tablespoons of the milk. In a saucepan, combine the remaining 1 cup milk, 30 grams (1 ounce) sugar, and 28 grams (1 ounce) butter. Split the vanilla bean lengthwise and scrape the "seeds" into the mixture. Bring the mixture to a boil over medium-high heat.

When the contents of the pan come to a boil, temper the yolks, while whisking, by ladling a small amount of the hot liquid into the yolk mixture, then gradually whisk in the rest in a slow, steady stream. Pour the

pastry cream back into the saucepan and cook over medium heat, whisking constantly, until it thickens and returns to a boil, then whisk on the heat for an additional minute to set the cream. Immediately strain the pastry cream through the prepared sieve into the bowl. Place plastic wrap directly on the pastry cream (to prevent a skin from forming), then chill it thoroughly, at least 2 hours.

To form and cook the doughnuts, line a baking sheet with parchment paper. Punch the dough down in the bowl, folding it in on itself to expel all the air, then turn it out onto a lightly floured surface. Let the dough relax for 5 to 10 minutes, then roll it into a rectangle about ½ inch thick. Cut the dough into rounds using a 2¾-inch cutter, dipping it in flour as you go and applying downward pressure without twisting. (Reroll any leftover dough and make doughnut holes with a 1-inch cutter). Arrange the doughnuts on the prepared baking sheet. Cover the doughnuts with plastic wrap and let them proof until they have risen again by half, about 25 minutes.

Heat about 3 inches of oil in a large, heavy pot to 350°F. Set a wire rack over a baking sheet near the stove. Working in small batches, fry the doughnuts until the edges brown, about 45 seconds, then flip them and fry the second sides until they, too, are golden brown, about 45 seconds more. Drain the doughnuts on the wire rack. When the doughnuts are cool enough to handle, dip one side of each in sugar, then set them aside to cool completely.

To fill the doughnuts, put the pastry cream into a piping bag. Make a small incision in the "equator" of each doughnut with a paring knife. Pipe a generous amount of cream into each doughnut before serving.

Variation 1: To make Chocolate Cream Doughnuts, prepare the doughnuts as above. Make the pastry cream as described but omit the vanilla bean. Melt 114 grams (4 ounces) chopped extra bitter chocolate in a bowl set over a pan of simmering water. Whisk the melted chocolate into the pastry cream, strain it through a fine sieve, then chill the pastry cream and pipe it into the doughnuts as above.

Variation 2: To make Jelly Doughnuts, make the doughnuts as above. Skip the pastry cream, instead filling each doughnut with about 1 tablespoon jelly or jam (avoid anything too chunky or it will be hard to pipe).

Variation 3: To make Dessert Minis, make the dough as above but cut rounds using a 1-inch cutter. Fry the mini doughnuts, let them drain and cool on a wire rack, then fill them or simply dust with confectioners' sugar and serve with a bowl of warm chocolate-and-espresso glaze (page 51) for dunking.

Maple and White Chocolate Skiffs

Makes about 30

I call these baked, yeasted sweet buns "skiffs." Filled with cream, they are inspired by the French "it dessert" *tarte tropézienne*. Like the original, an invention of a Polish baker with a shop in Saint-Tropez, I start with a brioche-style dough, then fill it with pastry cream. Unlike the classic, I cut my dough into buns (that look to me like dinghies or skiffs) and flavor my cream with maple sugar and white chocolate. Note this dough needs to rest in the refrigerator overnight before it is proofed. The pastry cream can be made a day ahead and must chill for at least 6 hours. For a riff on a Sicilian ice cream sandwich, see the Variation below.

Brioche:

350g	bread flour (12.4oz / 2¼ cups + 3 T), plus extra for dusting
25g	sugar (0.9oz / about 2 T)
10g	Diamond Crystal kosher salt (1 T)
6	large eggs
2 tsp	active dry yeast
283g	unsalted butter (10oz), chilled and very thinly sliced, plus extra for greasing
20g	walnuts (0.7oz / about ⅔ cup)
10g	maple sugar (0.4oz / about 1 T)
	Maple syrup, for brushing

Filling:

1 recipe	Maple and White Chocolate Cream (page 86)
½ cup + 2 T	heavy cream
½ cup + 2 T	crème fraîche
60g	maple sugar (2.1oz / about ¼ cup)
114g	white chocolate (4oz), chopped

To make the brioche, grease a large bowl with butter and set it aside. In the bowl of a stand mixer, whisk the flour with the sugar and salt. In a heatproof bowl, whisk the eggs with the yeast. Set the bowl over a pan of simmering water until the mixture is warm (about 100°F), 2 to 4 minutes. Add the warm egg mixture to the dry ingredients. Mix with the paddle attachment to combine the ingredients, then switch to the dough hook and knead on medium speed until the dough comes together around the hook, about 6 minutes. With the mixer still on medium, add the chilled butter, a couple slices at a time, letting it emulsify between each addition, about 18 minutes total. Transfer the dough to the buttered bowl, dust the dough with a little flour, then cover the bowl with plastic wrap

and set it aside to rise in a warm place until the dough doubles, about 2 hours. Sprinkle the dough with a little more flour and punch it down in the bowl, folding it in on itself. Re-cover it directly with plastic wrap and refrigerate overnight.

To make the filling, follow the instructions on page 86. Chill the cream for at least 6 hours.

To start the skiffs, turn the dough out onto a lightly floured piece of parchment. Dust with a little more flour and pat the dough into a squarish shape, forcing the air out as you go. Roll the dough into a rectangle about 10 × 12 inches and ¼ inch thick. Add a dusting of flour to both sides of the dough, slide the parchment and dough onto a baking sheet, and put it in the refrigerator to rest for at least 15 minutes.

To form the skiffs, trim the dough to even the edges, then, using a floured knife, cut out rectangles about ¾ × 3 inches. (Alternatively, you can cut the dough into 2-inch rounds, in which case your buns won't look anything like skiffs.) Line two baking sheets with parchment paper. Arrange the skiffs on the prepared baking sheets. Butter two sheets of plastic wrap, cover the skiffs, and set them aside to proof at room temperature until almost doubled, at least 1 hour.

To finish the skiffs, preheat the oven to 350°F. Combine the walnuts and maple sugar in a food processor and pulse until the mixture is medium-fine.

Remove the plastic and brush each skiff with maple syrup, then dust them all with the walnut mixture. Bake the skiffs for 7 minutes, then rotate the pan front to back and continue baking until they are golden brown, about 7 minutes more. Brush the skiffs with a little more maple syrup, transfer them to a wire rack, and set them aside to cool completely.

To finish the skiffs, by hand or with a mixer, whip the maple and white chocolate cream until it holds stiff peaks. Use a serrated knife to cut each skiff in half horizontally through the equator. Put the cream into a piping bag fitted with a star tip and pipe a generous amount of cream on the bottoms. (Alternatively, for a more rustic look, simply spoon the cream onto the pastry.) Replace the tops and serve.

Variation: To make Sicilian Ice Cream Sandwiches, follow the recipe above but omit the Maple and White Chocolate Cream and cut the dough a little larger, about 1½ × 3½ inches. Bake the buns until they are golden, about 17 minutes. Cool them thoroughly, then split the buns horizontally, brush both halves with a favorite liqueur, scoop ice cream on the bottoms (I like maple pecan or coffee), replace the tops, and serve immediately.

Strawberry Cassata

Makes one 9-inch cake

As a kid, I never liked cassata, a liqueur-soaked Sicilian classic garnished with candied fruit and often covered with marzipan, but I've found that with a few adjustments I am now very partial to this ricotta-filled dessert. I start mine with an orange-flavored cornmeal cake so tasty and full of brightness and texture that there is no need for a bath in alcohol. I include candied orange and a little chocolate—both typical—and then garnish it with fresh strawberries, probably a more American than Italian choice. I candy my own orange rinds (see page 275), but good commercially prepared candied fruit makes a fine substitute.

Cake:

226g	cake flour (8oz / about 2 cups)
56g	finely ground yellow cornmeal, preferably stone-ground (2oz / about 5 T)
2¼ tsp	baking powder
½ tsp	baking soda
1.5g	Diamond Crystal kosher salt (½ tsp)
6 T	fresh orange juice
2 tsp	vanilla paste or pure vanilla extract
2	large eggs
2	large egg yolks
142g	sugar (5oz / about ½ cup + 3½ T)
2 tsp	orange zest
1 cup	extra-virgin olive oil, plus extra for the pan

Garnish:

3½ T	chopped Candied Orange Rinds (page 275)
3	oranges

300g	sugar (10.6oz / about 1½ cups)
1 T	light corn syrup
525g	fresh strawberries (18.5oz)
18g	sugar (0.6oz / about 1¾ T)
30g	bittersweet chocolate, finely chopped (1oz)

Ricotta cream:

178g	ricotta cheese (6.3oz / about ¾ cup)
40g	confectioners' sugar (1.4oz / about ⅓ cup)
44g	mascarpone cheese (1.6oz / about 3½ T)
¼ tsp	ground cinnamon
	Seeds from 1-in piece of vanilla bean, or ¾ tsp vanilla paste or pure vanilla extract
¾ cup	heavy cream

To start the cake, preheat the oven to 350°F and brush a 5 × 9-inch loaf pan with olive oil. In a bowl, mix the cake flour with the cornmeal, baking powder, baking soda, and salt. In a smaller bowl, mix the orange juice with the vanilla.

In the bowl of a stand mixer, using the whisk attachment, whip the eggs and yolks with 142 grams (5 ounces) sugar and the zest on medium-high speed until the mixture reaches the ribbon stage—it becomes pale and thick enough so when the whisk is

lifted, "ribbons" of the batter trail to the bowl. With the mixer on high, drizzle in the olive oil. Whip until the batter looks like thin mayonnaise.

Remove the bowl from the mixer and, using a spatula, incorporate a third of the dry ingredients into the egg mixture. Follow with half of the orange juice mixture, then add the remaining flour in two additions, alternating with the remaining juice and finishing with the last third of the flour mixture. (This process ensures even distribution and prevents overmixing.) Spoon the cake batter into the prepared loaf pan.

Bake until the cake is golden, springy, and begins to pull from the sides of the pan, about 40 minutes. Cool the cake in the pan for 15 minutes, then turn it out and let it cool completely on a wire rack.

To start the garnish, candy the orange rinds, following the directions on page 275. When the rinds are cool, chop 3½ tablespoons; reserve the remainder for another purpose.

An hour or two before you plan to serve the cake, stem the strawberries and cut them lengthwise in half or quarters, depending on their size. Put the berries in a bowl, sprinkle them with 18 grams (0.6 ounces) sugar, and set them aside to macerate.

To make the ricotta cream, combine the ricotta, confectioners' sugar, mascarpone, cinnamon, and vanilla in a bowl and whisk until well combined. In a separate bowl, whip the cream until it holds stiff peaks (if you are using a mixer, switch when it holds medium peaks and finish whipping by hand to avoid overbeating). Fold the whipped cream into the ricotta mixture.

To assemble the cassata, trim off the top of the cake with a serrated knife so it is flat, then split the cake into 3 layers by cutting it horizontally in thirds. Put the bottom layer on a serving plate. Spread a little less than a third of the ricotta cream over the cake. Sprinkle with a third of the chocolate, a third of the candied orange rind, and a third of the strawberries (reserve the prettiest berries for the final layer). Repeat twice more, finishing with an extra-generous layer of cream and the nicest berries. Slice and serve.

Plum and Almond Cake

Makes one 9-inch cake

I've been making this almond cake since I was at Gramercy Tavern. It's Lindsey Shere's recipe, one of my favorites, from her book, *Chez Panisse Desserts*. It is easy and amenable to adaptation. The starting point is almond paste (be aware that marzipan is not the same thing and is not a substitute). I find it more efficient to grate the paste than to chop it. Here, I pair the cake with Italian prune plums. Other plums tend to be too juicy for this recipe. Figs or apricots will work in place of the plums.

70g	all-purpose flour (2.5oz / about ½ cup), plus extra for the pan
½ tsp	baking powder
	Pinch of Diamond Crystal kosher salt
100g	almond paste (3.5oz), grated
137g	sugar (4.8oz / about ½ cup + 3 T)
114g	unsalted butter (4oz), room temperature, plus extra for the pan
½ tsp	lemon zest
3	large eggs, room temperature
½ tsp	vanilla paste or pure vanilla extract
8	smallish Italian plums, stems trimmed, quartered lengthwise

Preheat the oven to 350°F. Butter and flour a 9-inch springform cake pan. Mix the flour, baking powder, and salt together in a bowl. In the bowl of a stand mixer and using the paddle attachment, beat the almond paste and sugar together on low speed until the ingredients come together into a grainy mixture, about 10 minutes.

Add the butter and the lemon zest to the almond mixture and beat on low speed until smooth, about 30 seconds, then increase the speed to high and whip until the mixture is light and fluffy, 1 to 2 minutes, scraping down the bowl as needed. Break the eggs into a measuring cup and add the vanilla but don't mix them. Lower the mixer speed to medium-high and beat in the eggs, one at a time, scraping down the bowl after each addition. Remove the bowl from the mixer.

Sift half of the flour mixture into the batter. Fold to incorporate the dry ingredients, then repeat, sifting and folding the remaining flour mixture into the batter. Spoon the batter into the prepared pan, spreading it evenly and smoothing the top. Arrange the plums cut-sides up in the batter.

Bake the cake until it is firm, the edges begin to pull from the pan, and a cake tester inserted in the center comes out clean; begin checking after 45 minutes but expect the cake to take closer to an hour. Allow the cake to cool in the pan. Remove it from the pan and serve at room temperature, topped with whipped cream or crème fraîche, if desired.

Quince Goat Cheese Cake

Makes one 8-inch cake

Goat cheese gives this cake a nuanced flavor, and my play with sweet and tart continues in the quince topping. Here, and whenever I make cheesecake, I prepare the pan by greasing it with cooking spray or oil then wrapping it with tinfoil. This prevents moisture from the water bath from seeping into the cake as it cooks. Because the salinity of goat cheese varies, I taste mine before incorporating it and adjust the amount of salt I add accordingly. Note that I combine the goat and cream cheeses in a food processor but whisk in the sour cream and eggs by hand. This leads to a more refined texture.

Poached quince:

1	Poached Quince and 1 cup poaching liquid (page 268) (½ recipe)
1	medium quince
150g	sugar (5.3oz / about ¾ cup)
½ cup	white wine
1	whole clove inserted into a piece of orange peel
¼	cinnamon stick
1	whole star anise

Cheese cake:

	Cooking spray or neutral oil, for the pan
286g	fresh goat cheese (10oz), room temperature
226g	cream cheese (8oz), room temperature
2-in piece	vanilla bean, split lengthwise
88g	sugar (3.1oz/ about ½ cup + 1 T)
	Pinch of Diamond Crystal kosher salt (optional, see headnote)
174g	sour cream (6.1oz / about ¾ cup)
4	large eggs, room temperature
2 tsp	orange zest

Poach the quince according to the directions on page 268. Quarter 1 quince lengthwise (reserve the other for another use), then slice each quarter about ½ inch thick. Reserve the sliced quince and poaching liquid separately.

To start the cake, preheat the oven to 325°F and prepare an 8-inch springform pan as directed in the headnote above. Combine the goat cheese and cream cheese in a food processor. Scrape the seeds from the vanilla bean into the machine, then add the sugar and a pinch of salt, if necessary (see headnote). Run the processor until the mixture is smooth, then transfer it to a bowl. Whisk in the sour cream, followed by all the eggs. Strain the batter through a fine sieve into a clean bowl. Stir in the zest. Spoon the batter into the prepared pan, spreading it evenly and smoothing the top.

Set the pan in a larger high-sided pan and add enough boiling water to come two-thirds up the sides of the springform pan. Bake the cake, uncovered, until the edges are set but the center is still a little jiggly, about 1 hour. Remove the cake from the water bath and allow it to cool in the pan. When the cake reaches room temperature, transfer it to the refrigerator and chill thoroughly, uncovered, at least 4 hours.

To finish the cake, in a medium skillet, reduce the quince poaching liquid over medium-high heat by about a third; it should be syrupy. Add the sliced quince to the glaze, lower the heat, and warm the quince, turning the slices to coat them evenly. Allow the quince to cool in the liquid, then arrange them on the cheesecake, drizzle with the quince syrup, slice, and serve.

Apple Crumb Cake

Makes one 12-inch cake

This is a cake that's appealing at any time of day. It works for breakfast with coffee, in the afternoon with tea, and it makes a nice dessert garnished with whipped crème fraîche. To avoid disturbing the crumb topping, I serve this cake in the cast-iron pan I like to cook it in. I bring that to the table or cut slices in the kitchen. I always make the whole crumble recipe, although this recipe calls for only a cup. I keep the extra in my freezer and use it to top fruit, pies, or ice cream (for specifics see the recipe).

Crumble:

1 cup	**Brown Butter Pecan Crumble (page 296)**
114g	unsalted butter (4oz)
45g	pecans (1.6oz / about ⅓ cup), chopped
110g	light brown sugar (3.9oz / about ½ cup)
50g	sugar (1.8oz / about ¼ cup)
180g	all-purpose flour (6.3oz / about 1¼ cups)
⅛ tsp	ground cardamom
¼ tsp	ground cinnamon
0.7g	Diamond Crystal kosher salt (¼ tsp)

Apple:

1	large slightly tart, crisp apple, such as Honeycrisp
28g	unsalted butter (1oz)
2-in piece	vanilla bean, split lengthwise
1 T	maple syrup
	Pinch of ground cinnamon

Cake:

245g	sour cream (8.6oz / about 1 cup)
6	large eggs
3	large egg yolks
2 T	vanilla paste or pure vanilla extract
420g	all-purpose flour (14.8oz / about 3 cups)
300g	sugar (10.6oz / about 1½ cups)
1½ tsp	baking soda
1½ tsp	baking powder
2.3g	Diamond Crystal kosher salt (¾ tsp)
255g	unsalted butter (8oz), room temperature, plus extra for the pan

Make the crumble according to the directions on page 296. Reserve 1 cup for this recipe and freeze the rest for future use.

Prepare the apple by peeling it, halving it lengthwise, and coring it. Cut each half lengthwise into quarters, then cut each quarter into ¼-inch-thick slices. Melt 28 grams (1 ounce) butter in a medium skillet over medium-high heat. Scrape the vanilla seeds into the butter and add the pod. Cook the butter until it is golden, about 7 minutes, then add the apple slices, arranging them in a single layer. Brown the apple slices, without moving them, about 5 minutes. Add the maple syrup and cinnamon to the pan and turn the apple slices over in the flavored butter. Continue to cook the apples until the syrup concentrates, about

1 minute longer. Pull the skillet off the heat and allow the apples to cool in the syrup.

To make the cake, preheat the oven to 350°F and butter the bottom and sides of a 10-inch cast-iron skillet or cake pan. In a bowl, mix the sour cream with the eggs, yolks, and vanilla. In the bowl of a stand mixer, combine the flour, sugar, baking soda, baking powder, and salt. Add 255 grams (8 ounces) butter and beat with the paddle until the mixture is crumbly. Add half the sour cream mixture, beating until it is incorporated, about 2 minutes. Scrape down the bowl, add the remaining sour cream mixture, and beat on high until the batter is fluffy, about 3 minutes more. Spoon two-thirds of the batter into the prepared skillet. Evenly distribute the apples over the batter. Spoon the remaining batter on top and smooth it with a spatula. Top the cake with the crumble.

Bake until the cake is golden, pulls from the sides of the pan, and a tester inserted in the center comes out clean, about 1 hour 15 minutes. Allow the cake to cool in the pan for at least 20 minutes, then serve warm or at room temperature.

Cornmeal and Olive Oil Cake

Makes one 9-inch loaf

This cake is an element in my Strawberry Cassata Cake (page 59), but it is so scrumptious I wanted to share the recipe separately. How to garnish it? That depends on the season. I like it with Poached Rhubarb (page 270) in the spring, berries or peaches and whipped cream in the summer, and Blood Oranges in Caramel (page 273) during the colder months.

226g	cake flour (8oz / about 1½ cups + 2 T)
56g	finely ground yellow cornmeal, preferably stone-ground (2oz / about 5 T)
2¼ tsp	baking powder
½ tsp	baking soda
1.5g	Diamond Crystal kosher salt (½ tsp)

6 T	fresh orange juice
1 tsp	vanilla paste or pure vanilla extract
2	large eggs, room temperature
2	large egg yolks, room temperature
142g	sugar (5oz / about ½ cup + 3½ T)
2 tsp	orange zest
1 cup	extra-virgin olive oil (use an everyday oil), plus extra for the pan

To start the cake, preheat the oven to 350°F and brush a 5 × 9-inch loaf pan with olive oil. In a bowl, mix the flour with the cornmeal, baking powder, baking soda, and salt. In a smaller bowl, mix the orange juice with the vanilla.

In the bowl of a stand mixer, use the whisk attachment on high speed to whip the eggs, yolks, sugar, and zest together until the mixture reaches the ribbon stage—it will become pale, aerated, and thickened enough so that when the whisk is lifted, "ribbons" of the batter trail to the bowl. With the mixer on high, drizzle in the olive oil, then whip until the batter looks like a thin mayonnaise.

Remove the bowl from the mixer and, using a spatula, stir a third of the dry ingredients into the egg mixture. Follow with half the orange juice mixture, then repeat, alternating with the remaining orange juice and finishing with the dry mixture. (This process ensures even distribution and prevents overmixing.) Spoon the batter evenly into the prepared pan and smooth the top.

Bake until the cake is golden and springy and begins to pull from the sides of the pan and a tester inserted in the center comes out clean, about 40 minutes. Cool the cake in the pan for 20 minutes, then turn it out and let it cool completely on a wire rack. Serve as is or with fresh or poached fruit, whipped cream, or crème fraîche.

Fennel Tea Cake with Pernod Whipped Cream

Makes one 9-inch loaf

Fennel and citrus, typically lemon or orange, is a flavor combination I grew up with. For this cake, I chose to use grapefruit instead, because I like the particular dynamics the fruit brings. I mix zest into the batter and garnish the cake with homemade Candied Grapefruit Rinds, although Candied Kumquats (page 271) are a nice alternative. Either way, I always add a little Pernod to the whipped cream. The anise flavor reinforces the licorce taste of the fennel seeds.

Cake:

1 T	fennel seeds
226g	unsalted butter (8oz), plus extra for the pan
5	large eggs, room temperature
200g	sugar (7oz / about 1 cup)
1 T	Pernod
180g	cake flour (6.3oz / about 1½ cups + 1½ T), plus extra for the pan
0.7g	Diamond Crystal kosher salt (¼ tsp)
1 T	grapefruit zest

Garnish:

½ cup	Candied Grapefruit Rinds (page 277) (¼ recipe) plus ¼ cup syrup (optional)
½	grapefruit, preferably pink
150g	sugar (5.3oz / about ¾ cup)
1½ tsp	light corn syrup
1 cup	heavy cream
15g	confectioners' sugar (0.5oz / about 2 T)
1 T	Pernod, or to taste

To start the cake, preheat the oven to 325°F and butter and flour a 5 × 9-inch loaf pan. Toast the fennel seeds in a skillet over medium-low heat until they smell toasty, about 8 minutes. Transfer the seeds to a cutting board and bruise them with the flat of a knife. Return the seeds to the skillet, add the butter, and melt it over medium-low heat. Turn off the burner but leave the pan on the stove to keep the butter a bit warm.

Combine the eggs, sugar, and 1 tablespoon of the Pernod in the bowl of a stand mixer. Using the whisk attachment, whip on high speed until the eggs look thicker and pale, about 5 minutes. In a separate bowl, whisk together the flour, salt, and zest. Fold the flour into the egg/sugar mixture one quarter at a time. Measure out 1 cup of the batter and put it in a separate bowl. Whisk the warm fennel butter into the cup of batter, then very gently fold this mixture into the rest of the batter. Spoon the batter into the prepared pan and smooth the top.

Bake the cake until the top is golden, the edges begin to pull from the sides, and a tester inserted in the center comes out clean, 40 to 45 minutes. Remove the cake from the oven and allow it to cool in the pan for 30 minutes, then unmold it.

If you're using the candied grapefruit, poke about 8 holes in the top of the cake with a toothpick. Brush the top and sides of the cake with the grapefruit syrup. Set the cake aside to cool completely.

To finish the cake, arrange candied grapefruit on top. Whip the cream with the confectioners' sugar and about 1 tablespoon Pernod. Slice the cake and serve with the Pernod whipped cream.

Coconut Layer Cake

Makes one 8-inch 3-layer cake

Inspired by chiffon cakes, I moisten this classic yellow cake by adding a little oil. Be sure to start with your in-gredients, specifically the eggs, at room temperature, and don't worry if the batter looks a little broken when you first mix in the coconut milk—it will come back together. I reserve any extra coconut milk in the can to use in the Coconut Custard filling (see note below). By the way, for a change-up, this cake is also good filled with XVOO Lemon Cream (page 233).

Cake:

360g	cake flour (12.7oz / about 3 cups + 3 T), plus extra for the pan
2 tsp	baking powder
½ tsp	baking soda
2.8g	Diamond Crystal kosher salt (1 tsp)
226g	unsalted butter (8oz), room temperature, plus extra for the pans
¼ cup	neutral oil, such as canola
400g	sugar (14.1oz / about 2 cups)
3	large eggs, room temperature
3	large egg yolks, room temperature
1 tsp	good-quality coconut extract
1 cup	unsweetened coconut milk (reserve any extra for the custard*)

Filling:

½ recipe	Coconut Custard (page 232)
80g	unsweetened flaked coconut (2.8oz / about 1 cup)
1 ½ cups + 2 T	milk*
4	large egg yolks

100g	sugar (3.5oz / about ½ cup)
0.7g	Diamond Crystal kosher salt (¼ tsp)
3 T	cornstarch
14g	unsalted butter (0.5oz), diced

Frosting:

1 recipe	Buttermilk "Ermine" Frosting (page 91)
50g	all-purpose flour (1.8oz / about 5¾ T)
1¼ cups	buttermilk
1¼ tsp	vanilla paste or pure vanilla extract
0.7g	Diamond Crystal kosher salt (¼ tsp)
285g	unsalted butter (10oz), room temperature
250g	sugar (8.8oz / about 1¼ cups)
2½ tsp	lemon zest
2 tsp	good-quality coconut extract

To start the cake, preheat the oven to 350°F. Butter the sides and bottoms of three 8-inch cake pans, line the bottoms with parchment paper, then butter and lightly flour the paper.

Sift the flour with baking powder, baking soda, and salt into a bowl. In a separate bowl, lightly beat the eggs with the yolks and vanilla.

In the bowl of a stand mixer, using the paddle attachment, cream the butter with the oil on high speed, about 3 minutes. Add the sugar and beat until the mixture is pale and fluffy, about 6 minutes. With the mixer still on high, add the egg mixture, a quarter at a time, scraping between each addition and adding the coconut extract with the last addition. Turn the mixer to low and add a third of the flour, mixing well, then drizzle in half the coconut milk. Repeat, alternating the flour mixture and coconut milk, scraping the bowl as you go, and ending with flour. (This process ensures even distribution and prevents overmixing.) Divide the batter evenly among the prepared pans. Smooth the batter on top and gently tap the pans on the counter to get rid of any air bubbles.

Bake the cakes until they are golden, springy, and beginning to pull away from the sides and a tester inserted in the center comes out clean, 25 to 30 minutes. Remove the cakes from the oven and set them aside to cool for 30 minutes, then remove them from the pans.

To make the coconut custard, follow the instructions on page 232.*

To make the frosting, follow the directions on page 91, but add 2 teaspoons coconut extract after you whip the base.

To assemble the cake, level the top of each cake using a serrated knife. Place one cake on a cake stand or cardboard round. Spread the cake with half of the coconut custard. Place a second cake on top and spread the remaining custard on it. Finish with the third cake. Using an offset spatula, begin frosting the sides. Fill your spatula with the buttermilk frosting and mound it on top of the cake. Smooth out the surface, then begin working your way around the sides of the cake, always in the same direction, refilling your spatula as you go and creating an evenly coated surface. Fill in any bare spots, smooth the sides, and smooth the top a final time. Garnish the cake with the reserved toasted coconut, patting it gently in an even layer around the sides and on the top. (For more about frosting cakes see page 83.) Slice and serve.

* The custard is delicious made with whole milk alone, but if I have extra coconut milk, I pour it into a measuring cup, top it off with milk, and proceed as described on page 232.

Devil's Food Cake with Earl Grey Cream

Makes one 9-inch 4-layer cake

This grownup chocolate cake is flavored with Earl Grey tea. I love the way the citrusy aroma, which comes from bergamot orange, pairs with chocolate (see notes). Although I am very fond of this combination, I think of the cream filling, the cake, and the frosting as separates and use them along with other fillings, cakes, and frostings in various combos defined by the occasion—so don't hesitate to mix and match. Be aware that the Earl Grey cream, like most cream fillings, must be chilled thoroughly before you can whip it.

Earl Grey cream:

102g	milk chocolate (3.6oz), chopped
2¼ cups	heavy cream
10g	loose Earl Grey tea (6 tea bags)

Cake:

286g	all-purpose flour (10oz / about 2 cups + 1½ tsp), plus extra for the pan
1½ tsp	baking soda
3 tsp	baking powder
10g	Diamond Crystal kosher salt (1 T)
172g	unsalted butter (6oz), room temperature, plus extra for the pans
342g	sugar (12oz / about 1½ cups + 3½ T)
2	eggs, room temperature

85g	natural (not Dutch-processed) unsweetened cocoa powder (3oz / about 1 cup)
1½ cups	buttermilk

Frosting:

1 recipe	Chocolate Buttercream (page 88)
228g	extra bitter chocolate (8oz), chopped
4	large egg whites
100g	sugar (3.5oz / about ½ cup)
1.5g	Diamond Crystal kosher salt (½ tsp)
226g	unsalted butter (8oz), room temperature

To start the Earl Grey cream, put the milk chocolate in a heatproof bowl. Combine the cream and tea in a saucepan and bring to a simmer over medium-high heat. Pour the hot flavored cream over the chocolate, let it sit until the chocolate begins to melt, about 1 minute, then whisk until the mixture is smooth. Set the mixture aside to steep for 30 minutes, then strain the cream through a fine sieve into a clean bowl. Cover the cream directly with plastic wrap (to prevent a skin from forming) and chill thoroughly, at least 8 hours and up to 24 hours.

To start the cake, preheat the oven to 350°F. Butter the bottoms and sides of two 9-inch cake pans, line them with parchment paper, then butter and lightly flour the paper.

Sift the flour with the baking soda, baking powder, and salt into a bowl. In the bowl of a stand mixer, using the paddle attachment, cream the butter with the sugar on medium-high speed until the mixture is light and fluffy, about 6 minutes, stopping periodically to scrape down the bowl.

(recipe continues)

With the mixer running, add the eggs one at a time, scraping the bowl after each addition. Turn off the mixer, scrape the bowl again, then add the cocoa powder. Mix on low until combined and scrape down again. Add a third of the flour mixture, mix on low until the flour is incorporated, then add ¾ cup of the buttermilk. Scrape the bowl and repeat, alternating dry ingredients and buttermilk, scraping in between, and ending with the flour mixture. (This process ensures even distribution and prevents overmixing.) Divide the batter evenly among the prepared pans and smooth the tops. Gently tap the pans on the counter to eliminate air bubbles.

Bake the cakes until they are springy, beginning to pull from the sides, and a cake tester inserted in the middle comes out clean, about 30 minutes. Cool the cakes in the pans for 30 minutes, then turn them out onto wire racks to cool completely.

To make the chocolate buttercream, follow the directions on page 88. To finish the Earl Grey cream, whip it until it is stiff.

To assemble the cake, trim the top of each layer with a serrated knife so it is level, then slice each cake in half horizontally to create 4 layers. Place the first layer on a cake stand or cardboard round. Spread the surface with a third of the Earl Grey cream. Place a second layer of cake on the first and spread it with another third of the cream. Repeat, topping it with the third cake and finishing with the remaining cream. Place the final layer on the cake, then, using an offset spatula, begin frosting the sides. Fill your spatula with buttercream and mound frosting on top of the cake. Smooth the surface, then begin working your way around the sides of the cake, always in the same direction, refilling your spatula as you go and creating an evenly coated surface. Fill in any bare spots, smooth the sides, then smooth the top a final time (For more about frosting cakes see page 83). Slice and serve.

Ginger-Stout Layer Cake
with Ermine Frosting

Makes one 8-inch 3-layer cake

I reworked my gingerbread recipe, published in *The Last Course*, and wound up with a delicious cake. I don't like too much frosting, so I'm happy with generously icing between the layers and then finishing the top, leaving the sides au naturel. If you feel as I do, a single recipe of Buttermilk "Ermine" Frosting will do the trick; if you like more, increase the recipe by half.

Cake:

1 cup	stout, such as Guinness
1 cup	molasses
1 T	freshly grated ginger
1 T	baking soda
	Cooking spray or unsalted butter, for the pans
3	large eggs, room temperature
100g	sugar (3.5oz / about ½ cup)
110g	dark brown sugar (3.9oz / about ½ cup)
¾ cup	neutral oil, such as canola
140g	all-purpose flour (4.9oz / about 1 cup), plus extra for the pans
1½ tsp	baking powder
2 T	ground ginger
¾ tsp	ground cinnamon
¼ tsp	ground cloves
⅛ tsp	ground cardamom
1.5g	Diamond Crystal kosher salt (½ tsp)

Frosting:

1 recipe	Buttermilk "Ermine" Frosting (page 91)
1¼ cups	buttermilk
1¼ tsp	vanilla paste or pure vanilla extract
0.7g	Diamond Crystal kosher salt (¼ tsp)
285g	unsalted butter (10oz), room temperature
250g	sugar (8.8oz / about 1¼ cups)
2½ tsp	lemon zest

To start the cake, preheat the oven to 350°F. Combine the stout and molasses in a large, deep saucepan that has plenty of room for the mixture to bubble up. Bring to a boil over medium-high heat. Pull the pan off the heat and whisk in the fresh ginger and then the baking soda. Set aside to cool.

Prepare three 8-inch cake pans by greasing each pan, lining the bottoms with parchment paper, then greasing and lightly flouring the paper. In the bowl of a stand mixer, use the whisk attachment to whip the eggs with the white and brown sugars on medium-high speed until they are combined. Drizzle in the oil, whisking to incorporate. In a separate bowl, whisk the flour with the baking powder, ground ginger, cinnamon, cloves, cardamom, and salt. Remove the bowl from the stand and stir the (cooled) stout mixture into the eggs and sugar. Stir the egg/stout mixture into the dry ingredients, a third at a time. Divide the batter evenly among the three pans.

Bake the cakes until they are springy, the edges begin to pull from the pan, and a cake tester inserted in the middle comes out clean, 25 to 30 minutes. Remove

the cakes from the oven and allow them to cool in the pans on a wire rack.

To make the frosting, follow the instructions on page 91.

To finish the cake, use a serrated knife to level the top of each cake. Place the first layer on a cake stand or cardboard round and spread the surface with frosting. Place a second layer of cake on top of the first and spread it with frosting; top with the remaining layer. Fill an offset spatula and mound frosting on top of the cake, then spread it in an even layer. Leave the sides bare. (For more about frosting cakes, see page 83.) Slice and serve.

White Cake with Plum Filling

Makes one 8-inch 2-layer cake

I start this classic white cake by "reverse creaming" the butter, a trick I learned from Rose Levy Beranbaum's classic cookbook, *The Cake Bible*. This method, which involves mixing diced butter into the dry ingredients, coats the flour with fat, thereby minimizing gluten formation. I add a little oil to my batter to further moisten the cake, which I find gives you a tender, finely crumbed cake. A pure white frosted cake is always stunning, but for a different effect, use a handheld torch to lightly brown the meringue frosting.

Cake:

8	large egg whites, room temperature
¾ cup	milk
1 T	vanilla paste or pure vanilla extract
511g	cake flour (18oz / about 4½ cups + 1½ tsp), plus extra for the pans
570g	sugar (20oz / about 2¾ cups + 1½ T)
4 tsp	baking powder
6g	Diamond Crystal kosher salt (2 tsp)
170g	unsalted butter (6oz), diced, room temperature, plus extra for the pans
⅓ cup	neutral oil, such as canola

Plum filling:

600g	plums (5.3oz), pitted and diced
300g	sugar (10.6oz / about 1½ cups)
1	vanilla bean
	Zest of 1 orange
1 T	yuzu juice (optional)

Frosting:

1 recipe	Italian Meringue (page 85)
208g	sugar (7.3oz / about 1 cup + 1½ tsp)
4¾ tsp	light corn syrup
4	large egg whites
½ tsp	cream of tartar

Preheat the oven to 350°F. Prepare three 8-inch cake pans by buttering them, covering the bottoms with parchment paper, and buttering and lightly flouring the paper. In a bowl, whisk together the egg whites, milk, and vanilla. In the bowl of a stand mixer, sift the flour with 570 grams (20 oz) sugar, baking powder, and salt.

Add the butter to the mixer bowl and, using the paddle attachment, mix on low speed until most of the butter has broken down, 2 to 3 minutes. Add the oil and mix until the mixture looks like coarse meal, 6 to 8 minutes. Add 4 of the egg whites (half) and beat on high for 90 seconds. Scrape down the bowl, then add the remaining 4 egg whites and beat on high for an-

other 30 seconds. Scrape down the bowl again, then beat for 30 seconds longer. Divide the batter evenly among the prepared pans. Smooth the tops, then gently tap the pans on the counter to eliminate large air bubbles.

Bake the cakes until they are golden, pulling away from the sides of the pans, and springy and a tester inserted in the center comes out clean, about 30 minutes. Cool the cakes for 30 minutes, then remove them from the pans and let them cool completely on wire racks.

To make the filling, combine the plums and 300 grams (10.6 oz) sugar in a glass bowl. Split the vanilla bean lengthwise and scrape the seeds into the plums. Stir in the zest. Set the plums aside to macerate at room temperature until they release their juices and the juice and sugar combine, at least 1 hour. Transfer the mixture to a saucepan and bring it to a boil over medium-high heat. Reduce the heat and simmer until the fruit breaks down and the jam reaches a temperature of 220°F on a candy thermometer. Strain the jam through a medium strainer. Stir in the yuzu juice (if using) and set aside to cool. Reserve 1 cup of jam for the filling; refrigerate any extra for another purpose.

Shortly before serving, make the Italian meringue as described on page 85.

To assemble the cake, use a serrated knife to level the top of each cake. Place a cake on a stand or cardboard round. Spread half of the filling on this first layer, top that with a second cake, then spread it with the remaining filling. Place the final layer on the cake and, using an offset spatula or a piping tip, begin frosting the sides of the cake. Fill your spatula (or piping bag) with meringue, mound it on top of the cake, and smooth the meringue. Work your way around the sides of the cake, always in the same direction, refilling your spatula as you go, and creating an evenly covered surface. Finish by going back around the sides to even them out and fill in any bare spots and smooth the top a final time. (For more about frosting cakes see page 83.) If you are so inclined, use a handheld kitchen torch to carefully brown the meringue. Slice and serve.

How to Frost a Cake

Back in the day, when bakers first started finishing cakes with a sweet top layer, the primary goal was to keep them fresh longer. Cooks mixed egg whites with sugar and made glazes they poured on their cakes before returning them to the oven to harden. The topping added sweet flavor, but more importantly, it "sealed" the cake, holding in moisture. "Frosting," which has become a catchall term for cake toppings in this country, started out as the name for a fluffy, creamy spread that didn't come into use until the twentieth century. Some bakers continue older traditions and "ice" cakes with fondant. I like to finish celebration cakes with meringue (see White Cake with Plum Filling, page 81) or a crown of whipped cream, unless it's for a birthday, then I almost always conclude with "frosting," usually a buttercream (for more on buttercream, see page 87).

Aesthetic considerations are of the utmost importance for most people when they frost a cake. For me, taste is paramount, but I do want my handiwork to look enticing. Practically speaking, this is how I get the sleek finish I prefer.

- I thoroughly cool my cake(s). You simply can't properly frost a warm cake. I let cake cool at least 2 hours, then I wrap it in plastic and hold it overnight in a cool place.
- I make sure my frosting is at room temperature.
- It is easiest to frost a cake on a rotating pedestal. Short of that, place the cake on a cake stand or put your cake on a cardboard round that measures a couple of inches bigger than the cake (so you can easily turn it) and elevate it as best you can. (Note: If I plan to ultimately move my cake, I always work on a cardboard round.)
- When I plan to transport my cake, I organize the equipment (the box or carrier). And I make sure the cardboard round fits inside.
- To keep things tidy, I line my serving stand or plate with parchment. I find that paper cut into strips beforehand are easy to remove at serving time.
- When I plan to divide a cake into layers, I use a serrated knife.
- Again using a serrated knife, I level my cakes by slicing off the rounded tops.
- When my prep is done, I put the first layer of cake on my stand or round and, with an offset spatula, spread frosting (or filling) over the surface. I carefully place the next layer on top and repeat, building the cake. I leave the top and sides clean.
- When I want things perfect, I put a layer of "primer" on the cake. I use milk or water to thin a little frosting, then spread an even layer around the sides—my goal is to seal any loose crumbs to the cake. Sometimes one layer of primer is enough; other times I need two. When I'm done, I chill the primed cake for at least 15 minutes.
- To finish, I mound un-thinned frosting on the top of the cake and spread it in an even layer. Next, I spread an even layer of frosting on the sides, turning the cake as I go, always moving around the sides in one direction and refilling my spatula to evenly coat the surface. I go back around the sides to smooth them, and then I smooth the top a final time. I remove the parchment strips underneath and the cake is ready to be served.

Italian Meringue (Frosting)

Makes about 4¾ cups

This recipe is one of a handful I consider most essential to my repertoire, because it is so versatile. When I want a truly white finish on a layer cake, this is what I choose. It is classic, elegant, airy, and gorgeous. I also use Italian meringue to finish pies, garnish custards, and to transform my Spumoni with Meringue and Caramelized Oranges (page 251) into a showstopper. My one word of warning: Be sure to add the hot syrup very slowly to the beating egg whites.

208g	sugar (7.3oz / about 1 cup + 1½ tsp)		4	large egg whites
4¾ tsp	light corn syrup		½ tsp	cream of tartar

Combine the sugar and corn syrup in a saucepan. Add ⅓ cup water and bring to a simmer over medium-high heat.

Meanwhile, put the egg whites in the bowl of a stand mixer. When the sugar mixture reaches 230°F on a candy thermometer, begin whipping the whites, with the whisk attachment, on high. When the sugar syrup reaches 248°F, remove the pan from the heat and begin very slowly streaming the sugar syrup into the egg whites as you continue whipping them. Beat the whites until they are shiny and stiff and the mixer bowl no longer feels warm, 5 to 10 minutes. I use meringue as soon as I make it.

Maple and White Chocolate Cream

Makes about 1¾ cups

This is not a buttercream but rather a delicious, flavored whipped cream I use to fill sweet buns, like the Maple Skiffs on page 56. It is also an excellent cake filling. Like most, this "cream" must be chilled before it is whipped, so I generally make it a day ahead.

½ cup + 2 T	heavy cream	60g	maple sugar (2.1oz / about ¼ cup)
½ cup + 2 T	crème fraîche	114g	white chocolate (4oz), chopped

To make the maple cream, combine the cream, crème fraîche, and maple sugar in a small saucepan and bring to a simmer over medium heat, stirring occasionally. Adjust the heat as necessary to maintain a simmer until the sugar dissolves. Meanwhile, put the chopped chocolate in a heatproof bowl that is large enough to hold the cream mixture. Pour the hot maple cream over the white chocolate, allow it to sit until the chocolate begins to melt, about 1 minute, then whisk until the mixture is smooth and homogeneous. Strain the cream through a fine sieve into a bowl. Cover the cream directly with plastic wrap (to prevent a skin from forming) and chill thoroughly, at least 6 hours. Shortly before using, whip the cream by hand or in a mixer until it holds stiff peaks.

The World of Buttercreams

"Buttercream" means something different to a professional pastry cook than it does to a novice baker. To me, the term signifies a family of cake frostings, not just one preparation or procedure. All feature an emulsification of butter and sugar, and most include eggs, either whites or yolks. When I want "buttercream," meaning a frosting full of rich buttery flavor, I generally make a Swiss buttercream. It is nicely white because it is made with egg whites, not yolks, it is relatively durable, even in hot weather, and it is the one buttercream with a cooked-egg base. (When I want a brighter white finish for a cake I frost with an Italian meringue; see page 85.) Although, in this book both of my buttercreams are Swiss buttercreams, over the years I have made various kinds. Each has advantages and disadvantages and is worth knowing about.

American buttercream is what you likely made as a kid. Butter is whipped until fluffy, and then confectioners' sugar, cream, and flavoring are added. It is easy, fluffy, and very sweet.

German buttercream begins with a custard that contains egg yolks and cornstarch. The custard is gradually added to beaten butter along with flavorings. Because it contains yolk, it is a little yellow. It is also thinner and softer than most other buttercreams.

French buttercream starts with *pâte à bombe* (sugar syrup drizzled into yolks as they are beaten). When the yolks thicken, butter is gradually incorporated. The yolks make this frosting a little yellow, but this, like the German buttercream, is a rich-tasting and delicious frosting.

Italian buttercream starts like a French buttercream, except that the base is an Italian meringue rather than a *pâte à bombe,* meaning here sugar syrup is drizzled into egg *whites* (not yolks) while beating. When the whites are stiff, butter is gradually added. This frosting is bright white. It is more stable than German or French buttercreams, less rich tasting than either, and, like the latter, can be tricky to make until you get the hang of it.

Swiss buttercream is my go-to. Egg whites are cooked with sugar, then whipped until firm and glossy, at which point butter is slowly added. See the recipes that follow for details.

Chocolate Buttercream

Makes about 5 cups

I start this frosting with a Swiss meringue—egg whites are whipped with sugar over a pot of simmering water until the sugar dissolves and the whites froth, at which point they are beaten off the heat. To keep dirty dishes to a minimum, I use the bowl from my mixer as the top of my makeshift double boiler.

456g	extra bitter chocolate (16oz), chopped		3g	Diamond Crystal kosher salt (1 tsp)
8	egg whites, room temperature		452g	unsalted butter (16oz), cut into a large dice, room temperature
200g	sugar (7oz / about 1 cup)			

Melt the chocolate in a heatproof bowl set over, but not touching, a pot of simmering water, stirring occasionally. Remove the chocolate from the heat and allow it to come to room temperature.

Combine the egg whites, sugar, and salt in the bowl of a stand mixer. Put the mixer bowl over the pot of simmering water (again, take care that the bowl doesn't touch the water). Whisk the mixture continuously until the sugar dissolves and the egg whites froth and whiten, about 6 minutes (the temperature will be about 150°F).

Replace the mixer bowl in the machine and, using the whisk attachment, whip the whites on medium-high until the outside of the bowl no longer feels warm and the whites are stiff and glossy, 5 to 10 minutes. Scrape down the bowl and switch to the paddle attachment.

With the mixer on high, add the butter, a piece or two at a time. When half of the butter has been incorporated, stop the mixer and scrape down the bowl, then resume mixing and add the remaining butter. (Expect that midway through, the mixture will look lumpy and broken, but continue gradually adding butter and the frosting will come together.) When all the butter has been added, turn off the mixer and scrape down the bowl.

Add the room-temperature melted chocolate. Mix on low, pausing to scrape the bowl as needed, then continue to mix in the chocolate. Use immediately or store in an airtight container at room temperature overnight, in the refrigerator for up to 5 days, or in the freezer for up to 3 months; always bring to room temperature and re-whip before using.

Vanilla Buttercream

Makes about 5 cups

Like Chocolate Buttercream (page 88), I begin this frosting by making a Swiss meringue. This is a creamy topping with a rich buttery flavor. Here again, I use my mixer bowl as the top of a double boiler to ease cleanup.

8	large egg whites, room temperature
200g	sugar (7oz / about 1 cup)
3g	Diamond Crystal kosher salt (1 tsp)
2 tsp	vanilla paste or pure vanilla extract
452g	unsalted butter (16oz), cut into a large dice, room temperature

Combine the egg whites, sugar, salt, and vanilla in the bowl of a stand mixer. Put the mixer bowl over a pot of simmering water (take care that the bowl doesn't touch the water). Whisk the mixture continuously until the sugar dissolves and the whites froth and whiten, about 6 minutes (the temperature will be about 150°F).

Place the bowl in the stand mixer and, using the whisk attachment, beat the whites on medium-high until the outside of the bowl no longer feels warm and the whites are stiff and glossy, 5 to 10 minutes. Scrape down the bowl and switch to the paddle attachment.

With the mixer on high, add the butter, a piece or two at a time. When half of the butter has been incorporated, stop the mixer and scrape down the bowl, then resume mixing and add the remaining butter. (Expect that halfway through, the mixture will look lumpy and broken. Continue gradually adding butter and the frosting will come together.) When all the butter has been added, turn off the mixer and scrape down the bowl. Use immediately or store in an airtight container at room temperature overnight, in the refrigerator for up to 5 days, or in the freezer for up to 3 months; always bring to room temperature and re-whip before using.

Buttermilk "Ermine" Frosting

I first tasted ermine frosting at my dear friend (and former business partner) Mary Maraz's house. Although she's not from the South, that is where you are most likely to find this cake topping. Made without eggs, ermine frosting is thickened with a base of milk cooked with flour. This base is whipped with butter and sugar to produce a frosting so airy and sumptuous that the comparison to silky white fur is not out of line. Because I like some tang, I use buttermilk in place of whole milk and add a little lemon zest.

50g	all-purpose flour (1.8oz / about 5¾ T)		285g	unsalted butter (10oz), room temperature
1¼ cups	buttermilk		250g	sugar (8.8oz / about 1¼ cups)
1¼ tsp	vanilla paste or pure vanilla extract		2½ tsp	lemon zest
0.7g	Diamond Crystal kosher salt (¼ tsp)			

Put the flour in a small saucepan, gradually whisk in the buttermilk, and cook over medium heat, whisking constantly, until the buttermilk thickens to the consistency of pudding, 5 to 10 minutes. Stir in the vanilla and salt. Transfer the buttermilk base to a bowl, place plastic wrap directly on the surface (to prevent a skin from forming), and set aside to cool.

Combine the butter with the sugar in the bowl of a stand mixer. Using the paddle attachment on medium speed, cream the butter with the sugar. Add the lemon zest, switch to the whisk attachment, and whip in the buttermilk base a little at a time, scraping down the bowl from time to time. Use immediately or store in an airtight container in the refrigerator for up to 3 days. Bring to room temperature and re-whip before using.

CHAPTER 3

Cookies

Seeking Deliciousness

I find cookies all but irresistible, and for me, their compact size is a big part of the appeal. Just a few bites deliver assertive flavor and engaging texture. Because they are small, they can deftly handle more intensity than would work in a larger dessert. That suits me fine. It is not hard to make a good cookie, however, in my experience, it is quite difficult to make a sublime one. I don't mean fancy; I mean a cookie that possesses what I think of as the essence of deliciousness—one that tastes special and satisfying and balanced all at once. Sugar plays a critical role in this, not just as a sweetener but also as a structural component.

Sugar, also known as granulated, table, or white sugar, was once exclusively made by processing sugarcane. Today, this sweetener is also made from sugar beets. In addition to white sugar, I use several other types. Brown sugar is white sugar recombined with molasses (which is typically extracted during processing)—more molasses for dark brown sugar, less for light brown. Confectioners' sugar, also known as 10X, powdered, or icing sugar, is finely ground sugar mixed with cornstarch. Turbinado and Demerara are less refined cane (not beet) sugars that retain some molasses. I use these mainly as finishing sugars.

I don't think of sugar as having a particularly strong flavor. It is sweet, of course, which makes it an ingredient that changes the overall taste of a dish, but it is otherwise neutral to me—unless it is overused. Honey, by contrast, has a powerfully distinctive flavor, so I use it infrequently. Maple sugar is also flavorful, but I am more drawn to the taste.

Sugars are not only flavorings but forces in the chemistry of cooking. Sugar helps with leavening, browning, and the creation of crunch and a tender crumb comes from sugar bonding with water to lock in moisture. Broadly speaking, it is the interplay between sugar and flour, fat, and liquid (transformed by heat) that determines whether a cookie will be crispy (like Pizzelles, page 109), cakey (like Molasses Ginger Cookies, page 124), or crumbly (like Maple Shortbread, page 123). In my baking, I try to manage my desire to sweeten in a way that permits other ingredients to shine. It is easy to be tempted away from the correct balance, but the secret to a truly delicious bite is approaching the bound without crossing it. That's how to get what I think of as a sweet-kitchen version of umami—my goal with all the cookies in this book.

I begin this chapter with choices inspired by European cookies, followed by those with roots in American favorites—I've organized things this way, because this is how I think of them. My experiments have left me confident that I have a measure of sugar in each that enhances the flavors and creates a harmony of taste.

Finally, most cookies are best freshly baked. Happily, many doughs keep well (sugar helps with that, too), so I roll excess dough into logs to keep "on ice." I either refrigerate rolled dough for a day or freeze it for up to a month. Getting into the nitty-gritty, once the dough is made, I form it into a cylinder (the diameter determined by how big I want my cookies) and wrap it in parchment paper. It is important that the log is uniform and best, for storage, to eliminate as much air as possible. I do this by beginning to wrap the parchment snugly, then I tighten the wrap by pressing the cylinder against my bench scraper as I roll to make the log as compact as I can get it. If I plan to bake my cookies within a day, I simply fold up the edges of the paper and refrigerate the dough. If, instead, the dough is destined for the freezer, I label the parchment, then wrap the cylinder in plastic.

Cooking Sugar

Sugar dissolves in water. At room temperature, 67 grams (almost ⅓ cup) of sugar will dissolve into ⅛ cup of water. If you add more sugar, it will not dissolve. Somewhere along the line, someone realized that you can dissolve more sugar when you add heat. The resulting syrup becomes supersaturated, meaning, among other things, that when it cools, it will no longer be granular and it will be either more or less solid, depending on the temperature it was brought to. This is the secret to fudge, jelly, and lollipops. It's magical but not as easy as it sounds. Unfortunately, sugar (aka sucrose) is unstable when heated and inclined to crystallize. Crystals make preserves grainy and candy taste sandy. How to prevent unwanted crystals from forming? Avoid stirring sugar as it heats and, when possible, add either an acid—lemon juice or cream of tartar—or a non-sucrose sugar such as corn syrup. Below is a summary of what happens to sugar at an ascending scale of cooking temperatures, along with the corresponding old-fashioned "water tests" that generations relied on to make preserves and candy. I find all of this interesting generally and useful specifically when I am making the Grapefruit and Poppy Seed Rugelach (page 101), Raspberry and Cranberry Linzer Cookies (page 105), and Toffee (page 113) in this chapter and the semifreddos and candied fruit and preserves later in the book. Although I've included the traditional tests, be assured that I check the temperature with a candy thermometer.

Thread Stage

230°F to 235°F

Sugar concentration: 80%

Water test: Drop melted sugar syrup into cold water and a semi-liquid thread will form.

Applications: Syrups and preserves

Soft-Ball Stage

235°F to 240°F

Sugar concentration: 85%

Water test: Dropped into cold water, the syrup will form a soft malleable ball that can easily be flattened.

Applications: Fondant, fudge, and praline

Firm-Ball Stage

245°F to 250°F

Sugar concentration: 87%

Water test: Drop syrup in cold water and it will form a firm ball that will retain its shape when removed from the water unless it's squeezed.

Application: Italian meringue

Hard-Ball Stage

250°F to 265°F

Sugar concentration: 92%

Water test: Syrup will form thick, "ropy" threads as it drips from the spoon, then form a ball when dropped into the water; the ball will be too hard to flatten.

Application: Soft candy

Soft-Crack Stage

270°F to 290°F

Sugar concentration: 95%

Water test: Drop molten syrup into cold water and it forms solid threads that will bend a little before snapping.

Application: Toffee

Hard-Crack Stage

300°F to 310°F

Sugar concentration: 99%

Water test: Drop molten syrup into cold water and it will form brittle threads.

Applications: Brittles, hard candy, and lollipops

Keep going and you will be on your way to creating caramelized sugar (the brown liquid stage—338°F), which I use in my Kumquat Tatin (page 163).

Fig Bars

Makes about 32 cookies

These cookies owe a debt of inspiration to Fig Newtons' British predecessor, fig rolls. I like to add apple to my filling. The applesauce recipe below yields a little more than you need here, which is not a problem for me because I like to have applesauce in the fridge—if you feel the same, you might even want to make a double batch.

Dough:	
150g	all-purpose flour (5.3oz / about 1 cup + 1 T)
75g	whole-wheat flour (2.6oz / about ½ cup)
56g	light brown sugar (2oz / about ¼ cup)
Rounded ½ tsp	baking soda
⅛ tsp	ground cinnamon
1 tsp	orange zest
0.7g	Diamond Crystal kosher salt (¼ tsp)
140g	unsalted butter (5oz), chilled and diced
1 T	honey
1 T	milk
3	large egg yolks

Applesauce:	
1	medium tart apple, peeled and diced
	Strip of orange peel

Fig jam:	
32g	walnuts (1.1oz / about 4½ T)
225g	dried Black Mission figs (7.9oz / about 1½ cups), stemmed and halved
	Peel of a ¼ orange, pith removed
½-inch	cinnamon stick
½	vanilla bean
1¼ T	honey
¾ cup	fruity red wine, such as merlot
1¼ T	orange juice
1	large egg, beaten, for egg wash

To start the dough, combine the all-purpose and whole-wheat flours in a food processor. Add the brown sugar, baking soda, cinnamon, orange zest, and salt and pulse to mix. Add the butter and process until the dough resembles coarse meal. In a measuring cup, mix the honey with the milk and egg yolks. Stream the honey mixture into the machine, processing just until the dough is homogeneous. Turn the dough out onto a lightly floured surface and gather it into a rectangle. Wrap it in plastic, flatten it so it is about an inch thick, and chill it thoroughly, at least 30 minutes.

To make the applesauce, combine the apple and orange peel in a small saucepan. Add ¼ cup water, cover, and simmer over medium-low heat until the apple is very soft, about 20 minutes. Remove the lid, mash the apple with a fork, then simmer, adjusting the heat if necessary, until the water evaporates, about 10 minutes longer. Allow it to cool, remove the orange peel, and puree the applesauce in a food processor.

To start the fig jam, preheat the oven to 325°F. Roast the walnuts in a small ovenproof skillet until they smell toasty, about 12 minutes. Remove the walnuts from the oven and set them aside to cool.

Put the figs in a small saucepan with the orange peel and cinnamon stick. Split the vanilla bean lengthwise and scrape the seeds into the pan. Add the vanilla pod and the honey, wine, and just enough water to cover the figs. Bring the fig jam to a boil over medium-high heat, then reduce the heat to low, cover the pan, and simmer the figs until they are soft, about 20 minutes. Remove the lid, mash the figs with a fork, then simmer the jam, adjusting the heat as necessary, until the liquid has reduced and concentrated to a syrup, about 20 minutes. Let the jam cool to room temperature, then remove the orange peel, cinnamon stick, and vanilla pod. Put the fig jam in a food processor.

Process the fig jam with 1 tablespoon of the orange juice and 2½ tablespoons of the applesauce. Add the toasted walnuts and process until they are finely ground.

To make the cookies, preheat the oven to 350°F and line a baking sheet with parchment paper. Roll out the dough between two pieces of parchment into a 12 × 16-inch rectangle. Arrange the dough so the long edges are at the top and bottom. Trim the dough to even it, then cut it crosswise into four strips, each about 3 × 16 inches. Working with one strip at a time, pipe a ribbon of filling along the center. Brush the bottom edge with the egg wash and, starting at the opposite long edge, roll the dough from the top to the bottom around the filling, forming a tight log. Press to seal the seam and place the log on the prepared baking sheet, seam-side down. Continue rolling and filling the remaining dough. Brush the rolled logs with beaten egg.

Bake the logs for 7 minutes, then rotate the pan front to back and continue baking until the pastry feels firm and looks nicely browned, about 8 minutes more. Immediately, cut each log into 2-inch-thick cookies. Transfer the cookies to a wire rack to cool, then serve.

Grapefruit and Poppy Seed Rugelach

Makes about 32 cookies

While I stick close to tradition and use a cream cheese dough for my version of this eastern European treat, I followed a whim and filled these rugelach with a homemade grapefruit conserve. It is delicious, so I highly recommend it, but store-bought marmalade will also work.

Filling:

¾ cup	Grapefruit Conserve (page 279)
2	small to medium pink grapefruits, peeled
About 200g	sugar (7oz / about 1 cup)
1 tsp	freshly squeezed lemon juice
½ cup	minced Candied Grapefruit Rinds (page 277)
70g	**poppy seeds (2.5oz / about ½ cup), ground (a clean coffee grinder works for this)**

Rugelach dough:

1 recipe	Cream Cheese Dough (page 174)
140g	all-purpose flour (4.9oz / about 1 cup)
0.7g	Diamond Crystal kosher salt (¼ tsp)
114g	unsalted butter (4oz), chilled and diced
114g	cream cheese (4oz / about ½ cup)
1	**large egg, lightly beaten**
About 12g	**crystallized sugar, such as turbinado, Demerara, or Sugar In The Raw (0.4oz / 2½ tsp)**

To start the filling, make the conserve according to the instructions on page 279. Measure out ¾ cup and refrigerate the rest for another use.

To make the rugelach, prepare the dough according to the instructions on page 174. Preheat the oven to 350°F and line a baking sheet with parchment paper. Roll out half of the dough on a lightly floured surface into a round about ⅛ inch thick. Spread the dough with half of the conserve and top with half of the ground poppy seeds. Cut the dough into 16 wedges—like a pizza (see facing page). Starting at the wider base, roll each dough triangle toward the point, forming a little spiraled crescent. Arrange the rugelach about 1½ inches apart on the prepared baking sheet. Repeat with the remaining dough, rolling and forming 15 additional rugelach. Brush all the rugelach with beaten egg and sprinkle with crystallized sugar.

Bake the rugelach for 10 minutes, then rotate the pan front to back and continue baking until the pastry is golden brown, about 10 minutes more. Transfer the rugelach to a wire rack to cool, then serve.

Crisps

Makes about 24 cookies

I tend to make these sweet crispy cookies, my version of French *palmiers*, when I have leftover Rough Puff Pastry, but they are so tasty that making a batch of dough with these in mind would be effort well spent. To make savory cheese crisps, simply brush the rolled dough with a little water and top it with a mix of grated Cheddar and Parmigiano (instead of the sugar), then finish with more cheese.

½ recipe	Rough Puff Pastry (page 179), or 245g store-bought puff pastry, thawed if frozen	63g	sugar (2.2oz / about ¼ cup + 1 T), plus extra for finishing
114g	all-purpose flour (4oz / about ¾ cup)	½ tsp	ground cinnamon (optional)
2.3g	Diamond Crystal kosher salt (¾ tsp)		
114g	unsalted butter (4oz)		

To start the crisps, prepare the puff pastry according to the instructions on page 179. Put the sugar in a small bowl and stir in the cinnamon, if using.

Roll the dough between two pieces of parchment paper into a 10 × 12-inch rectangle about ⅛ inch thick. Carefully lift the top piece of parchment and spread half of the sugar (with or without cinnamon) over the dough. Replace the parchment and slide the dough onto a baking sheet. Chill the dough until it is firm, about 15 minutes. Carefully turn the dough over (so the sugared side is now on the bottom), lift the parchment, and cover the dough with the remaining sugar. Replace the parchment, then, using a rolling pin, press the sugar into the dough; return it to the refrigerator for at least 15 minutes.

To form the crisps, remove the top piece of parchment. Arrange the rectangle so the long sides are at the top and bottom. Using your hands, roll the dough up from the bottom into a tight spiral, stopping in the middle of the sheet of dough. Turn the dough around and roll the other half of the dough to meet the spiral in the center (to me, the rolls look like the curls on an English barrister's wig). Press the spiraled dough gently with the rolling pin, then chill the dough until it is firm, at least 1 hour.

Preheat the oven to 375°F and line a baking sheet with parchment paper. Slice the dough crosswise into cookies about ½ inch thick. Dip each in sugar (I prefer to finish the cookies with plain sugar). Arrange the crisps on the prepared baking sheet, and bake for 10 minutes. Rotate the pan front to back and continue baking until the crisps are golden brown, about 10 minutes more. Transfer the crisps to a wire rack to cool, then serve.

Pecan Olive Shortbread

Makes about 40 cookies

These cookies, my version of a Provençal snack that walks the line between savory and sweet, are good with an aperitif or a dessert wine. My one caution: Make sure your pecans are fresh and your cured olives tasty— bottled olives won't work here. These cookies freeze well. I keep a log in the freezer and slice to bake as needed.

60g	pecan pieces (2.1oz / about ½ cup)
140g	all-purpose flour (4.9oz / about 1 cup)
0.7g	Diamond Crystal kosher salt (¼ tsp)
½ tsp	baking powder
114g	unsalted butter (4oz), room temperature
40g	confectioners' sugar (1.4oz / about 5 T)
1 T	extra-virgin olive oil
24	pitted oil-cured black olives (about 50g), chopped

Preheat the oven to 325°F and line a baking sheet with parchment paper. Roast the pecan pieces in a small ovenproof skillet until they smell toasty, about 12 minutes. Remove the pecans from the oven (do not turn off the oven), allow them to cool, then put them in a food processor. Add 40 grams (1.4 ounces) of the flour and finely grind the mixture. Add the remaining 100 grams (3.5 ounces) flour, the salt, and baking powder and pulse to mix. In the bowl of a stand mixer and using the paddle attachment, cream the butter with the sugar on medium-high. With the mixer on low, drizzle in the olive oil. Add half of the flour and mix. Scrape the bowl and mix in the remaining flour, then the olives.

Turn the dough out onto a piece of parchment. Form 2 logs, each about 1½ inches thick, rolling and then shaping and wrapping the dough in the parchment. Chill the dough until it is firm, at least 30 minutes. (For more on rolling and storing dough, see page 95.)

Slice the number of cookies you want ¼ inch thick and arrange them on the prepared baking sheet (return the dough to the refrigerator or freeze it for later). Working in batches if necessary, bake the cookies for 7 minutes (at 325°F), then rotate the pan front to back and continue baking until the cookies are firm and lightly browned, about 8 minutes more. Transfer the cookies to a rack to cool, then serve.

Pignoli Cookies

Makes about 12 cookies

These traditional Italian cookies are quick and easy and sensational when freshly made. I add a little lemon zest to my dough to perk up the flavors.

2	large egg whites
200g	sugar (7oz / about 1 cup)
200g	almond flour (7oz / about 2 cups)
	Zest of 1 lemon

0.7g	Diamond Crystal kosher salt (¼ tsp)
About 226g	pine nuts (8oz / about 1½ cups)
	Confectioners' sugar, for dusting

Preheat the oven to 350°F and line a baking sheet with parchment paper. In the bowl of a stand mixer, use the whisk attachment on medium-high to whip the egg whites until they are foamy. Continue whipping and gradually add the sugar, then keep going until the whites are stiff (be forewarned that the sugar will not fully dissolve). In another bowl, mix the almond flour with the zest and salt. Gently fold the flour mixture into the whites.

Put the pine nuts in a bowl. Using a 1-ounce scoop (or a heaping tablespoon), drop small balls of dough into the pine nuts. Turn the cookies to coat them evenly, then arrange them about 1½ inches apart on the prepared baking sheet.

Bake the cookies for 5 minutes, rotate the pan front to back, and continue baking until they are firm and color slightly. Cool the cookies on a wire rack. Dust them with confectioners' sugar before serving.

Raspberry and Cranberry Linzer Cookies

Makes about 12 cookies

I like the filling of these cookies to be shiny and gemlike, so I strain the preserves. But the truth is, the preserves are so good unstrained that I sometimes make a big batch and keep half as is to eat on toast. This dough also makes delicious chocolate ganache–filled cookies and unfilled almond and hazelnut cookies—see the Variations below.

Filling:

100g	fresh or frozen raspberries (3.5oz / about ¾ cup)
50g	fresh or frozen cranberries (1.7oz / about ½ cup)
150g	sugar (5.3oz / about ¾ cup)
	Zest of ½ orange

Cookies:

60g	almonds (2.1oz / about ¾ cup)
50g	hazelnuts (1.8oz / about 6½ T)
280g	all-purpose flour (9.9oz / about 2 cups)
3g	Diamond Crystal kosher salt (1 tsp)
2 tsp	ground cinnamon
90g	confectioners' sugar (3.2oz / about ¾ cup), plus extra for dusting
228g	unsalted butter (8oz), room temperature
2 tsp	vanilla paste or pure vanilla extract

To make the filling, combine the raspberries, cranberries, sugar, and zest in a bowl. Mix to distribute the sugar and set the berries aside to macerate at room temperature for 1 hour. Transfer the mixture to a saucepan and bring it to a rapid simmer over medium-high heat, then reduce the heat so the mixture just simmers. Cook, stirring occasionally, until the preserves reach a temperature of 220°F on a candy thermometer, 15 to 20 minutes. Press the preserves through a fine sieve into a bowl, discard the seeds, then cover the bowl with plastic wrap and chill the jelly thoroughly, at least 1 hour.

To start the cookies, preheat the oven to 325°F and roast the almonds and hazelnuts in an ovenproof skillet until they smell toasty, about 12 minutes. Remove the nuts from the oven and set them aside to cool.

In a food processor, combine the nuts and the flour and process until the mixture is finely ground. Add the salt and cinnamon and pulse to mix. In the bowl of a stand mixer and using the paddle attachment, cream the confectioners' sugar with the butter on medium-high speed. Add the vanilla, turn the mixer to low, and add the flour mixture. Mix until the dough is homogeneous, scraping the bowl as necessary. Form the dough into a disk, wrap it in plastic, and chill it until it is firm, about 30 minutes.

To bake the cookies, preheat the oven to 325°F and line a baking sheet with parchment paper. Roll out the dough between two pieces of lightly floured parchment—this dough is a little sticky and you want it nice and thin for sandwich cookies—about ⅛ inch thick. Be sure to loosen the dough from the paper

from time to time, adding a little more flour if necessary. Cut out cookies: hearts, rounds, or squares. I like to use a cutter that is 2 inches across. Arrange the cookies in a single layer on the prepared baking sheet. Dock the dough with a fork and chill in the refrigerator for at least 15 minutes. Using a ¾-inch cutter, punch out the centers of half the cookies; these will be the tops. (I bake the cute little cookie "holes," cool them, then serve them dusted with confectioners' sugar).

Bake all the cookies for 6 minutes, then rotate the pan front to back and continue baking until the bottoms and edges are lightly browned, about 6 minutes more. Let the cookies cool completely on the baking sheet, then dust the top halves—the cookies with the holes—with confectioners' sugar.

Heat the jelly in a small pan over low heat (or warm it in the microwave) just until it "loosens" (this makes the jelly extra shiny when it sets). Spoon a little jelly onto each base—the uncut, un-sugared cookies. Let the jelly set for about 5 minutes, then, using an offset spatula, gently top with the other cookies, sugared-sides up. Let the jelly set completely before serving.

Variation 1: To make Chocolate-Filled Hazelnut Almond Cookies, roll, cut, and bake the dough as described above. While the cookies cool, make a ganache (see page 110): Chop 57 grams (2 ounces) chocolate and put it in a bowl. Bring ½ cup heavy cream to a simmer over medium-high heat, pour the cream over the chocolate, and let it sit for 1 minute, then whisk until the mixture is smooth and emulsified. Allow the ganache to cool enough so it thickens and is the consistency of frosting. Pipe (or spoon) quarter-size dollops of ganache onto half the cookies (these will be the bottoms). Carefully lift the cut cookies onto the chocolate (I use an offset spatula). Set the cookies aside to allow the chocolate to set. Serve at room temperature.

Variation 2: To make Hazelnut Almond Cookies, prepare the dough as above but roll it out to ¼-inch thickness for these unfilled cookies. Cut the cookies into the desired shapes. Chill and bake them as described above. Cool then serve dusted with confectioners' sugar, if desired.

Pizzelles

Makes about 25 cookies

Every holiday, my grandmother Anna DiMarco made what seemed like hundreds of these crisp cookies. She used an old-fashioned stovetop pizzelle iron. I have an electric iron (not at all hard to find). You can play with the flavoring; my aunts liked Cointreau and anise. I like pizzelles every which way, but my absolute favorite, then and now, is to use a couple of pizzelles to make the best ice cream sandwich ever.

230g	all-purpose flour (8.1oz / about 1⅔ cups)	150g	sugar (5.3oz / about ¾ cup)
1½ tsp	baking powder	1½ tsp	vanilla paste or pure vanilla extract
0.7g	Diamond Crystal kosher salt (¼ tsp)	114g	unsalted butter (4oz), melted and cooled
3	large eggs		Cooking spray

Heat a pizzelle iron. Sift the flour with the baking powder and salt into a bowl. In another bowl, beat the eggs with the sugar and vanilla, then whisk in the melted butter. Using a wooden spoon, mix the wet ingredients into the flour to form a stiff batter.

Spray the pizzelle iron with cooking spray (you only need to do this before the first cookie). Spoon a teaspoonful of the batter onto the heated iron (I use a dinner spoon, not a measuring spoon, and mist it with cooking spray so it is easier to get the batter off). Lower the top and cook the pizzelle until it is golden, about 45 seconds. Remove the pizzelle and repeat, wiping off the iron if it begins to look greasy. (Expect to sacrifice the first couple of pizzelles; as when cooking pancakes, it takes a minute to get the temperature and cooking surface just right.) Cool the pizzelles on a rack, then serve. Stored in an airtight container, pizzelles will keep for up to a week.

Melted Chocolate: Ganache and Tempered Chocolate

Melted chocolate is a pastry kitchen workhorse, though at times a temperamental one. I use two classic techniques in this book to make chocolate sauces and glazes. The easier of them is ganache. It is what I use in the recipe for the Chocolate Doughnuts with Espresso Glaze (page 51) and in a variation of the linzer cookies on page 105. To make ganache, put finely chopped chocolate in a heatproof bowl. Bring heavy cream to a simmer, then pour it over the chocolate. I usually let the two sit together until the chocolate begins to melt, about 1 minute, then whisk until smooth. I always cover the ganache directly with plastic (to prevent a skin from forming) and set it aside to cool until it is the consistency of heavy cream (this happens when it is about 85°F); expect this to take up to an hour. The ganache will remain liquid for another hour or so and then will solidify. Once solid, ganache can be brought back to the desired consistency by reheating it in a bain-marie (a bowl over a pot of simmering water). As is evident in the doughnut recipe, sometimes I add other flavors. Ganache is chocolaty and delicious; it does not, however, have the luster and clean-breakable texture of tempered chocolate.

When I want a shiny, snappable finish, I temper my chocolate. That is what is required for Dad's Favorite Cookie (page 118) and chocolate-covered Toffee (page 113). I'll be frank: Tempering can be tricky. It entails melting chocolate so the molecules shift to produce a glossy, crisply solid coating. The recipe below is my method. I start with couverture chocolate—chocolate that is ground more finely during production and contains a higher percentage of cocoa butter (31% to 38%). It has a superior flavor and texture after tempering.

I usually work by observation and feel, but if you are new to tempering, definitely use an instant-read thermometer. Be aware that it is easier to temper large batches of chocolate. The quantity in the following recipe is as small as you can safely go. You can, however, reuse the leftovers to make ganache, or you can re-temper the chocolate. Finally, keep in mind that tempering doesn't affect the taste of chocolate, so if your first efforts aren't perfect, don't despair. Have some chopped nuts handy to prettily disguise any near misses.

Tempered Chocolate Glaze

Makes about 2 cups

500g **extra bitter couverture chocolate (17.6oz), finely chopped**

Melt 300 grams (10.6 ounces) of the chopped chocolate in a small metal bowl and set it over a pot of steaming water (make sure the bowl isn't in direct contact with the water). Let the chocolate melt completely and reach a temperature of 115°F. Remove the bowl from the heat, wiping the bottom with a kitchen towel to remove condensation.

Using a spatula, stir in the remaining 200 grams (7 ounces) chocolate. Continue stirring until the temperature falls to 85°F—be patient, this can take a few minutes. At this point, a bit of chocolate touched to your lower lip on the end of a knife will feel neutral, neither warm nor cool. Also, a smear on the side of the bowl will hold a defined line and lose only a little gloss as it dries. The chocolate is now ready to use. Work quickly to glaze your cookies or confections, then put them aside to set in a cool place. The ideal temperature for setting chocolate is between 65°F and 70°F; on a hot summer day, it may be necessary to put chocolate-glazed confections in the refrigerator briefly—for 5 minutes—to bring down the temperature.

To save leftover tempered chocolate, pour it onto a piece of parchment paper. Let it cool—in the winter, room temperature is fine, but on warm days, put it in the refrigerator until it is solid. Chop the chocolate and keep it in an airtight container at room temperature.

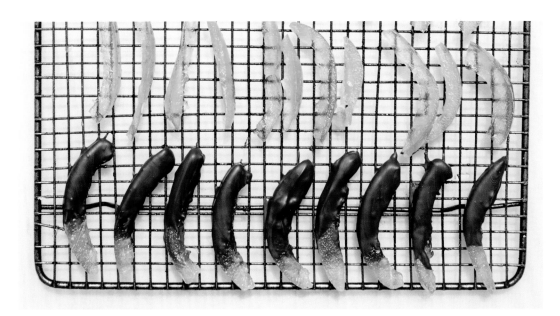

Toffee

Toffee is more a candy than a cookie, but it lives on the same shelf at my house. It is made by heating butter and sugar together to a high temperature—just short of the hard-crack stage (see page 96 for more about cooking sugar). I top toffee with tempered chocolate and then usually garnish it with crushed peppermint sticks, pretzel bits, or chopped nuts—depending on what I have at hand and feel in the mood for.

450g	unsalted butter (15.9oz), sliced
450g	sugar (15.9oz / about 2¼ cups)
3g	Diamond Crystal kosher salt (1 tsp)
3½ tsp	vanilla paste or pure vanilla extract
About 1 cup	Tempered Chocolate Glaze (page 111)
500g	extra bitter couverture chocolate (17.6oz), finely chopped
About 1 cup	chopped nuts, pretzels, or peppermint, for garnish (optional)

Line a 13 × 18-inch jelly-roll pan (sided baking sheet) with parchment paper. In a deep saucepan, melt the butter over medium heat. Add 6 tablespoons water and the sugar. Raise the heat to medium-high and, stirring constantly, bring the toffee to a boil. Continue stirring, adjusting the temperature if necessary to prevent the mixture from boiling over, and cook until the temperature of the toffee reaches 295°F; the toffee will be pale gold. Remove the pan from the heat and carefully stir in the salt and vanilla. When they are incorporated, immediately and carefully pour the toffee onto the prepared pan. Working quickly, spread the toffee out to the desired thickness with an offset spatula—I like mine thin.

Cool the toffee at room temperature until it is hard, at least 1 hour. Pour a thin layer of tempered chocolate over the toffee and spread it thinly and evenly with an offset spatula. Garnish, if desired, then let the chocolate cool completely and harden. To serve, crack the toffee into pieces by whacking it with the back of a knife.

Almond and Walnut Brownies

Makes 8 midsize or 16 small brownies

Is there an ultimate brownie? I don't think so. My current favorite version happens to be gluten-free. I use almond flour instead of wheat, the typical binder. These need time to settle because nut flour melds with fat and moisture a bit more gradually, so I let them rest at least 8 hours before serving—it's worth the wait.

114g	unsalted butter (4oz), diced, plus extra for the pan
114g	unsweetened chocolate (4oz), chopped
350g	sugar (12.3oz / about 1¾ cups)
3g	Diamond Crystal kosher salt (1 tsp)
4	large eggs
1 tsp	vanilla paste or pure vanilla extract
114g	almond flour (4oz / about 1 cup + 2½ T), plus extra for the pan
½ tsp	baking powder
100g	walnuts (3.5oz / about ¾ cup), chopped

Preheat the oven to 325°F. Butter an 8-inch square baking pan, line it with parchment paper, then butter and lightly dust the paper with almond flour. Put the diced butter in a heatproof bowl. Add the chocolate and set the bowl over a saucepan of gently simmering water to melt (take care that the bottom of the bowl doesn't touch the water). Stir the chocolate with the butter so they blend. When the mixture is smooth, take it off the heat and allow it to cool slightly.

In the bowl of a stand mixer fitted with the paddle attachment, combine the sugar, salt, and eggs. Add the vanilla and beat on medium speed until the mixture is pale and thickens, about 3 minutes. Remove the bowl from the mixer and stir in the melted chocolate mixture. Mix thoroughly. Put the flour and baking powder in a fine sieve and sift them into the batter. Stir to combine, then fold in the walnuts.

Spoon the batter evenly into the prepared pan and smooth the top. Bake the brownies for 25 minutes, the rotate the pan front to back and continue baking until the brownies are firm and the edges darken and begin to pull from the sides, about 25 minutes more. Allow the brownies to cool, then let them settle for at least 8 hours before cutting and serving.

Food Truck Chocolate Chip Cookies

Makes about 34 cookies

Chocolate chip cookies are so good, so seemingly simple, and so familiar that you'd think this recipe would be a toss off. Quite the opposite is true. I made many versions until I got a cookie I felt comfortable enough with to serve at the North Fork Table food truck. Then I went through the process again at home, making sure that my oven yielded a bake as tasty as those we produced for the truck. Like most chocolate chip cookies, these are best the day they are made, so bake what you need, then roll the rest of the dough into logs (see page 95) for another day.

140g	all-purpose flour (4.9oz / about 1 cup)
140g	bread flour (4.9oz / about 1 cup)
10g	Diamond Crystal kosher salt (1 T)
1 tsp	baking soda
285g	extra bitter chocolate (10oz), chopped

228g	unsalted butter (8oz), room temperature
175g	sugar (6.1oz / about ¾ cup + 2 T)
125g	light brown sugar (4.4oz / about ½ cup)
2	large eggs, room temperature
1 T	vanilla paste or pure vanilla extract

Put the all-purpose and bread flours, salt, and baking soda in a large bowl and whisk to combine. Add the chopped chocolate and mix well. In the bowl of a stand mixer, use the paddle attachment to cream the butter with the white and brown sugars on medium-high, scraping down the bowl as you go. Mix the eggs with the vanilla in a measuring cup. With the mixer running, add half the eggs, stop and scrape down the bowl, then add the remaining eggs. Scrape the bowl again. Reduce the mixer speed to low, add the dry ingredients, and mix until the dough is homogeneous.

Cover the bowl with plastic and chill until the dough is firm, at least 1 hour.

Preheat the oven to 375°F and line a baking sheet with parchment paper. Drop heaping teaspoonfuls of batter (just the number you want in the short term) onto the prepared baking sheet. Bake the cookies for 6 minutes, then rotate the pan front to back and continue cooking until the cookies are nicely browned and smell done, about 6 minutes more. Transfer the cookies to a wire rack to cool, then serve.

Dad's Favorite Cookie

Makes 40 cookies

These cookies were inspired by Mallomars, a cookie my father loved. I started making my own—the graham-cracker cookie base, the marshmallow, and the tempered chocolate glaze—at my husband Gerry's restaurant Amuse, then I continued to serve them at the North Fork Table. Be warned this is a technical recipe that is significantly harder to get right in hot weather, so I suggest you consider these cookies a cool weather treat—after all, that's what Nabisco does; they only sell them from September to March.

Graham crackers:

58g	whole-wheat flour (2oz / about 6 T)
119g	all-purpose flour (4.2g / about ¾ cup + 2 T)
1.5g	Diamond Crystal kosher salt (½ tsp)
½ tsp	baking soda
¼ tsp	ground cinnamon
85g	unsalted butter (3oz), diced, room temperature
72g	light brown sugar (2.5oz / about ⅓ cup)
2 T	honey

Marshmallows:

1 T	powdered gelatin
150g	sugar (5.3oz / about ¾ cup)
½ cup	light corn syrup
4	large egg whites, room temperature
1.5g	Diamond Crystal kosher salt (½ tsp)
2 tsp	vanilla paste or pure vanilla extract

Chocolate coating:

1 recipe	Tempered Chocolate Glaze (page 111)
500g	bittersweet couverture chocolate (17.6oz), chopped

To start the graham crackers, combine the whole-wheat and all-purpose flours in a bowl, then whisk in the salt, baking soda, and cinnamon. In the bowl of a stand mixer, combine the butter, brown sugar, and honey. Using the paddle attachment, cream the mixture on medium-high speed, scraping down the sides of the bowl as necessary. Turn the mixer speed to low, add the dry ingredients, and mix until the dough is homogeneous. Turn the dough out onto a lightly floured work surface. Gather it into a rectangle, wrap it in plastic, and chill until firm, at least 1 hour.

Roll out the dough between two very lightly floured pieces of parchment—this makes it easier to roll the crackers out thinly, but this is already a dry dough and you want to avoid adding unnecessary flour. Roll the dough so it is not much thicker than a nickel, carefully loosening the dough and flipping it over whenever it begins to stick to the parchment paper. Slide the parchment (and dough) onto a baking sheet. Refrigerate the dough until it is firm, an hour or so.

Carefully remove the top sheet of parchment. Using a floured 1½-inch round cutter, cut out the cookies. Arrange the cookies on the parchment-lined baking sheet and chill again for at least 30 minutes.

Preheat the oven to 325°F. Bake the cookies for 6 minutes, then rotate the pan front to back and continue baking until they are firm and well browned, about 6 minutes more. Allow the cookies to cool on the baking sheet.

To make the marshmallow, put ¼ cup cold water in a small bowl, sprinkle the gelatin over it, and set it aside to "bloom." Put ¼ cup plus 2 teaspoons water in a small saucepan. Add the sugar and corn syrup and heat on medium-high. Meanwhile, put the egg whites in the bowl of a stand mixer fitted with the whisk attachment. Add the salt and whip until the whites are opaque. Check the sugar temperature with a candy thermometer. When it reaches 232°F, pull the pan off the heat and whisk in the gelatin. With the mixer on medium-high, slowly stream the hot syrup into the whites, then add the vanilla. Continue beating on high speed until the mixer bowl is cool to the touch and the meringue is stiff and glossy but retains some elasticity, 5 to 10 minutes.

Put the marshmallow into a piping bag with a ⅝-inch tip (I use an Ateco no. 808). Pipe the marshmallow at a 90-degree angle onto each cookie (hold the bag so the tip is in contact with a cookie, which makes for a concentrated, rounded dollop). Twist the piping bag to create a nipple before releasing the tip and moving on to the next cookie. (If your marshmallow is soft and doesn't hold its shape, set the mixture aside for 15 more minutes to allow the gelatin to work, then try again.) Once the cookies are topped with marshmallow set them aside to dry for at least an hour.

Make the tempered chocolate glaze according to the instructions on page 111.

To finish the cookies, dampen a kitchen towel (to use to wipe your fingers between cookies). Set the bowl of chocolate glaze so it is slightly tipped and the chocolate pools. Lift a cookie, grabbing the base between your fingers. Dip the marshmallow into the chocolate and gently shake it about five times, until the chocolate stops dripping. Replace the cookie on the baking sheet, wipe your fingers on the towel, and repeat, dipping the remaining cookies in chocolate. The cookies need to cool to 68°F; if your room is warmer than that, once you have dipped all the cookies, refrigerate them for 5 minutes. Serve immediately or store them in an airtight container for up to 3 days.

Espresso Shortbread with Cacao Nibs

Makes about 60 cookies

Over the years, I've made many kinds of shortbread cookies because I love their buttery crumble. This version boasts espresso and chocolate and is a good cookie to serve at the end of a meal. For a slightly sweeter and smoother effect, substitute chopped bitter chocolate for the cacao nibs. This is a big recipe, but I very rarely bake more than one baking sheet at a time. You can halve the recipe, but I prefer to wrap the extra dough in parchment, then refrigerate or freeze it to use later instead (see page 95).

280g	all-purpose flour (9.9oz / about 2 cups)		90g	confectioners' sugar (3.2oz / about ¾ cup)
3 T	instant espresso		2 tsp	pure vanilla paste or extract
2.3g	Diamond Crystal kosher salt (¾ tsp)		30g	crystallized sugar, such as turbinado, Demerara, or Sugar In The Raw (1oz / about 2 T)
50g	cacao nibs (1.8oz / about ½ cup)			
228g	unsalted butter, room temperature (8oz)			

Whisk the flour with the espresso, salt, and cacao nibs in a bowl. In the bowl of a stand mixer and using the paddle attachment, cream the butter and sugar on medium-high speed, about 2 minutes. Mix in the vanilla, then turn the mixer speed to low, add the dry ingredients, and mix until the dough is homogeneous.

Divide the dough in half and form two 16-inch logs, rolling each in parchment paper and pressing out as much air as possible. Chill the dough until it is firm, at least 2 hours.

Preheat the oven to 325°F and line a baking sheet with parchment paper. Slice the dough into ¼-inch-thick rounds. Arrange the cookies about 1½ inches apart on the prepared baking sheet.

Bake the cookies for 7 minutes, then rotate the pan front to back and continue cooking until the bottoms are firm and darker and the cookies smell done, about 8 minutes more. Transfer the cookies to a wire rack to cool, then serve.

Maple Shortbread

Makes about 48 cookies

Packaged maple sugar varies. Some is dry and granulated, and some moister—more like brown sugar in texture. Either will work for this recipe, but I prefer the latter. I find it has a richer taste.

280g	all-purpose flour (9.9oz / about 2 cups)		170g	maple sugar (6oz / about ¾ cup + 1 T)
4.5g	Diamond Crystal kosher salt (1½ tsp)		2 tsp	vanilla paste or pure vanilla extract
228g	unsalted butter (8oz), room temperature			

In a bowl, whisk the flour with the salt. In the bowl of a stand mixer and using the paddle attachment, cream the butter with the sugar on medium-high speed, about 2 minutes. Mix in the vanilla, then turn the mixer speed to low, add the dry ingredients, and mix until the dough is homogeneous.

Divide the dough in half and form two 12-inch logs. Wrap the dough in parchment paper, pressing out as much air as possible (see page 95). Chill the dough until firm, at least 2 hours.

Preheat the oven to 325°F and line a baking sheet with parchment paper. (I usually bake cookies as I need them, no more than one sheet at a time; I keep the extra dough in the refrigerator or freezer.) Remove the dough to be baked from the refrigerator and let it warm slightly—just enough so the sugar will stick to the cookies, about 10 minutes. Roll the logs in crystallized sugar, then slice each into ¼-inch-thick rounds and arrange the cookies about 1½ inches apart on the prepared baking sheet.

Bake the cookies for 6 minutes, then rotate the pan front to back and continue baking until the bottoms are firm and golden and the cookies smell done, about 7 minutes more. Transfer the cookies to a wire rack to cool, then serve.

Molasses Ginger Cookies

Makes about 24 cookies

This recipe has deep ginger flavor. I incorporate it in three forms—dry, crystallized, and fresh.

Unless otherwise specified, I always bake with room-temperature eggs. It helps with emulsification. That's especially important in this dough. If you haven't planned ahead, simply put a chilled egg in warm water. It will take the chill off quickly.

260g	all-purpose flour (9.2oz / about 1¾ cups + 2 T)
2 tsp	baking soda
1 T	ground ginger
1½ tsp	ground cinnamon
1.5g	Diamond Crystal kosher salt (½ tsp)
⅛ tsp	ground white pepper
	Pinch of ground cloves
70g	crystallized ginger (2.5oz / about ⅓ cup), minced
114g	unsalted butter (4oz), melted and cooled
75g	sugar (2.6oz / about 6 T)
75g	dark brown sugar (2.6oz / about ⅓ cup)
⅓ cup	molasses
1 T	freshly grated ginger
1 tsp	lemon zest
1	large egg, room temperature
About 60g	crystallized sugar, such as turbinado, Demerara, or Sugar In The Raw (2.1oz / about ¼ cup)

In the bowl of a stand mixer, combine the flour, baking soda, ground ginger, cinnamon, salt, pepper, and cloves. Whisk the dry ingredients together, then mix in the minced crystallized ginger. In a separate bowl, combine the melted butter with the white and brown sugars, molasses, fresh ginger, lemon zest, and egg and mix together.

Using the paddle attachment on low speed, stream the butter mixture into the dry ingredients. Mix until a homogeneous dough forms, pausing and scraping the bowl as necessary. Cover the bowl with plastic wrap and chill for at least 2 hours (this makes the dough easier to work and allows the flavors to blend).

Preheat the oven to 350°F and line a baking sheet with parchment paper. Using a 2-ounce ice cream scoop or a large spoon, drop cookies onto the prepared baking sheet, leaving at least 2 inches between them. Top each with crystallized sugar—I put the sugar in a bowl, then dip the cookies in it, and return them to the baking sheet. Bake the cookies for 6 minutes, then rotate the pan front to back and continue baking until the cookies are firm throughout and smell done, about 6 minutes more. Cool on a wire rack, then serve.

Oatmeal Cookies with Sour Cherries

Makes about 16 cookies

Like chocolate chip cookies (see page 117), oatmeal cookies are a homey favorite. They are hard to screw up but even harder to make exactly how you want them. This version, for me, hits that mark. I usually double the recipe, roll it into logs (see page 95), and freeze the dough. Then I have cookies ready to slice and bake—my preferred approach because these are best eaten within hours of baking.

120g	dried sour cherries (4.2oz / about ¾ cup + 2 T)		2.3g	Diamond Crystal kosher salt (¾ tsp)
1½ tsp	lemon juice		114g	unsalted butter (4oz), room temperature
65g	all-purpose flour (2.3oz / about ⅓ cup + 2 T)		½ tsp	lemon zest
65g	bread flour (2.3oz / about ⅓ cup + 2 T)		112g	light brown sugar (4oz / about ½ cup)
½ tsp	ground cinnamon		75g	sugar (2.6oz / about 6 T)
½ tsp	baking soda		½ tsp	vanilla paste or pure vanilla extract
			1	large egg
			80g	rolled oats (2.8oz / about 7 T)

Put the cherries in a bowl and cover them with very hot water. Add the lemon juice and set the cherries aside to rehydrate for at least 15 minutes. Drain the cherries and lay them on paper towels to dry.

Whisk together the all-purpose and bread flours, cinnamon, baking soda, and salt in a large bowl. Put the butter in the bowl of a stand mixer with the lemon zest and the brown and white sugars and using the paddle attachment, cream the mixture until it is smooth and fluffy, scraping down as necessary, about 2 minutes on medium. Stir the vanilla into the egg in a measuring cup and with the mixer running pour the egg into the mixer. With the mixer on low, add the dry ingredients and mix until a homogeneous dough forms, scraping the bowl as necessary. Add the oats and rehydrated cherries to the dough and mix on low just until combined.

Preheat the oven to 350°F and line a baking sheet with parchment paper. Drop the dough by teaspoonfuls onto the prepared baking sheet—just the number of cookies you want to eat in the short term. Wrap the remaining dough in parchment and refrigerate or freeze for future use (see page 95).

Bake the cookies for 6 minutes, then rotate the pan front to back and continue baking until they are browned and crisping around the edges, about 6 minutes more. Allow the cookies to cool on a wire rack, then serve.

CHAPTER 4

Pies

Careful with the Crust

My hands run cold, and though that is annoying much of the time, it is an advantage in pastry. Dough, a mingling of starch, liquid, and fat, is temperature sensitive—pie dough especially. Every good baker knows that keeping everything cool is the secret to tender, flaky crust, so I refrigerate (or freeze) butter before I mix it with the flour and I hydrate my dough with ice water. I am lucky that my touch doesn't warm things up much. Occasionally I've wondered if the ease my icy fingers give me with dough explains my fondness for this branch of the dessert family. Perhaps, but when I reflect on my mom's altogether very good baking, I remember it was her tarts (and amazing cookies) that excited me most, so I think it more probable that I like good pies and tarts because, though they can seem homey, they are in fact artful, balanced desserts.

Putting my fondness (and fingers) aside, what is the difference between a pie and a tart? Per the dictionary, it seems that all tarts are pies but not all pies are tarts. Interesting—maybe—but not very helpful. Looking at things from my own angle, tarts are pastries associated with French and Italian traditions. They are distinguished from pies by crusts that have snap and crumble. My tarts are single crusted, straight sided, and removed from the cooking vessel before serving. They are baked in thin metal pans, usually with removable bottoms. The metal conducts the heat to the dough quickly and allows the cooked crust to cool fast. They can be sweet or savory. In this chapter, I focus on the former (but see chapter 5, Savories, for the latter). Some of my tart crusts owe their delicate crisp to extra sugar or an egg, and some contain almonds, hazelnuts, or chocolate. All tarts once baked are fragile, but beforehand the dough is forgiving—I appreciate that because I can re-roll or patch as I need to.

When I see the word *pie,* I think of an American pastry-crusted dessert that has roots in England. Pies ideally have a flaky crust that is firm but not cookie-crisp. Like tarts, the fillings can be sweet or savory, but unlike tarts, pies can be single or double crusted. Either way, American-style pies are baked and served in slope-sided "plates" or "tins" (in England, crust is made of sterner stuff so pies are often removed from their pan and plated—or even eaten in hand). I bake most pies in heatproof glass (Pyrex). I find glass conducts the heat well, gives me a view into what's going on during cooking, and allows the crust to cool at a rate that does not cause steam accumulation. Metal pie pans also work well, but be forewarned that unless otherwise specified, these recipes were tested in glass, and using metal may impact the cooking time.

In the next pages, I share not only my favorite pies and tarts (arranged seasonally, starting with spring) but also a tatin and a crisp. The link is the combination of a filling (or topping) and a crust (or crumble—a deconstructed crust). I have also included recipes for peach and plum cobblers. In those, the fruit is teamed with a biscuit topping, and because they strike me as similar to many of the recipes in this chapter, I have placed them here.

Returning to the subject of temperature, I chill my doughs before I roll them out, then usually again afterward. This allows the dough to rest, which prevents gluten development and keeps the fat from melting into the flour prior to baking—both essential for a great crust. Your hands run warm? Not a problem. A quick bath in ice water will bring their temperature down.

Rhubarb and Strawberry Pie

Makes one 10-inch double-crust pie

Although some bakers like to feature strawberries in this classic flavor duet, I prefer to flip the script and show-case the briefly available taste of rhubarb—botanically a vegetable—in my pie. I use the berries (and a little ginger) to underscore its simultaneously tart and sweet fruity taste.

Crust:		
Double recipe	**Basic Butter Pie Dough (page 170)**	
350g	all-purpose flour (12.3oz / about 2 ½ cups)	
24g	sugar (0.8oz / about 2 T)	
4.5g	Diamond Crystal kosher salt (1½ tsp)	
228g	unsalted butter (8oz), diced and frozen	

Filling:	
340g	**rhubarb (12oz), trimmed and cut into 1-inch chunks**
226g	**strawberries (8oz), hulled and halved (or quartered if large)**
56g	**sugar (2oz / about 4½ T)**
1 T	**finely grated fresh ginger**
2 T	**cornstarch**
About 2 T	**buttermilk, heavy cream, or milk**
About 10g	**crystallized sugar, such as turbinado, Demerara, or Sugar In The Raw (0.4oz / about 2 tsp)**

To prepare the crust, double the recipe and follow the instructions on page 170, dividing the dough in half, gathering it into 2 balls, flattening them into disks, wrapping them in plastic, and refrigerating. Roll out one of the disks on a lightly floured surface so it is about 12 inches across and ⅛ inch thick. Fit it into a 10-inch pie pan. Using a sharp knife, trim away the excess crust. Chill this bottom crust in the refrigerator for at least 30 minutes. Meanwhile, on a lightly floured piece of parchment paper, roll out the second disk (the top crust) also about 12 inches in diameter and ⅛ inch thick. Transfer the parchment (and dough) to a baking sheet and chill the dough for 15 minutes in the freezer or at least 30 minutes in the refrigerator.

To start the filling, put the rhubarb and strawberries in a large bowl. Add the sugar, ginger, and cornstarch and mix until just combined. Set the fruit aside to macerate at room temperature until the rhubarb and berries release their juices and the cornstarch and sugar dissolve, about 30 minutes.

To assemble and bake the pie, preheat the oven to 400°F. Spoon the rhubarb, strawberries, and accumulated juices into the chilled bottom crust. Cut out a hole about an inch in diameter in the center of the top crust and, using a razor or sharp knife, make 6 good-size slashes so the steam can vent. Lift the top crust onto the pie, centering the hole. Trim the excess dough, pinch the two crusts together, and crimp the edges. Brush the top crust and the rim of the pie with buttermilk (or cream or milk) and sprinkle with crystallized sugar.

Bake the pie 15 minutes, then lower the oven temperature to 350°F, rotate the pan front to back, and continue baking until the crust is golden brown and the fruit within is bubbling; start checking after 30 minutes but expect that it may take 10 or so minutes more. Allow the pie to cool completely. Slice and serve with ice cream or whipped cream, if desired.

Blueberry, Blueberry, Blueberry Tart

Makes one 9-inch tart

This is a celebration of blueberries that doesn't hold back. If you can find tiny wild blueberries, use them for the topping, but be assured that easier-to-come-by cultivated berries work just fine. The reduction can even be made with frozen berries. I bake this hybrid of a tart and a pie in a shallow, slope-sided metal tin I inherited; if you can find one, snag it. In any event, avoid a deep-dish pie plate for this.

Crust:

1 recipe	**Cornmeal Buttermilk Dough, page 172**
34g	finely ground cornmeal (1.2oz / about 3 T)
210g	all-purpose flour (7.4oz / about 1½ cups)
12g	sugar (.4oz / about 1 T)
2.3g	Diamond Crystal kosher salt (¾ tsp)
143g	unsalted butter (5oz), diced and frozen
¼ cup	buttermilk

Reduction:

165g	blueberries (5.8oz / about 1 cup), fresh or frozen, stemmed if necessary
16g	sugar (0.6oz / about 1¼ T)
1	whole star anise, bruised
1 tsp	lemon zest

Filling:

300g	fresh blueberries (10. 6oz / about 1¾ cups), stemmed
50g	sugar (1.8oz / about ¼ cup)
1 tsp	cornstarch

Whipped yogurt "cream" and topping:

½ cup	heavy cream
8g	confectioners' sugar (0.3oz / about 1 T)
½ tsp	vanilla paste or pure vanilla extract
¼ cup	plain yogurt, stirred if separated
150g	fresh blueberries (5.3oz / about ¾ cup + 2 T), stemmed

To make the crust, follow the instructions on page 172. Roll the dough out between two pieces of parchment paper or on a lightly floured surface into a 12-inch round about ⅛ inch thick. Fit the dough into a shallow 9-inch pie pan. Don't trim the excess; instead, roll it under to form a thicker-edged crust, then crimp it. Chill the crust thoroughly for 15 minutes in the freezer or at least 30 minutes in the refrigerator.

To blind-bake the crust, preheat the oven to 375°F. Line the crust with foil and fill it with pie weights (dried beans or rice work). Bake the crust until it looks set, about 10 minutes, then remove the foil and weights and continue baking to dry out the bottom of the crust, about 5 minutes more. Remove the tart shell from the oven and let it cool completely. Reduce the oven temperature to 325°F.

To make the blueberry reduction, combine 165 grams (5.8 ounces) blueberries and 16 grams (0.6 ounces) sugar in a small saucepan. Add the star anise and zest, stir, and cook over medium heat until the sugar dissolves and the berries begin to pop. Remove the pan from the heat and allow the mixture to cool for at least 15 minutes. Strain the reduction through a fine sieve into a bowl, reserving the syrup and discarding the pulp.

To make the filling, put 300 grams (10.6 ounces) blueberries, 50 grams (1.8 ounces) sugar, and the cornstarch in a bowl. Toss to combine, spoon the berries and any juices into the blind-baked tart shell, then bake the tart until the filling is bubbling and the crust is golden brown, 30 to 40 minutes. Set the tart on a wire rack to cool thoroughly.

To make the whipped yogurt "cream," beat the cream with the confectioners' sugar and vanilla either by hand or in a stand mixer with the whisk attachment until it holds medium peaks. Gently fold in the yogurt. (The yogurt cream can be prepared, covered, and held in the refrigerator for up to 1 hour).

To finish the tart, spread an even layer of the yogurt cream over the blueberry filling. Put the remaining 150 grams (5.3 ounces) berries in a bowl. Add about 2 tablespoons of the berry reduction and mix to coat the fresh berries. Spoon the berries on top of the tart, drizzle with additional reduction, and serve.

Blueberry Turnovers

Turnovers, or old-fashioned hand pies, are easy to make. I love this blueberry version (made with the same cornmeal and buttermilk dough I use for the tart on page 135), but when the seasons change, so does my choice of fruit. Try a different berry or apricots or Italian plums, using this recipe as a template; my proportions here will work as a guide.

Crust:

1 recipe	**Cornmeal Buttermilk Dough (page 172)**
34g	finely ground cornmeal (1.2oz / about 3 T)
210g	all-purpose flour (7.4oz / about 1½ cups)
12g	sugar (0.4oz / about 1 T)
2.3g	Diamond Crystal kosher salt (¾ tsp)
143g	unsalted butter (5oz), diced and frozen
¼ cup	buttermilk, plus extra for brushing the crust

Filling:

31g	sugar (1.1oz / about 2 T)
½ tsp	lime zest
2 T	finely chopped candied ginger
285g	fresh blueberries (10oz / about 1¾ cups), stemmed
1 T	fresh lime juice
4 tsp	cornstarch
About 10g	crystallized sugar, such as turbinado, Demerara, or Sugar In The Raw (0.4oz / about 2 tsp)

To make the dough, follow the instructions on page 172. Roll the dough on a lightly floured piece of parchment paper into a rectangle about 12 × 15 inches and ⅛ inch thick. Put the parchment (and dough) on a baking sheet and chill the dough for 15 minutes in the freezer or at least 30 minutes in the refrigerator.

To make the filling, combine the sugar, lime zest, and ginger in a small saucepan. Stir to evenly distribute the zest and ginger. Add 63 grams (2.2 ounces) of the berries, the lime juice, and cornstarch and bring to a simmer over medium heat, crushing the berries with a wooden spoon as they soften. When the mixture is bubbly, pull the pan off the heat and fold in the remaining 222 grams (7.8 ounces) blueberries. Allow the filling to cool, then transfer it to a container, cover it, and chill for at least 30 minutes. The filling will keep in the refrigerator for several days.

To make the turnovers, preheat the oven to 400°F. Trim the dough to even it and cut 6 rectangles, each about 2 × 2½ inches. Brush the perimeter of each with buttermilk. Spoon a sixth of the berry mixture (about 3½ tablespoons) into the middle of each rectangle. Working one at a time, fold the long side of the dough over the filling to meet its opposite, forming rectangular turnovers. Pinch the edges to seal, then crimp them with a fork. Chill the turnovers on the parchment-lined baking sheet in the freezer for 15 minutes or the refrigerator for at least 30 minutes.

(recipe continues)

Brush the tops of the turnovers with buttermilk and sprinkle them with crystallized sugar. Using a razor or sharp knife, cut 3 slits in the top of each to vent the steam. Bake the turnovers for 15 minutes, then reduce the heat to 375°F, rotate the baking sheet front to back, and continue baking until the turnovers are golden brown and the filling bubbles through the slits, about 15 minutes more. Cool the turnovers on a wire rack, then serve.

Peach and Blackberry Cobbler
with **Ricotta Biscuits**

Serves 8

You could top this cobbler with shortcake biscuit dough (see Variation below), though I rather like ricotta biscuits for this recipe. The cheese adds a richness and tang that I think works nicely with sweet summer peaches. I used blackberries here, but feel free to substitute another berry—either raspberries or blueberries would be nice.

Fruit:

567g	peaches (20oz), pitted and sliced thickly (cut smallish peaches into 8 slices each)
57g	sugar (2oz / about ½ cup + 2 tsp)
2 T	cornstarch
144g	blackberries (5oz / about 1 cup)

Ricotta biscuits:

114g	all-purpose flour (4oz / about ¾ cup + 1 T)
28g	semolina flour (1oz / about 2⅔ cups)
28g	sugar (1oz / about 2 T)
2½ tsp	baking powder
1 tsp	lemon zest
0.4g	Diamond Crystal kosher salt (⅛ tsp)
42g	unsalted butter (1.5oz), cut into ½-inch dice and frozen
227g	ricotta (8oz / about ¾ cup + 2 T), drained if wet
About 1 T	heavy cream or buttermilk
About 5g	crystallized sugar, such as turbinado, Demerara, or Sugar In The Raw (0.2oz / about 1 tsp)

To macerate the peaches, put them in a bowl with 57 grams (2 ounces) sugar and the cornstarch. Stir and set aside at room temperature until the peaches release their juices and the cornstarch and sugar dissolve, about 30 minutes.

To start the ricotta biscuits, preheat the oven to 350°F. In a food processor, combine the all-purpose and semolina flours with 28 grams (1 ounce) sugar, the baking powder, lemon zest, and salt. Pulse to mix. Add the butter and process until the mixture is the texture of coarse meal, about 15 seconds (when it's right, the butter will no longer sound rumbly in the processor and the largest bits will be no bigger than a lentil), about 15 seconds. Add the ricotta and pulse until the ingredients are combined and the dough comes together into a shaggy mass.

To assemble the cobbler, add the berries to the peaches and mix gently to evenly distribute them. Spoon the fruit and juices into a deep-dish 9½-inch pie pan or baking dish with at least 2-inch-high sides. Using a floured ⅓-cup measure or a large spoon, drop 8 biscuits evenly onto the fruit. Brush the biscuits with cream or buttermilk and sprinkle them with crystallized sugar.

Bake the cobbler until the biscuits are golden, about 35 minutes. Rotate the pan from front to back, cover the biscuits with foil, and continue baking until the juices in the cobbler are bubbling (the center takes the longest to heat), about 20 minutes more. Serve warm or at room temperature with ice cream, if desired.

Variation: To make Peach Cobbler with Shortcake Biscuits, make a half recipe of shortcake biscuit dough (see page 16). Roll the dough out on a lightly floured surface about an inch thick, cut out 8 biscuits, and arrange them on top of the peach/berry filling. Brush the biscuits with heavy cream or buttermilk, sprinkle with crystallized sugar, and bake until the filling is bubbly and the biscuits are golden; begin checking after 30 minutes and cover the biscuits with foil per the instructions above.

Peach and Raspberry Crostata

Makes one 10-inch crostata

I don't know if crostatas are any simpler to make than pies or tarts, but the relaxed, unfussed feel of the pastry makes them my preferred summertime dessert. I don't peel the peaches for this; if you prefer to, I recommend you add a little extra cornstarch to the filling so it doesn't wind up too juicy. I cool all crostatas on a wire rack to prevent the crusts from steaming and softening. Note: This recipe calls for only ¾ cup of the crumble, but I make the whole batch and freeze the rest for later.

Crust:

1 recipe	**Crostata Dough (page 175)**
143g	unsalted butter (5oz), chilled
210g	all-purpose flour (7.4oz / about 1½ cups)
12g	white sugar (0.4oz / about 1 T)
3g	Diamond Crystal kosher salt (1 tsp)

Crumble topping:

1 cup	**Brown Butter Pecan Crumble (page 296)**
142g	unsalted butter (5.2oz)
45g	pecans (1.6oz / about 6 T), chopped
110g	light brown sugar (3.9oz / about ½ cup)
50g	sugar (1.8oz / about ¼ cup)

180g	all-purpose flour (6.3oz / about 1¼ cups)
⅛ tsp	ground cardamom
¼ tsp	ground cinnamon
0.7g	Diamond Crystal kosher salt (¼ tsp)

Filling:

4	**medium peaches (about 600g), halved, pitted, and thickly sliced**
60g	sugar
1 tsp	vanilla paste or pure vanilla extract
1½ tsp	cornstarch
1	large egg, lightly beaten
75g	raspberries (2.6oz)
About 8g	**crystallized sugar, such as turbinado, Demerara, or Sugar In The Raw (0.3oz / about 1½ tsp)**

To start the crust, follow the instructions on page 175. Roll out the crostata dough on a piece of parchment into a round about 13 inches across. Put the parchment (and dough) on a baking sheet and chill the dough for 15 minutes in the freezer or at least 30 minutes in the refrigerator.

To prepare the crumble, follow the directions on page 296. Measure ¾ cup of crumble then freeze the rest for future use.

To start the crostata and filling, preheat the oven to 400°F. In a large bowl, combine the peaches, sugar, vanilla, and cornstarch and set aside for about 5 minutes. Take the dough out of the refrigerator, leaving it on the baking sheet. Brush a 2-inch border around the perimeter with the beaten egg. Spoon the peaches and their juices onto the dough, avoiding the egg-washed border. Scatter the raspberries over the peaches. Form the crostata's sides by working a section of dough at a time, lifting it up and over the fill-

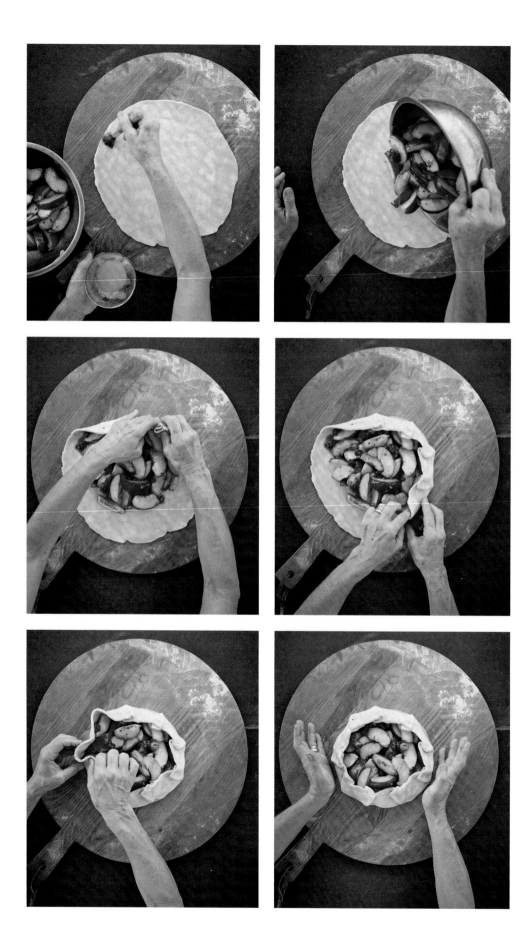

ing and pinching and folding it, pleating the dough and forming the edge. Spoon the crumble evenly over the exposed fruit in the center of the crostata. Brush the top and sides of the pastry with egg, then sprinkle the crust with crystallized sugar.

Bake the crostata on the baking sheet until the crust begins to color, about 15 minutes. Reduce the oven temperature to 350°F and continue baking until the crust is nicely browned and the filling is bubbly, about 35 minutes more. Remove the crostata from the oven, transfer it to a wire rack (this is done most easily by sliding the parchment with the crostata onto the rack). Allow the crostata to cool, then slice and serve it with ice cream or whipped cream, if desired.

Caramelized Nectarine and Fig Tart

Makes one 9-inch tart

Nectarine season on the North Fork runs from mid-July through September. Local fresh figs aren't available until late August. I confess I like the combination of these fruits so much that I often stretch the season and buy out-of-state figs. I recommend starting this tart a day ahead, a necessity if you plan to do as I do and make the pastry, which is not difficult to prepare, but is time consuming. Store-bought puff pastry is a fine substitute.

Filling:

115g	cream cheese (4oz / about ½ cup), room temperature
60g	fresh goat cheese (2.1oz / about ⅓ cup), room temperature
75g	Greek yogurt (2.6oz / about 5 T), or 100g plain yogurt (3.5oz), drained through a fine sieve overnight
½ cup	heavy cream
½ tsp	lemon zest
16g	confectioners' sugar (0.6oz / about 2 T)
½ tsp	vanilla paste or pure vanilla extract

Tart shell:

½ recipe	Rough Puff Pastry (page 179), or 245g store-bought puff pastry, thawed if frozen
114g	all-purpose flour (4oz / about ¾ cup), plus extra for dusting
2.3g	Diamond Crystal kosher salt (¾ tsp)
114g	unsalted butter (4oz)
1	large egg, lightly beaten

Fruit and caramel:

2	medium nectarines (about 302g / 10.7oz), pitted and cut into 16 segments
5	figs, preferably Black Mission (about 285g / 10oz), quartered
100g	sugar (3.5oz / about ½ cup)
½ cup	pinot noir or other medium-bodied dry red wine
42g	shelled pistachios (1.5oz / about 4½ T), chopped

To make the filling, combine the cream cheese, goat cheese, yogurt, heavy cream, zest, confectioners' sugar, and vanilla in the bowl of a stand mixer and use the whisk attachment on low to whip until smooth. Increase the speed to medium-high and whip until the mixture holds firm peaks, then transfer it to a covered container. Chill thoroughly, for at least 2 hours.

To start the tart shell, make the dough according to the instructions on page 179. On a lightly floured piece of parchment, roll out the pastry into a 12-inch square about ⅛ inch thick. Transfer the parchment (and dough) to a baking sheet and chill for at least 15 minutes. Trim the dough to even the square, then cut a 1-inch strip of dough from each side. Brush the perimeter of the square with beaten egg, then lay the strips of dough on the four edges to build a raised rim. Dock the dough all over, including where the sides meet the bottom. Return the dough to the refrigerator and chill at least 30 minutes.

To blind-bake the crust, preheat the oven to 425°F. Line the tart with foil, then fill it with pie weights (dried beans or rice work). Bake the tart for 15 minutes. Lower the oven tempertaure to 350°F, remove the foil and weights, and bake the crust until it is golden, about 50 minutes. Set the tart shell aside to cool completely.

To prepare the fruit and caramel, put the nectarines and figs in a heatproof bowl. Combine ¼ cup water and the sugar in a small skillet and set it over medium-high heat. Cook, without disturbing the mixture, until it comes to a boil. Reduce the heat to medium-low and cook until the caramel turns a pale gold, swirling the pan occasionally so the sugar heats evenly. Pull the pan off the heat and add the wine—this will cause the caramel to seize. Return the pan to the stovetop and heat it over medium-high to liquefy the caramel. Simmer until it reduces to a syrup, 3 to 5 minutes. (Note: If you go too far and the caramel becomes too thick to pour, add a tablespoon of water.) Pour the hot caramel over the fruit. Toss to mix and set aside for at least 15 minutes, tossing once or twice more as the caramel cools.

To finish the tart, spoon the chilled cheese filling mixture into the tart shell. Strain the fruit into a clean bowl, reserving the caramel (which will have mixed with the fruit juices). Arrange the nectarines and figs on the tart. Heat the caramel in a small saucepan and let it boil just long enough so it concentrates to a glaze consistency, about 2 minutes. Let the caramel cool for 5 to 10 minutes, then spoon it over the fruit. Sprinkle the glazed tart with pistachios, slice, and serve.

Raspberry, Rose, and White Chocolate Tart

Makes one 9-inch tart

This white chocolate tart offers intense berry flavor mellowed with a hint of rose. The secret: I toss fresh berries with a quickly cooked raspberry sauce. Because frozen raspberries are often more flavorful than supermarket berries, and always less expensive, I generally make the sauce from frozen berries.

Tart shell:

½ recipe	**Rough Puff Pastry (page 179), or 245g store-bought puff pastry, thawed if frozen**
114g	all-purpose flour (4oz / about ¾ cup), plus more for dusting
2.3g	Diamond Crystal kosher salt (¾ tsp)
114g	unsalted butter (4oz)

Garnish:

¼ cup	**Sugared Almonds (page 291)**
100g	sliced almonds (3.5oz / about 1 cup + 1½ T)
2 tsp	light corn syrup
1.5g	Diamond Crystal kosher salt (½ tsp)
30g	crystallized sugar, such as turbinado, Demerara, or Sugar In The Raw (1oz / about 2 T)
About 1 tsp	dried rose petals (optional)

White chocolate cream:

1¼ cups	heavy cream
115g	good-quality white chocolate (4oz), chopped
½ tsp	rose water

Raspberry sauce:

170g	frozen raspberries (6oz / about 1⅓ cups)
30g	sugar (1oz / about 2½ T)
⅛ tsp	rose water
240g	fresh raspberries (8.5oz / about 2 cups)

To prepare the tart shell, make the dough according to the instructions on page 179. Preheat the oven to 425°F. On a lightly floured piece of parchment, roll the pastry out into a circle about 12 inches across and ⅛ inch thick. Slide the parchment (and dough) onto a baking sheet and chill for at least 30 minutes.

Remove the dough from the refrigerator and dock it all over with a fork. Fit the dough into a 9-inch tart pan with a removable bottom. (The easiest approach: Slide the bottom of the pan under the rolled-out dough, fold it loosely over the edges, drop the bottom into the pan, then unfold the dough and fit it to the pan.) Trim the tart shell (saving the trimmings to make the Crisps on page 102). Line the crust with tinfoil and fill it with pie weights (dried beans or rice work).

Blind-bake the tart until the crust is set, about 15 minutes, then remove the foil and weights, lower the temperature to 325°F, and bake the crust until it is fully cooked and golden, about 50 minutes more. Allow the pastry to cool completely in the pan on a wire rack.

To start the garnish, prepare the sugared almonds according to the instructions on page 291. Allow the almonds to cool, then reserve ¼ cup. Store the remaining almonds in an airtight container for future use.

To start the white chocolate cream, heat 1 cup of the cream over medium-high. Put the chopped chocolate in a bowl. When the cream mixture comes to a simmer, pour it over the chocolate. Allow the mixture to sit undisturbed until the chocolate begins to melt, about 1 minute, then whisk until the mixture is smooth. Cover the chocolate directly with plastic wrap (to prevent a skin from forming) and chill it thoroughly, at least 1 hour.

To make the raspberry sauce, combine the frozen berries, sugar, and ⅛ teaspoon rose water in a bowl. Set the berries aside to macerate until the sugar dissolves, about 15 minutes. Transfer the berry mixture to a saucepan and bring to a simmer over medium heat. Cook until the berries break down and the mixture thickens a little, about 5 minutes. Press the sauce through a fine sieve into a bowl and chill it; discard the pulp.

To finish the white chocolate cream and assemble the tart, combine ½ teaspoon rose water and the remaining ¼ cup heavy cream with the white chocolate mixture in a bowl and whisk the mixture until it holds medium peaks (I prefer to whisk small amounts of cream by hand). Spoon the cream into the tart shell, spreading it evenly and smoothing the top. Toss the fresh berries with the chilled sauce and spoon them over the cream. Garnish with sugared almonds and dried rose petals (if desired).

Ricotta Tart with Roasted Cherries

Makes one 9-inch tart

You can make this tart with easy-to-find cow's milk ricotta, or you can use small-batch sheep's milk ricotta, which tastes even better. Just remember, if the cheese is watery, you need to drain it in a cheesecloth-lined sieve set over a bowl until it is no longer releasing liquid. I add orange zest and fennel seeds to my filling, a nod to favorite Sicilian flavors. I reinforce the effect by adding a little Pernod to my cherries when I roast them, then a bit more just before serving.

Tart shell:

1 recipe	**Sweet Almond Tart Dough**
165g	all-purpose flour (5.8oz / about 1 cup + 3 T)
20g	almond flour (0.7oz / about 3 T)
65g	confectioners' sugar (2.3oz / about ½ cup)
0.7g	Diamond Crystal kosher salt (¼ tsp)
100g	unsalted butter (3.5oz), diced and chilled
1	large egg, lightly beaten

Garnish:

About 2 T	**Sugared Almonds (page 291)**
100g	sliced almonds (3.5oz / about 1 cup + 1½ T)
2 tsp	light corn syrup
1.4g	Diamond Crystal kosher salt (½ tsp)
30g	crystallized sugar, such as turbinado, Demerara, or Sugar In The Raw (1oz / about 2 T)

Ricotta filling:

1 tsp	fennel seeds
454g	ricotta cheese (16oz / about 1¾ cups)
1 tsp	orange zest
75g	sugar (2.6oz / about 6 T)
1 tsp	orange blossom water
1	large egg
1	large egg yolk

Cherry topping:

465g	sweet red cherries (16.4oz), halved and pitted
90g	sugar (3.2oz / about ¼ cup + 3 T)
½	vanilla bean, split lengthwise
2 T + 1 tsp	Pernod

To prepare the crust, follow the instructions on page 180. On a floured work surface, roll out the dough into a round about 12 inches across and ⅛ inch thick. Dock the dough all over with a fork. Fit the dough into a 9-inch tart shell. (The easiest approach: Slide the bottom of the pan under the rolled-out dough, fold it loosely over the edges, drop the bottom into the pan, then unfold the dough and fit it to the pan.) Trim the edges and chill the dough in the freezer for 15 minutes or in the refrigerator for at least 30 minutes.

Preheat the oven to 325°F. Line the tart shell with tinfoil and fill it with pie weights (dried beans or rice work). Blind-bake the crust until it looks set, about 15 minutes, then remove the weights and foil and bake the tart until it looks dry, about 10 minutes more. Remove the crust from the oven and allow it to cool completely in the pan on a wire rack.

Meanwhile, make the garnish. Prepare the sugared almonds according to the instructions on page 291. Allow the almonds to cool, then reserve about 2 tablespoons. Store the remaining almonds in an airtight container for future use.

To make the ricotta filling and bake the tart, preheat the oven to 325°. Roast the fennel seeds in an ovenproof skillet until they are fragrant, about 12 minutes. Remove the seeds from the oven, allow them to cool, then grind them in a mortar or with a spice grinder. Increase the oven temperature to 400°F.

Put the ground fennel in a food processor. Add the ricotta, zest, 75 grams (2.6 ounces) sugar, and orange blossom water and process until the mixture is smooth. Transfer the ricotta mixture to a large bowl. Whisk in the egg and yolk, then pour the filling into the cooled tart shell.

Put the tart pan on a baking sheet (this just makes things easier) and bake it until the filling is set, about 30 minutes. Allow the tart to cool fully in the pan on a wire rack.

To make the roasted cherry topping, combine the pitted cherries and 90 grams (3.2 ounces) sugar in a small skillet with a lid. Mix well, then scrape the vanilla seeds into the pan and add the pod and 2 tablespoons of the Pernod. Cover the skillet and roast the cherries until the sugar dissolves and mixes with the fruit juices and the cherries have softened, about 20 minutes. Remove the cherries from the oven, uncover, and allow them to cool in the pan juices.

Shortly before serving, strain the cherries, reserving the fruit and juices separately. Return the juices to the skillet and bring them to a simmer over medium-high heat. Reduce the cherry juice until it is slightly syrupy, 5 to 7 minutes. Take the skillet off the heat and add the remaining teaspoon Pernod. Allow the sauce to cool completely.

To serve, mound the cherries on the tart. Spoon the reserved syrup over the cherries, top with the sugared almonds, slice, and serve.

Plum Cobbler with Cornmeal Biscuits

Serves 8

Italian plums, also known as prune plums, are my favorite for baking. They are delicious and not as soft or juicy as most other commonly available varieties, so they keep their shape and texture when cooked. Their arrival signals the end of the plum season and the beginning of fall. Always greedy for a last taste of summer, I opt for cornmeal biscuits in this cobbler, but ricotta dumplings (page 139) or shortcake biscuit dumplings (page 16) also work nicely.

Cornmeal biscuits:

262g	all-purpose flour (9.2oz / about 1¾ cups + 2 T)
50g	sugar (1.8oz / about ¼ cup)
60g	medium-grind cornmeal (2.1oz / about 7 T)
1 T	baking powder
0.7g	Diamond Crystal kosher salt (¼ tsp)
85g	unsalted butter (30oz), cut into ½-inch dice and frozen
1 cup + 2 T	heavy cream, plus extra for brushing

Filling:

680g	Italian plums (1½ lb), pitted and halved (or quartered if large)
130g	sugar (4.6oz / about ½ cup + 2½ T)
½ tsp	ground cardamom
1 tsp	orange zest
1 T	cornstarch
About 10g	crystallized sugar, such as turbinado, Demerara, or Sugar In The Raw (0.4oz / about 2 tsp)

To start the biscuits, combine the flour, 50 grams (1.8 ounces) sugar, the cornmeal, baking powder, and salt in a food processor and pulse to mix. Add the butter and process until the mixture is the texture of coarse meal, about 15 seconds. Add the cream and pulse just until a dough forms.

Turn the dough out onto a piece of parchment paper. Gather it into a ball, then shape it into a square. Roll it out so it is about 1 inch thick, fold the parchment around it, and wrap it in plastic; chill the dough for at least 30 minutes.

To prepare the filling, put the plums in a bowl. Add 130 grams (4.6 ounces) sugar, the cardamom, and orange zest. Mix well and set aside to macerate at room temperature until the plums begin to release their juices, at least 15 minutes. Add the cornstarch and mix thoroughly. Spoon the plums and their juices into a 9-inch deep-dish pie plate or baking dish with sides at least 2 inches high.

To finish the cobbler, preheat the oven to 350°F. Loosen the dough from the parchment and, using a 1½-inch round pastry cutter (or sharp knife), cut out 8 biscuits and arrange them. Brush each biscuit with a little cream and sprinkle with crystallized sugar.

Bake the cobbler until the biscuits are golden brown and the filling bubbly, about 50 minutes, covering the biscuits with foil once they are nicely colored. Allow the cobbler to cool on a wire rack for at least 1 hour. Serve warm or at room temperature, topped with ice cream, if desired.

Italian Plum and Hazelnut Tart

Makes one 9-inch tart

I admit that the shaved Pecorino and black pepper garnish seem unusual in this recipe, but when you think about how well plums, nuts, and salty cheese go together, I think you'll see where I got the idea. I use hazelnuts in both the crust and the cake-like filling; you can toast all the nuts together or do them separately.

Tart shell:

1 recipe	Hazelnut Dough (page 178)
25g	hazelnuts (0.9oz / about 3 T)
160g	all-purpose flour (5.6oz / about 1 cup + 2½ T)
60g	hazelnut flour (2.1oz / about ½ cup + 2 T)
	Pinch of Diamond Crystal kosher salt
150g	unsalted butter (5.3oz), room temperature
40g	confectioners' sugar (1.4oz / about ⅓ cup)
1	large egg yolk

Hazelnut filling:

145g	hazelnuts (5.1oz / about 1 cup + 3 T)
35g	all-purpose flour (1.2oz / about ¼ cup)
	Pinch of Diamond Crystal kosher salt
1	large egg
1	large egg yolk
114g	unsalted butter (4oz), room temperature
125g	sugar (4.4oz / about ½ cup + 2 T)
1 tsp	orange zest
¼ tsp	vanilla paste or pure vanilla extract

Plums:

430g	Italian plums (15oz / about 15), halved and pitted
2 T	light brown sugar

Topping:

30g	Pecorino (1oz) (optional)
	Freshly ground black pepper (optional)

To prepare the dough, follow the instructions on page 178. On a lightly floured surface, roll the dough out into a round about 12 inches across and ⅛ inch thick. Dock the dough all over with a fork. Fit the dough into a 9-inch tart pan. (The easiest approach: Slide the bottom of the pan under the rolled-out dough, fold it loosely over the edges, drop the bottom into the pan, then unfold the dough and fit it to the pan.) Trim the edges, then thoroughly chill the crust for 15 minutes in the freezer or at least 30 minutes in the refrigerator.

Preheat the oven to 325°F. Line the tart shell with tinfoil and fill it with pie weights (dried beans or rice work). Blind-bake the tart until the crust is set, about 15 minutes, then remove the foil and weights and bake until the bottom of the crust appears dry, 5 to 10 minutes more. Set the crust aside to cool. Do not turn off the oven.

To prepare the hazelnut filling, roast the hazelnuts in a small ovenproof skillet until they smell toasty, about 12 minutes. Remove the hazelnuts from the oven and allow them to cool completely. Combine them in a food processor with 35 grams (1.2 ounces) all-purpose flour and the salt. Process until the nuts are finely ground. Transfer the nut mixture to a bowl; wipe out the processor. Mix the egg with the egg yolk in a measuring cup and reserve.

In the food processor, cream the butter with the sugar, zest, and vanilla. With the machine running, stream in the egg mixture. Add the hazelnut mixture and pulse to combine. Spoon the hazelnut filling into the tart shell, smoothing it with an offset spatula (or the filling can be stored in the refrigerator for up to 2 days).

To prepare the plums, put them in a bowl, sprinkle them with brown sugar, toss to mix, and set aside to macerate at room temperature until the plums begin to release their juices, 10 to 15 minutes.

To finish the tart, preheat the oven to 350°F. Arrange the plums, cut-sides up, over the filling. Drizzle the tart with any accumulated fruit juices, then bake it until the crust is nicely browned and the cakey filling is golden and beginning to pull from the crust, about 50 minutes.

Allow the tart to cool for 10 minutes, then remove the sides of the tart pan. While the tart is still warm, shave the cheese over the top and sprinkle it with pepper, if desired. Serve the tart warm or at room temperature.

Apple Tartlets

Makes 4 tartlets

These individual free-form tarts are a perfect dinner party dessert because there is no cutting and serving required. They also make an elegant addition to a fall picnic lunch. You only need ½ cup of the apple butter in the filling; the recipe yields a quart. You could make less, but I'd go ahead and do the whole batch—it keeps beautifully and is delicious on toast or stirred into yogurt. I make Cinnamon Sugar Crisps with any extra dough; see the Variation below.

Filling:

½ cup	Apple Butter (page 278)
1125g	apples (2½ lb), a mixture works well, but avoid Macintosh
230g	light brown sugar (8.1oz / about 1 cup)
1 cup	apple cider
2 T	apple cider vinegar
1	cinnamon stick
4	whole cloves
	Peel of ½ orange
1	vanilla bean, split lengthwise
2 large or 3 medium	**tart, juicy apples, such as Mutsu, Honeycrisp, or Granny Smith, peeled, cored, and halved**
1	**large egg, beaten**

Crust:

1 recipe	Cream Cheese Dough (page 174)
140g	all-purpose flour (5oz / about 1 cup)
0.7g	Diamond Crystal kosher salt (¼ tsp)
114g	unsalted butter (4oz), diced and chilled
114g	cream cheese (4oz)

Topping:

4 tsp	**crème fraîche**
17g	**crystallized sugar, such as turbinado, Demerara, or Sugar In The Raw (0.6oz / about 4 tsp)**

To start the filling, make the apple butter according to the instructions on page 278. Measure out ½ cup. Store the rest in a covered container in the refrigerator; it will last several weeks.

To start the crust, make the dough according to the instructions on page 174. Line a baking sheet with parchment paper, then, working on a lightly floured surface, roll out the dough into a rectangle about 8 × 16 inches and ⅛ inch thick. Using a 6-inch round cutter or a knife, cut out 4 circles. Put the rounds on a parchment-lined baking sheet and chill the dough for 15 minutes in the freezer or at least 30 minutes in the refrigerator.

To assemble the tartlets, preheat the oven to 400°F. Cut the apple halves into ⅛-inch-thick slices, leaving the end pieces a little thicker and keeping the slices of each half apple together. Working on the parchment-lined baking sheet, top each pastry round with an even layer of apple butter, leaving a 1-inch border around the outside. Brush the border with beaten egg. Fan slices of half an apple on each tart on top of the apple butter. Build the tarts' rims by lifting and pinching the dough up and around the outermost sliced apple, pleating and creating an even pastry edge.

Brush the crust of each tart with beaten egg and bake until the dough begins to look dry and set, about 10 minutes, then reduce the oven temperature to 375°F and bake until the crust is nicely browned and the apples have softened, 20 minutes more. Remove the tartlets from the oven.

Heat the broiler. Make a "collar" out of tinfoil for each tart and fit it over the edges of the crust to prevent them from burning. Spread the exposed apple slices with crème fraîche and sprinkle them with crystallized sugar. Carefully caramelize the apple slices under the broiler, cooking just until the topping browns, about 2 minutes. Allow the tarts to cool on a wire rack. Serve warm or at room temperature with whipped crème fraîche or ice cream, if desired.

Variation: To make Cinnamon Sugar Crisps, preheat the oven to 375°F and line a baking sheet with parchment paper. Mix 30 grams (1 ounce) sugar with ¼ teaspoon ground cinnamon in a bowl. On a lightly floured surface, reroll any scraps of the cream cheese dough into a rectangle about ⅛ inch thick. Sprinkle the cinnamon sugar on the dough, turn it over, then sprinkle it on the other side. Roll the sugared dough into a tight log, slice it into ½-inch-thick cookies, arrange them on the baking sheet, and bake until they are golden; begin checking after 8 minutes.

Apple and Raspberry Crisp

Makes one 9-inch crisp

I top this crisp with an oat crumble. As always, I make a full recipe of crumble, which is about twice as much topping as I need here, and freeze the rest. As far as apples go, I like to mix different kinds. I usually include Honeycrisp and Granny Smith but almost any variety except Macintosh will work.

Crumble:

About 1¼ cups	Oat Crumble (page 298)
100g	sugar (3.5oz / about ½ cup)
110g	light brown sugar (4oz / about ½ cup)
105g	all-purpose flour (3.7oz / about ¾ cup)
80g	rolled oats (2.8oz / about ¼ cup + 3 T)
½ tsp	ground cinnamon
0.7g	Diamond Crystal kosher salt (¼ tsp)
141g	unsalted butter (5oz), melted and cooled

Filling:

760g	mixed tart and sweet apples (see headnote) (1lb 10oz), cored, peeled, and sliced about 1 inch thick
24g	light brown sugar (0.8oz / about 1¾ T)
50g	sugar (1.8oz / about ¼ cup)
1 tsp	lemon zest
2 T	lemon juice
1 T	cornstarch
80g	fresh raspberries (3oz / about ½ cup)

To prepare the crumble, follow the directions on page 298. Put half the topping aside to use in this recipe. Seal the rest in a plastic bag and freeze for later.

To start the filling and make the crisp, preheat the oven to 350°F. In a bowl, mix the apples with the brown and white sugars, lemon zest, and lemon juice. Toss to mix and set aside to macerate at room temperature until the apples release their juices, about 15 minutes. Pour the accumulated liquid into a small bowl. Stir the cornstarch into the juice. When the starch has dissolved, pour the mixture over the apples.

Spoon the apple mixture into a 9-inch deep-dish glass or ceramic pie pan or baking dish with sides at least 2 inches high (avoid a tin pan; it will react with the fruit). Arrange the raspberries over the apples then top with the crumble. Bake the crisp until the top is golden and the apples bubbly, about 1 hour. Serve warm or at room temperature topped with ice cream, if desired.

Lemon Pie with Coconut

Makes one 9-inch pie

This double-crust pie was inspired by Shaker lemon pie, but it ultimately bears it only a slight resemblance. The traditional version is typically made by macerating sliced whole lemons in sugar, then baking them in a flaky crust. I had difficulty getting the filling where I wanted it, so I decided to experiment. In the end, I minced a combination of whole and peeled lemons, macerated them, then added coconut—not a staple in the Shaker pantry, but quite delicious.

Filling:	
4	medium lemons, scrubbed
400g	sugar (1.4oz / about 2 cups)
2 T	grated fresh ginger
36g	shredded unsweetened coconut (1.3oz / about ½ cup)
6 T	coconut milk
4	large eggs
1	large egg white, lightly beaten
About 10g	crystallized sugar, such as turbinado, Demerara, or Sugar In The Raw (0.4oz / about 2 tsp)

Crust:	
Double recipe	**Basic Butter Pie Dough (page 170)**
350g	all-purpose flour (12.3oz / about 2½ cups)
24g	sugar (0.8oz / about 2 T)
4.5g	Diamond Crystal kosher salt (1 ½ tsp)
226g	unsalted butter (8oz)

The day before baking, cut 2 of the lemons into thick slices, remove and discard the seeds, and put the slices in a food processor. Peel the remaining 2 lemons, removing the membranes, pith, and the seeds from the sections. Add the lemon sections to the processor along with the sugar and fresh ginger. Process until the mixture is coarsely ground and transfer it to a bowl. Cover the bowl with plastic and allow the lemon mixture to sit at room temperature overnight.

To prepare the crust, double the recipe and follow the instructions on page 170. Divide the dough in half, gathering it into 2 balls, flattening them into disks, wrapping them in plastic, and chilling them thoroughly. Roll out the dough on lightly floured parchment paper into 2 rounds, each about 12 inches across and ⅛ inch thick. Fit one round into a 9-inch pie plate to form the bottom crust. Transfer the other crust (on the parchment) to a baking sheet. Chill both crusts for 15 minutes in the freezer or at least 30 minutes in the refrigerator.

To finish the pie, preheat the oven to 450°F. Strain the macerated lemon through a fine sieve, reserving the pulp and syrupy juice in separate bowls. Mix the shredded coconut into the lemon pulp and spoon the mixture into the chilled bottom crust. Beat the eggs in a medium bowl and whisk in the coconut milk and reserved lemon syrup to form a custard. Pour the custard mixture into the pie crust.

Using a sharp knife, cut a hole about an inch in diameter in the center of the top crust. Make 8 slashes in the dough with a sharp knife to vent steam and place the crust on top of the pie, centering the hole. Trim away the excess dough from the edge of the pie. Press the edges together to seal the pie. Form the rim by rolling the lip of the dough outward and under, then crimp the edge. Brush the crust with beaten egg white and dust it with crystallized sugar.

Bake the pie until it begins to color, about 15 minutes. Reduce the oven temperature to 350°F and continue baking. Check the pie after 15 minutes more to see if the rim is getting too dark. If it is, cover it with a tinfoil "collar" and continue baking until the rest of the crust is nicely browned and a knife inserted through an air vent into the custard comes out clean, about 15 minutes more (45 minutes in total). Remove the pie from the oven. Discard the foil and let the pie cool completely on a wire rack. Serve at room temperature, topped with coconut or vanilla ice cream, if desired.

Lemon Tart

This tart, filled with a vibrant olive oil–enriched lemon cream, is a perfect expression of my point of view these days. It reflects my inherited Italian sensibility and my French training, as well as my American inclination to merge the two.

Filling:

1 recipe	**XVOO Lemon Cream (page 233)**
200g	sugar (7oz / about 1 cup)
	Zest of 4 lemons
4	large eggs
¾ cup	freshly squeezed lemon juice
1.5g	Diamond Crystal kosher salt (½ tsp)
142g	unsalted butter (5oz), diced, room temperature
170g	extra-virgin olive oil

Crust:

½ recipe	**Sweet Tart Dough (page 181), made with lemon zest**
150g	all-purpose flour (5.3oz / about 1 cup)
50g	sugar (1.8oz / about ¼ cup)
½ tsp	lemon zest
0.7g	Diamond Crystal kosher salt (¼ tsp)
100g	unsalted butter (3.5oz), diced and chilled
1	large egg
½ tsp	vanilla paste or pure vanilla extract

To make the filling, follow the directions on page 233. Cover the lemon cream directly with plastic wrap and chill for at least 6 hours.

To start the tart shell, make the dough, adding lemon zest according to the instructions on page 181. On a lightly floured piece of parchment, roll the dough out into a round about 12 inches across and ⅛ inch thick. Transfer the dough to a 9-inch tart pan with a removable bottom. (The easiest approach: Slide the bottom of the pan under the rolled-out dough, fold it loosely over the edges, drop the bottom to the pan, then unfold the dough and fit it to the pan.) Chill the dough for 15 minutes in the freezer or at least 30 in the refrigerator.

To blind-bake the crust, preheat the oven to 350°F. Line the tart shell with tinfoil and fill it with pie weights (beans or rice work). Bake until the dough is set, about 15 minutes, remove the foil and weights, and continue baking until the crust is fully cooked and golden, 15 to 20 minutes longer. Allow the tart shell to cool completely on a wire rack.

To finish the tart, whisk the lemon cream to loosen it, pour it evenly into the tart shell, and smooth the surface with an offset spatula. Refrigerate the tart until the filling is set, at least 1 hour. Slice and serve.

Kumquat Tatin

Makes one 9-inch tart

Thinking about Shaker lemon pie (see page 159) got me wondering about cooking other fruits more or less whole. Kumquats sprang to mind, and the idea of featuring them in a tatin followed shortly. I make a single large tatin here, but you can also make individual tatins (just remember the cooking time will be shorter). Either way, be forewarned that seeding the fruit is tiresome. Although some people don't think you need to, I feel you must if you want to ensure your jewel-like dessert tastes as good as it looks.

Crust:

½ recipe	Rough Puff Pastry (page 179), or 245g of store-bought puff pastry, thawed if frozen
114g	all-purpose flour (4oz / about ¾ cup)
2.3g	Diamond Crystal kosher salt (¾ tsp)
114g	unsalted butter (4oz)

Filling:

1 T	light corn syrup
200g	sugar (7oz / about 1 cup)
56g	unsalted butter (2oz), diced
500g	kumquats (17.6oz), scrubbed

To start the crust, make the dough according to the instructions on page 179. Roll the pastry out on a sheet of lightly floured parchment into a round about 12 inches across and ⅛ inch thick. Slide the parchment (and dough) onto a baking sheet and chill the dough for 15 minutes in the freezer or at least 30 minutes in the refrigerator. Trim the dough down to an 11-inch round and return it to the refrigerator. (Reroll the trimmings to make the Crisps on page 102.)

Make the caramel by combining ¼ cup water with the corn syrup and sugar in a heavy-bottomed saucepan. Heat over medium-high without stirring until the sugar dissolves and the liquid turns light amber, about 15 minutes. Remove the pan from the heat and whisk in the butter, a piece at a time, taking care that the caramel doesn't bubble over. Pour the hot caramel into a 9-inch cake pan or cast-iron skillet and set it aside to cool. This may be done hours in advance.

To prepare the kumquats and make the tatin, preheat the oven to 425°F. Trim off the stem ends of the kumquats and halve them lengthwise. Using a paring knife, remove the seeds. Arrange the kumquats, cut-sides up, on the caramel. Dock the dough all over with a fork and place it over the kumquats, tucking in the sides.

Bake the tatin until the dough begins to color, about 20 minutes, then reduce the oven temperature to 375°F and bake until the crust is golden brown, about 30 minutes more. Let the tart cool completely in the pan on a wire rack, at least an hour. Shortly before serving, preheat the oven to 350°F. Put the tart in the oven just long enough to loosen the caramel, about 2 minutes. Carefully invert the tart out onto a plate and serve it topped with whipped crème fraîche, if desired.

Chocolate Caramel Tart
with **Peanuts**

I started making this tart when I was working at Gramercy Tavern. It's so good that I've never stopped. I did, however, try something new: I added salted peanuts to the filling. What took me so long?

Chocolate crust:

1 recipe	**Chocolate Dough (page 171)**
114g	unsalted butter (4oz)
120g	all-purpose flour (4.2oz / about ¾ cup + 2 T)
0.7g	Diamond Crystal kosher salt (¼ tsp)
20g	good-quality Dutch-processed cocoa powder, such as Cacao Barry Extra Brute (0.7oz / about ¼ cup)
65g	confectioners' sugar (2.3oz / about ½ cup)
1	large egg yolk

Filling:

3 T	light corn syrup
300g	sugar (10.6oz / about 1½ cups)
85g	unsalted butter (3oz), diced, room temperature
½ cup	crème fraîche
	Pinch of Diamond Crystal kosher salt
¾ tsp	vanilla paste or pure vanilla extract
100g	salted peanuts (3.5oz / about ⅔ cup), coarsely chopped

Ganache:

½ cup	heavy cream
113g	bittersweet chocolate (4oz), chopped

To start the crust, follow the instructions on page 171. Roll the dough out between two pieces of parchment paper into a thin round about 12 inches across and no thicker than ⅛ inch. Gently release the dough from time to time as you work. Fit the dough into a 9-inch tart pan with a removable bottom. (The easiest approach: Slide the bottom of the pan under the rolled-out dough, fold it loosely over the edges, drop the bottom into the pan, then unfold the dough and fit it to the pan.) Trim the dough, using the trimmings to patch any thin spots. Chill the crust for 15 minutes in the freezer or at least 30 minutes in the refrigerator.

To blind-bake the crust, preheat the oven to 325°F. Line the crust with tinfoil and then fill it with pie weights (dried beans or rice work). Bake the crust until it looks set, about 20 minutes. Remove the foil and weights and bake until the crust is fully cooked, about 20 minutes more. Allow the crust to cool completely in the pan on a wire rack.

To start the filling, first make a caramel by putting the corn syrup in a heavy-bottomed saucepan and cooking it over medium heat until bubbles appear around the edges. Stir in a third (100 grams / 3.5 ounces) of the sugar. When it begins to look like wet sand, add another third (100 grams / 3.5 ounces) of the sugar; continue cooking until that begins to dissolve, then add the remaining 100 grams (3.5 ounces) sugar. Cook the caramel without stirring until it turns deep amber, 15 to 20 minutes. Remove the pan from the heat and carefully whisk in the butter, a piece at a time. Whisk in the crème fraîche, salt, and vanilla. Whisk the caramel until it is smooth. Stir in the peanuts and immediately pour the caramel into the tart shell. Set it aside to cool to room temperature.

Make the ganache by bringing the cream to a simmer in a saucepan over medium-high heat. Put the chopped chocolate in a liquid measuring cup. Using a rubber spatula—not a whisk, because it is important here to avoid incorporating air bubbles—fold the cream into the chocolate and stir just until the ganache is smooth and shiny. Pour the ganache evenly over the cooled caramel. Allow the tart to set for at least an hour before slicing and serving.

Pastiera (Grain Pie)

Makes one 10-inch pie

This is my version of my uncle Frank's grain pie. He was a great cook. Unlike my family, Frank's people, the Ibertis, were from the north of Italy. Frank and my mother enjoyed a friendly regional, culinary rivalry. Because it is a Neapolitan classic, you would think this dessert would have fallen in my mom's territory, but in fact, it was Frank who made this every Easter. He got his recipe from a Polly-O cheese recipe book. I went on from there. Be warned that if you are starting with dried wheat berries, they need to soak overnight (see below).

Filling:

65g	dried wheat berries* (2.3oz / about 5¼ T)
1½ cups	milk
½ stick	cinnamon
	Peel from ¼ medium navel orange, pith removed
1.5g	Diamond Crystal kosher salt (½ tsp)
⅓ cup	diced Candied Orange Rinds (page 275)
3	medium navel oranges
300g	sugar (10.6oz / about 1½ cups)
1 T	light corn syrup
600g	ricotta cheese (1lb 5oz / about 2½ cups), drained
200g	sugar (7oz / about 1 cup)
1 T	orange flower water
1 tsp	vanilla paste or pure vanilla extract
1 tsp	orange zest
3	large eggs
2	large egg yolks

Crust:

1 recipe	Sweet Tart Dough (page 181) (made with orange zest)
300g	all-purpose flour, plus extra for the pan (10.6oz / about 2 cups + 2 ½ T)
100g	sugar (3.5oz / about ½ cup)
1 tsp	orange zest
1.5g	Diamond Crystal kosher salt (½ tsp)
200g	butter (7oz), diced and chilled, plus extra for the pan
1	large egg
1	large egg yolk
1 tsp	vanilla paste or pure vanilla extract

---

*   In Naples (and Italian American homes), bakers save time and begin with canned, presoaked wheat berries—Asti is the brand to look for if you want to go that way. I, however, prepare my own. My supermarket carries Nature's Earthly Choice. Because they are "quick cooking," meaning first steamed and then dried, they require only a quick 30-minute soak in boiling water before draining and cooking. If you are using raw dried berries, plan to soak them until you see the berries expand and "bloom," about 12 hours. Either way, simmer the soaked berries in water until they are very soft, 30 to 60 minutes, drain them, and then cook them in milk as described in the recipe. White wheat berries are traditional, but red wheat berries—easier to find—will work for this recipe.

To start the filling, put the wheat berries in a heat-proof bowl. Cover them with boiling water and set them aside to soak until they expand (see note). Drain the soaked wheat berries and put them in a saucepan with 1 cup water. Bring the water to a simmer and cook the wheat until it is very soft, 30 to 60 minutes, depending on the type of wheat berries you start with. Drain the wheat berries and return them to the pan. Add the milk, cinnamon, orange peel, and 0.7 grams (¼ teaspoon) of the salt and bring to a simmer over medium heat. Cook, stirring occasionally, until the milk is absorbed and the wheat forms a porridge, about 45 minutes. Remove the pan from the heat and allow the wheat berries to cool to room temperature. Discard the cinnamon stick and orange peel. (The wheat berries may be cooked a day in advance.)

Prepare the candied orange rinds according to the instructions on page 275. Dice enough to equal ⅓ cup and reserve them. Store the remainder in an airtight container for another use.

To prepare the crust, make the dough according to the instructions on page 181 (using orange zest), but divide it into a slightly larger and smaller ball. Roll the larger dough ball on a lightly floured surface into a 14-inch round about ⅛ inch thick. Fit the rolled dough into a buttered and floured deep-dish 10-inch pie or tart pan. Trim the crust's edge and chill the pie shell for at least 30 minutes. Roll out the smaller portion of dough on a lightly floured surface or piece of parchment into a round about 10 inches across and ⅛ inch thick. This will be the top crust. Line a baking sheet with parchment, transfer the top crust to the baking sheet, and chill for at least 30 minutes.

To continue the filling, combine the ricotta and 150 grams (5.3 ounces) of the sugar in a food processor. Add the orange flower water, vanilla, and zest and process until smooth. Transfer the mixture to a bowl. Separate the 3 whole eggs; reserve the whites at room temperature. Add the yolks plus 2 additional yolks to the ricotta mixture. Whisk to form a custard, then stir in the candied orange rinds and the wheat berry porridge; cover and chill thoroughly, at least 1 hour.

To finish the pie, preheat the oven to 350°F. In the bowl of a stand mixer and using the whisk attachment, beat the reserved egg whites until they hold soft peaks. While whisking, gradually stream in the remaining 50 grams (1.7 ounces) sugar and 0.7 grams (¼ teaspoon) salt. Whip the whites until they hold stiff peaks. Fold the whites into the chilled grain mixture and spoon the mixture into the chilled crust. Cut the 10-inch dough round into ¾-inch-wide strips and weave them into a lattice over the filling. Trim the edges of the lattice to fit the pie, pinch them together with the bottom crust, and crimp to seal. Bake the pie until the filling is set and the crust is golden, about 2 hours. Allow the pie to cool for at least 30 minutes, then serve warm or at room temperature.

Basic Butter Pie Dough

Makes one 9-inch pie crust

I prefer to make this dough by hand because it gives me more control, which I think leads to a lighter, flakier result. That said, there are times (like steamy summer days) when a food processor is the way to go. Either way, handle the dough less rather than more, just enough so the ingredients come together. If you are making a double-crust pie, refer to the ingredient amounts in brackets below. For savory pies, reduce the sugar to 6 grams (0.2 ounces / about 1½ tsp).

114g	unsalted butter (4oz), diced and frozen [228g / 8oz]	12g	sugar (0.4oz / about 1 T) [24g / 0.8oz]
175g	all-purpose flour (6.2oz / about 1¼ cups) [350g / 12.4oz]	2.3g	Diamond Crystal kosher salt (¾ tsp) [4.6g / 1½ tsp]

To make the dough by hand, cut half the butter into ½-inch dice and the remaining butter into 1-inch dice, then chill it all while you gather the remaining ingredients.

In a bowl, mix the flour with the sugar and salt. Add the butter and, working quickly and gently, use your fingers to massage the butter into the flour, pinching it bit by bit and coating each piece of butter with flour. Work just until all the butter pieces have been pinched and flattened. Sprinkle the dough with ¼ cup ice water. Using a fork, mix the water into the dough until it is evenly distributed, adding more ice water if the dough seems too dry to hold together. Turn the dough out onto a lightly floured work surface. Gather the dough into a ball, wrap it in plastic, then flatten it into a disk. Refrigerate the dough until it is firm, at least 1 hour and up to 2 days, or freeze it for up to a month.

To make the dough in a food processor, cut the butter as described above and freeze it. Combine the flour, sugar, and salt in the food processor and pulse to combine. Add the frozen butter and process until the biggest pieces are the size of peas, about 10 seconds. Add ¼ cup ice water and process until the water is evenly distributed and the dough holds together when pinched (add a little more ice water if the dough is too dry). Turn the dough out onto a lightly floured work surface. Gather the dough into a ball, wrap it in plastic, then flatten it into a disk. Refrigerate the dough until it is firm, at least 1 hour and up to 2 days, or freeze it for up to a month.

Chocolate Dough

I use this dough to make the Chocolate Caramel Tart (page 165). I like it quite thin, so I usually roll it out between pieces of parchment.

114g	unsalted butter (4oz), diced, room temperature
120g	all-purpose flour (4.2oz / about ¾ cup + 2 T)
0.7g	Diamond Crystal kosher salt (¼ tsp)

20g	good-quality Dutch-processed cocoa powder, such as Cacao Barry Extra Brute (0.7oz / about ¼ cup)
65g	confectioners' sugar (2.3oz / about ½ cup)
1	large egg yolk

Put the butter in the bowl of a stand mixer fitted with the paddle attachment. In a separate bowl, mix the flour with the salt and cocoa powder. Sift the confectioners' sugar into the mixer bowl, then cream the butter and sugar together. Scrape down the bowl, then add the yolk; scrape down again, then, with the mixer on low, add the flour mixture a third at a time, scraping down as necessary.

Turn the dough out onto a lightly floured work surface (expect it to be quite soft). Gather it together into a ball, wrap it in plastic, then flatten it into a disk. Chill the dough until it is firm, at least 1 hour and up to 2 days in the refrigerator, or freeze it for up to a month.

Cornmeal Buttermilk Dough

Makes one 9-inch pie crust or crusts for 6 turnovers

This flavorful dough is what I use for my blueberry tart on page 135 and for the turnovers on page 137. I love coarse stone-ground corn for lots of things, but this recipe is not one of them. Here, I want the taste of corn in a dough that gives me a light, flaky crust, so I use finely ground cornmeal.

34g	finely ground cornmeal (1.2oz / about 3 T)	2.3g	Diamond Crystal kosher salt (¾ tsp)
210g	all-purpose flour (7.4oz / about 1½ cups)	143g	unsalted butter (5oz), diced and frozen
12g	sugar (0.4oz / about 1 T)	¼ cup	buttermilk

Combine the cornmeal, flour, sugar, and salt in a food processor and pulse to mix. Add the butter and process until the mixture is the texture of coarse meal (the largest pieces of butter are no bigger than a pea). Add the buttermilk and 1 tablespoon ice water and process until the liquid is evenly distributed and the dough holds together when pinched. Turn the dough out onto a floured work surface. Gather the dough into a ball, wrap it in plastic, then flatten it into a disk. Refrigerate the dough until it is firm, at least 1 hour and up to 2 days, or freeze it for up to a month.

Cheddar Crostata Dough

I like extra-sharp cheese in this dough, the crust I use for my Tomato Crostata (page 203). It doesn't matter if the cheese is white or orange. The only difference between the two is a little annatto—added to give the cheese a consistent orange color over the course of a year, when otherwise the hue would traditionally vary with the season and the herds' diets.

210g	all-purpose flour (7.4oz / about 1½ cups)		88g	extra-sharp cheddar cheese (3.1oz / about 1¼ cups), grated and frozen
1.5g	Diamond Crystal kosher salt (½ tsp)		88g	unsalted butter (3.1oz), cut into ½-inch dice and frozen

Combine the flour and salt in a food processor and pulse to mix. Add the frozen butter and cheese and process until the mixture is the texture of coarse meal. Add ¼ cup ice water and process until the water is evenly distributed and the dough is clumpy and holds together when pinched (add a little more ice water if the dough is too dry). Turn the dough out onto a lightly floured work surface. Gather the dough into a ball, wrap it in plastic, then flatten it into a disk. Refrigerate the dough until it is firm, at least 1 hour and up to 2 days, or freeze it for up to a month.

Cream Cheese Dough

Makes four 6-inch tartlets

This easy-to-make dough is an adaptation of a recipe my friend Nancy Silverton developed. She "turns" the dough, as you would puff pastry. Instead, I use the same technique here that I do to make biscuits. I cut my dough in quarters and pile it up before I roll it out. I use this dough in many ways, including to make cookies and nibbles such as Grapefruit and Poppy Seed Rugelach (page 101), Onion and Poppy Seed Kiffles (page 212), and Cheese Kiffles (page 210).

140g	all-purpose flour (5oz / about 1 cup)		114g	unsalted butter (4oz), diced and chilled
0.7g	Diamond Crystal kosher salt (¼ tsp)		114g	cream cheese (4oz)

Combine the flour and salt in a food processor and pulse to mix. Add the butter and process until it is the size of peas. Add the cream cheese and process until the mixture is the texture of coarse meal. Turn the dough out onto a lightly floured work surface and shape it into a 6-inch square. Cut the square into quarters, then stack them on top of one another. If you are making Grapefruit and Poppy Seed Rugelach, Onion and Poppy Seed Kiffles, or Cheese Kiffles, cut the stacked dough in half, evening the sides of each portion by tapping them against the work surface. Wrap both halves in plastic, round the edges to form disks, and flatten them. On the other hand, if you are making tartlets, leave the dough in one piece and wrap it in plastic. Either way, chill it for at least 1 hour and up to 2 days, or freeze for up to a month.

Crostata Dough

This is essentially the same dough as the Basic Butter Pie Dough (page 170), but I've increased the recipe so it works for a crostata, which I like to make a bit larger. I use this dough for sweets and savories, though I reduce the amount of sugar for the latter. You can make this in the food processor, but I prefer to do it by hand. Either way, I cut the butter into different sizes to create extra flakiness in the finished crust. See amounts in brackets for making a double-crust crostata, like Mrs. Stasi's Escarole Pie (page 190).

143g	unsalted butter (5oz), chilled [286g / 2½oz]	12g	sugar* (see note) (0.4oz / about 1 T) [24g / 0.8oz / about 2 T]
210g	all-purpose flour (7.4oz / about 1½ cups) [420g / 14.8oz / about 3 cups]	3g	Diamond Crystal kosher salt (1 tsp) [6g / 2 tsp]

To make the dough by hand, cut half of the butter in a ½-inch dice and the remaining butter in a 1-inch dice, then chill it all while you gather the remaining ingredients. In a bowl, mix the flour with the sugar and salt. Add the butter and, working quickly, use your fingers to massage the butter with the flour, pinching it bit by bit and coating each piece of butter with flour. Work just until all the butter pieces have been pinched and flattened. Sprinkle the dough with ¼ cup ice water. Using a fork, mix the water into the dough until it is evenly distributed and the dough holds together (add a little more ice water if the dough seems too dry). Turn the dough out onto a floured work surface. Gather the dough into a ball, wrap it in plastic, then flatten it into a disk. Refrigerate the dough until it is firm, at least 1 hour and up to 2 days, or freeze it for up to a month.

To make the dough in a food processor, cut the butter as described above and freeze it. Combine the flour, sugar, and salt in the food processor and pulse to combine. Add the frozen butter and process until the biggest pieces are the size of peas, about 10 seconds. Add ¼ cup ice water and process until the water is evenly distributed and the dough holds together when pinched; add a little more water if the dough seems too dry. Turn the dough out onto a floured work surface. Gather the dough into a ball, wrap it in plastic, then flatten it into a disk. Refrigerate the dough until it is firm, at least 1 hour and up to 2 days, or freeze it for up to a month.

---

* To make a single-crust savory dough, reduce the sugar to 6 grams (0.2 ounces / about 1½ teaspoons); for a double crust, use 12 grams (0.4 ounces / about 1 tablespoon) sugar. This is also delicious with Pecorino cheese incorporated in the dough. For a double crust, add 12 grams (0.4 ounces) Pecorino cheese, grated (about 2¼ tablespoons) to the flour/sugar/salt mixture.

Cast-Iron Pizza Dough

Makes two 10-inch pizzas

I don't have a pizza stone, but I find my old 12-inch cast-iron skillet works fine as a substitute—if I heat it up properly. I like the fact that it has a handle that allows me to easily get it in and out of the oven. I use a half recipe of this dough for my Potato Flambé Tart (page 197) and have included those ingredient amounts in brackets below. In addition to the tart and pizza, I also use this to make dessert, topping it with crème fraîche, blackberries, and brown sugar (see photo on facing page).

1 ¼ tsp	active dry yeast [heaping ½ tsp]	3g	Diamond Crystal kosher salt (1 tsp) [1.5g / ½ tsp]
332g	bread flour (11.7oz / about 2 cups + 5 T) [166g / 5.9oz / about 1 cup + 2½ T]	About 4 T	extra-virgin olive oil [2 T], plus extra for greasing

In the bowl of a stand mixer fitted with the paddle attachment, dissolve the yeast in 1 cup plus 1 table-spoon room-temperature water. Set the yeast aside until it activates and looks creamy, about 10 minutes. In a medium bowl, whisk the flour with the salt. Add the flour mixture to the yeast and mix on medium speed until the liquid and dry ingredients are combined. Switch to the dough hook and knead the dough until it is smooth (expect it to be moist and a little sticky), about 15 minutes.

Grease a large bowl with olive oil. Put the dough in the bowl. To ensure a good structure, fold the dough ball in on itself and make a "four corner fold" by folding a pinch of dough at a time into the center to create a tighter, smaller ball. Flip the dough over, cover the bowl loosely with plastic wrap, and set it aside until the dough has doubled (at least 2 hours in a warm kitchen, but I prefer overnight in the refrigerator).

To shape the dough, turn it out onto a lightly floured surface, punch it down, then divide it in half (don't divide the dough if you are making a half recipe) and shape the dough into balls. Put the dough on an oiled baking sheet, cover with a kitchen towel, and let rest for 1 hour at room temperature or at least 4 hours in the refrigerator (overnight is also okay).

To make pizza, preheat the oven to 500°F. Put a large 12-inch cast-iron skillet in the oven for at least 20 minutes and get your toppings ready to go. I like fresh tomatoes, mozzarella, and oregano; or tomato sauce, Parmigiano-Reggiano, and Pecorino cheese; or olive oil, anchovies, sliced garlic, and hot pepper. Working with one ball at a time, roll or stretch the dough into a thin 10-inch round, letting it rest if it begins to re-sist. Transfer the dough to a floured plate. Carefully take the hot skillet out of the oven and put it on top of the stove. Put 2 tablespoons of the olive oil in the pan and, quickly but again carefully, slide the dough from the plate into the skillet. Top the pizza as desired and cook it until the crust is bubbly and browned, about 12 minutes. Allow the pizza to cool in the pan for 3 minutes, then transfer it to a wire rack while you prepare the second pizza. Serve warm.

Hazelnut Dough

Makes one 9-inch tart shell

I use this dough for my Italian Plum and Hazelnut Tart (page 152) but like it with any custard or fruit tart where you want hazelnut flavor.

25g	hazelnuts (0.9oz / about 3 T)
160g	all-purpose flour (5.6oz / about 1 cup + 2½ T)
60g	hazelnut flour (2.1oz / about ½ cup + 2 T)
	Pinch of Diamond Crystal kosher salt
150g	butter (5.3oz), room temperature
40g	confectioners' sugar (1.4oz / about ⅓ cup)
1	large egg yolk

To start the tart shell, preheat the oven to 325°F. Coarsely chop the hazelnuts, spread them in a single layer in a small ovenproof skillet, and roast them until they smell nutty, about 12 minutes. Remove them from the oven and allow them to cool. Put the toasted nuts, all-purpose flour, hazelnut flour, and salt in a food processor. Process until the nuts are finely ground, then transfer the mixture to a bowl. Combine the butter and confectioners' sugar in the processor and cream the two together. Add the hazelnut/flour mixture and pulse until the mixture is the texture of coarse meal. With the processor running, add the egg yolk and process until the dough comes together.

Turn the dough out onto a floured work surface (expect it to be quite soft). Gather it into a ball, wrap it in plastic, then flatten it into a disk. Chill the dough until it is firm, at least 1 hour and up to 2 days in the refrigerator, or freeze for up to a month.

Rough Puff Pastry

Makes about 570g, or 2 tart shells

This is a laminated dough, meaning it is extra flaky because butter has been carefully folded between the layers. It is not quite as finicky as traditional French puff pastry and makes a great substitute when you want a crust with light lacquered layers. Though it is more forgiving than the original, this recipe is difficult to get right when it is hot and humid, and the process can't be rushed—you must let the dough chill in between steps (I spread the work over two days). A trick: When the edges of my dough get uneven, I cut the messy side and put the strip of extra dough in between folds. Another trick: Even if I need only one crust, I always make the full recipe so I have some in the freezer.

227g	all-purpose flour (8oz / about 1½ cups + 2 T)	5g	Diamond Crystal kosher salt (1½ tsp)
227g	unsalted butter (8oz), cut in ½- to 1-inch dice and frozen		

Combine the flour and frozen butter in a food processor and process until the mixture is integrated and the largest pieces of butter are no bigger than a shelled peanut. Transfer this mixture to a bowl and, using a fork, stir in ½ cup ice water. Turn the dough out onto a lightly floured work surface or a piece of parchment and, working with your hands, make sure the wet ingredients are evenly incorporated. Form the dough into a rectangle about 6 × 8 inches. Loosely wrap the dough in plastic and roll it into a rectangle about 6 × 12 inches and ½ inch thick. Seal the plastic and chill the dough thoroughly, at least 1 hour.

Working on a lightly floured surface or floured parchment paper, roll the dough out so it is 6 × 18 inches. Arrange the dough so the short sides are at the top and bottom. Fold the dough like a letter, the uppermost third over the middle, then the bottom third over that. Rotate the dough a quarter turn so the edge that looks like the binding of a book is on the left. Repeat, rolling the dough out again to 6 × 18 inches and folding it in thirds. Wrap the dough in plastic, use a marker to indicate that two turns have been completed, and refrigerate the dough for another hour.

Remove the dough from the refrigerator, lay it on a lightly floured work surface or parchment with the "bound" side once again on the left. Roll the dough so it is 6 × 18 inches, then fold it in thirds again, top to middle, then bottom over top. Make a quarter turn, and repeat. Rewrap the dough, mark four turns done, and chill the dough for another hour before repeating for the final two turns—a total of six in all. At this point, I usually divide the dough in half before wrapping it in plastic and refrigerating or freezing it until I need it. It can be refrigerated for up to 2 days or frozen for 3 months.

Sweet Almond Tart Dough

Makes a 9-inch tart shell

This dough is a classic for a reason. I use it in my Ricotta Tart with Roasted Cherries, page 149, but it works anytime you want the flavor of almond in your tart, which I find I often do.

165g	all-purpose flour (5.8oz / about 1 cup + 3 T)		0.7g	Diamond Crystal kosher salt (¼ tsp)
20g	almond flour (0.7oz / about 3 T)		100g	unsalted butter (3.5oz), diced and chilled
65g	confectioners' sugar (2.3oz / about ½ cup)		1	large egg, lightly beaten

Combine the all-purpose and almond flours in a food processor. Add the confectioners' sugar and salt and pulse to mix. Add the butter and process until the mixture is the texture of fine meal. With the motor running, add the egg and process just until it is incorporated. Turn the dough out onto a floured work surface (expect it to be quite soft). Gather it together into a ball, wrap it in plastic, then flatten it into a disc. Chill the dough until it is firm, at least 1 hour and up to 2 days in the refrigerator (or freeze it for up to a month).

Sweet Tart Dough

Makes two 9-inch pie crusts

This is the dough I use to make Pastiera (page 167), a double-crust Neopolitan classic. Italian tart dough is a touch sweeter and even crispier than French tart dough. For a single-crust pie or tart, refer to the quantities in brackets.

300g	all-purpose flour (10.6oz / about 2 cups + 2½ T) [150g / 5.3oz]
100g	sugar (3.5oz / about ½ cup) [50g / 1.75oz / about ¼ cup]
1 tsp	lemon or orange zest, depending on the recipe [½ tsp]
1.5g	Diamond Crystal kosher salt (½ tsp) [0.7g / ¼ tsp]

200g	unsalted butter, diced and chilled (7oz) [100g / 3.5oz]
1	large egg [1 egg]
1	large egg yolk [omit]
1 tsp	vanilla paste or pure vanilla extract [½ tsp]

Combine the flour, sugar, zest, and salt in a food processor and pulse to mix. Add the butter and process until the mixture is the texture of coarse meal. Mix the egg, yolk, and vanilla together in a mixing cup or bowl. Stir in 1 teaspoon ice water. Add the egg mixture to the machine and process until the liquid is incorporated (if you are making a half recipe don't add ice water initially. Process the egg, then add ice water, ¼ teaspoon at a time, as necessary). Turn the dough out onto a lightly floured work surface. Gather it into a ball, wrap it in plastic, then flatten it into a disk. Chill the dough until it is firm, at least 1 hour and up to 2 days in the refrigerator, or freeze it for up to a month.

CHAPTER 5

Savories

A Taste for Savories

When I want a snack, I usually reach for something salty. Though I like sweets, I am discriminating about them. Honestly, what calls to me most loudly are plates full of umami—ironically, I confess I sometimes prefer to end a meal with cheese. But I believe my reserved relationship to sugar serves me well. It has impelled me to train my attention on balancing flavors rather than defining my vision by sweetness, even as I work within a canon of sugar-filled desserts. It has also led me (and others similarly inclined) to look beyond the usual spices and flavorings and borrow ingredients from the savory side of the kitchen.

Cooking at home, free to follow my whims, I started doing more savory baking. I made hors d'oeuvres and snacks, sometimes working on a classic (like the Pretzels on page 215) and other times continuing my professional habit of pilfering, but reversing things, stealing from the sweet world to create something savory. When I came upon a recipe for kiffles—an eastern European pastry made with a cream cheese dough that is often filled with jam or chocolate—my mind turned to pairing the tender pastry with a mixture of onions and poppy seeds (see page 212). I guessed the resulting nibble would be great with a drink, and so it is. I borrowed again when I lifted the brioche-like dough from my Chocolate Babka Buns (page 31) and used it to make a snack inspired by pork buns I ate at Momofuku Noodle Bar. I used my dough and technique but chose ingredients that I imagine I might find in David Chang's pantry. I wound up with Shiitake Sticky Buns (page 193) that satisfy me in much the same way Chang's *bao*-style buns do, making them an ideal meal on late Sunday morning, with or without eggs on the side.

Living on the North Fork for fifteen years, I have been surrounded by great ingredients and become part of a community of people who love food. When we gather, it naturally falls to me to bring the cake for the birthdays and make pies when the fruit is at its peak, but, as a changeup, I have also always liked taking a turn with the main course, particularly when a vegetable tart fits the bill. With more free time, I perfected some of the savory treats I have been sharing with friends for years, created a couple of new ones, and rediscovered several savory pies I'd almost forgotten. I had fun with the Eggplant Caponata Tart (page 187). It is not a traditional dish, though I think it tastes like it is. It reminds me of our Sunday lunches when I was growing up. Looking back, it seems like there was often a ricotta tart on our table at home. It served as the anchor for the rest of the meal, which in the late summer always included eggplant caponata. I'd eat a bite of the flaky, cheesy tart and use the caponata as a condiment. Why shouldn't the two be combined into one unified dish? No reason, so that's what I did, and I wound up with a tart that brings out the best in both.

Eggplant Caponata Tart

Makes one 9-inch tart

This recipe is a bit of a production, but it is worth the effort (and you can spread the work out). I like caponata so much I always make a double batch, and that larger quantity is provided on page 281, but I indicate how much I need for this tart in brackets there and below.

Tart shell:

½ recipe	Rough Puff Pastry (page 179), or 245g store-bought puff pastry, thawed if frozen
114g	all-purpose flour (4oz / about ¾ cup)
2.3g	Diamond Crystal kosher salt (¾ tsp)
114g	unsalted butter (4oz)

Caponata:

1	red or yellow bell pepper
About ⅓ cup	extra-virgin olive oil
1	medium eggplant (about 450g / 1lb), trimmed and cut in 1½-inch dice
About 4.5g	Diamond Crystal kosher salt (1½ tsp)
About ½ tsp	freshly ground black pepper
1	medium onion, peeled and diced
2	celery ribs, sliced on a diagonal
2	garlic cloves, peeled and sliced
	Pinch of crushed red pepper flakes, or to taste
12g	sugar (0.4oz / about 1 T)
1½ tsp	tomato paste
6 T	red wine vinegar
2 T	white wine

½ cup	green olives, pitted and chopped
2 T	capers, rinsed
2 tsp	chopped fresh parsley
2 T	chopped fresh basil

Ricotta cream:

114g	ricotta cheese (4oz / about 1½ cups), drained
1	large egg yolk
10g	Parmigiano-Reggiano (0.4oz / about 1¾ T), grated
6g	Pecorino cheese (0.2oz / about 1 T), grated
0.7g	Diamond Crystal kosher salt (¼ tsp)
¼ tsp	freshly ground black pepper
1½ tsp	chopped fresh parsley
1½ tsp	chopped fresh basil

Garnish:

About 200g	cherry or grape tomatoes (7oz / about 25—enough to cover the tart), halved
1 ½ to 2 T	crème fraîche
About 115g	Parmigiano-Reggiano (4oz / about 1½ cups), freshly grated
	Basil Oil (page 288) (optional)

To start the tart shell, make the dough according to the instructions on page 179. Preheat the oven to 425°F. On a lightly floured surface, roll out the dough into a 10-inch square about ⅛ inch thick. Dock the pastry, poking holes all over it with a fork, and then chill it in the freezer for 15 minutes or the refrigerator for at least 30 minutes.

Fit the dough into a 9-inch square tart pan with a removable bottom (or place the dough on a parchment-lined baking sheet with an edge). Line the crust with tinfoil and fill it with pie weights (dried beans or rice work).

Bake the tart shell until the dough looks set and the edges begin to color, about 15 minutes, then remove the weights and foil. Lower the oven temperature to 325°F and bake until the crust is cooked through but still pale gold, about 50 minutes. Set the crust aside to cool on a wire rack.

To start the filling, make a half batch of eggplant caponata, according to the instructions on page 281 (the correct quantities for this recipe are indicated above and in brackets there). Adjust the seasoning to taste and chill the caponata for at least 30 minutes.

To make the ricotta cream, in a large bowl, mix the ricotta with the egg yolk. Stir in 10 grams (0.4 ounces) Parmigiano, the Pecorino, salt, black pepper, parsley, and basil.

Preheat the oven to 375°F. To assemble the tart, spoon the caponata into the tart shell, spreading it out evenly, then cover it with the ricotta cream. Arrange the halved tomatoes, cut-sides down, over the entire tart. Whisk the crème fraîche in a bowl to loosen it, then spoon it over the tomatoes. Sprinkle 115 grams (4 ounces) Parmigiano on top. Bake the tart until the crust is golden brown, the tomatoes have softened, and the cheese has melted, about 20 minutes. Remove the tart from the oven and heat the broiler. Brown the tomatoes under the broiler, about 1 minute, then rotate the tart front to back and broil so it is evenly colored, about 30 seconds more. Allow the tart to cool for at least 15 minutes. Serve warm or at room temperature, topped with basil oil, if desired.

Mrs. Stasi's Escarole Pie

Makes one 12-inch pie

Escarole pie reminds me of my friend Deborah. Her family always ate it for breakfast on Christmas morning—big slices at room temperature. It's funny, but it wasn't until years later when Deborah started making the pie herself that she realized how good it is just out of the oven.

Crust:

Double	**Crostata Dough (page 175) (made with Pecorino cheese)**
286g	unsalted butter (10.1oz), chilled
420g	all-purpose flour (14.8oz / about 3 cups)
12g	Pecorino cheese (0.4oz / about 2¼ T), grated
12g	sugar (0.4oz / about 1 T)
6g	Diamond Crystal kosher salt (2 tsp)

Filling:

¼ cup	extra-virgin olive oil, plus extra for drizzling
6 to 8	anchovies, to taste
2 T	minced garlic
½ tsp	crushed red pepper flakes
900g	escarole (2lb / about 2 large heads), chopped and cleaned
6g	Diamond Crystal kosher salt (2 tsp)
6	green olives, pitted and chopped
12	kalamata olives, pitted and chopped
40g	Pecorino cheese (1.4oz / about ½ cup), grated
1	large egg, lightly beaten

To prepare the crust, double the recipe following the instructions on page 175, adding 12 grams (0.4 ounces) grated Pecorino to the flour mixture. Divide the dough in half, wrap it in plastic, flatten it into disks, and refrigerate.

To make the filling, heat the oil in a large, high-sided skillet or Dutch oven over low. Add the anchovies and cook until they soften, about 4 minutes. Break up the anchovies with a fork and add the garlic. Cook, stirring occasionally, until fragrant, about 3 minutes. Add the red pepper flakes and stir to evenly distribute. Increase the heat to medium and add a third of the escarole. Cook, stirring from time to time, and when the escarole wilts, add enough to refill the pan. Repeat until all the escarole has been added, then add the salt, cover the pot, and cook until the escarole is soft and has released its juices, about 8 minutes more. Remove the lid and simmer the escarole in its juices, stirring occasionally and cooking until the pan is almost dry, about 40 minutes. Remove the pan from the heat and stir in the olives. Let the filling cool, then stir in the cheese.

Preheat the oven to 400°F. Roll out one ball of dough into a 12-inch circle on a lightly floured piece of parchment. Roll the second ball a little thinner into a slightly bit bigger round on the same piece of parchment. Put the parchment paper (and dough) on a baking sheet and chill the dough for 15 minutes in the freezer or at least 30 minutes in the refrigerator.

Paint a 2-inch border around the outside of the smaller dough round (the bottom crust) with the beaten egg. Spread the escarole filling evenly on the dough, stopping short of the egg-washed perimeter. Cut a 1-inch hole in the center of the larger round with a sharp knife. Lay this round of dough over the filling, centering the hole. Press the edges of the dough rounds together. Trim away any excess so the crust is even, then roll and crimp the edges. Brush the top crust with beaten egg, then, using a sharp knife, cut 8 slits in the crust to vent steam.

Bake the pie on the baking sheet until the crust is golden brown, about 40 minutes. Allow the pie to cool for at least 15 minutes, then serve warm or at room temperature.

Shiitake Sticky Buns

Makes 6 buns

These soft, slightly sweet buns filled with mushrooms and flavored with miso, soy sauce, and pork were inspired by Chinese *bao*, but in a break with tradition, I used an American sticky bun as my jumping-off point. The recipe is time consuming but not hard, and you can spread out the work. The buns are best eaten within hours of baking, but once assembled they freeze well. For more about beginning a dough with a sponge, see page 26.

Sponge:
2 tsp	active dry yeast
25g	all-purpose flour (0.9oz / about 3 T)

Dough:
200g	all-purpose flour (7oz / about 1 cup + 7 T)
25g	sugar (0.9oz / about 2 T)
0.7g	Diamond Crystal kosher salt (¼ tsp)
1	large egg
30g	unsalted butter (1oz), cut into 6 pieces, room temperature
	Cooking spray or neutral oil

Pickled shallots:
½ cup	rice wine vinegar
½ cup	sake
31g	sugar (1.1oz / about 2½ T)
1.5g	Diamond Crystal kosher salt (½ tsp)
	Pinch of crushed red pepper flakes
	Peel of ¼ lemon
140g	shallots (5oz / about 3 large), peeled and sliced lengthwise

Mushroom filling:
125g	fresh shiitake mushrooms (4.4oz), stemmed and sliced (about 100g / 3.5oz stemmed)
About 2 T	canola or other neutral oil
35g	dried shiitakes (1.2oz) (Note: If you are using dried mushrooms without stems, start closer to 28g / 1oz.)
28g	good-quality bacon (1oz), slab or thick sliced, tough outer skin removed if necessary
¼ cup	soy sauce
¼ cup	sake
¼ cup	mirin
½ cup	chicken stock
1	scallion, minced (white and tender green parts)

Miso mayonnaise:
¼ cup	mayonnaise
1½ tsp	white miso
1 dash	sriracha or Tabasco sauce

Glaze and garnish:
½ cup	honey
4 tsp	soy sauce
	Dash or two of sriracha or Tabasco sauce
	Quick-Pickled Cucumbers (page 283) (optional)

To make the sponge, in a medium bowl, mix the yeast with 3 tablespoons warm water. Set the mixture aside until the yeast looks creamy and activates, about 10 minutes. Mix in 25 grams (0.9 ounces) flour, cover the bowl with plastic wrap, and set it aside in a warm place until the sponge doubles in volume, about 1 hour.

To start the dough, combine 200 grams (7 ounces) flour, 25 grams (0.9 ounces) sugar, and 0.7 grams (¼ teaspoon) salt in a bowl and whisk to blend. In the bowl of a stand mixer and using the whisk attachment, whip the egg with 6 tablespoons water until frothy. Switch to the paddle attachment and add the sponge. Beat on medium until the sponge is integrated, then add the flour mixture all at once and beat until the dough comes together. Switch to the hook and knead the dough until it is smooth and begins to pull away from the sides of the bowl, about 5 minutes. Add the butter, a piece at a time, kneading until fully incorporated before adding another. Continue kneading until the dough starts to slap against the sides of the bowl, about 5 minutes more. Grease a square or rectangular container (it is easier to roll the dough into a rectangle later if it rises in that shape) with cooking spray or neutral oil, put the dough in the container, then lightly coat a piece of plastic with cooking spray or oil and use it to cover the dough. Refrigerate the dough until it doubles, at least 4 hours but overnight is fine.

To pickle the shallots, combine the vinegar, ½ cup sake, 31 grams (1.1 ounces) sugar, 1.5 grams (½ teaspoon) salt, red pepper flakes, and lemon peel in a saucepan. Add ½ cup water and bring to a boil. Add the shallots, adjust the heat, and simmer until they are just tender, about 4 minutes. Take the pot off the heat and allow the shallots to cool in the pickling liquid. Discard the lemon peel. The shallots and liquid are ready to use but will keep in a covered container in the refrigerator for several weeks.

To start the mushroom filling, preheat the oven to 250°F and line a baking sheet with parchment paper. Toss the fresh shiitakes with 1 tablespoon oil and arrange them on the prepared baking sheet. Roast the shiitakes until they are browned and crisping at the edges, 1 to 1½ hours. Cool the mushrooms, then chop and reserve them.

Meanwhile, rehydrate the dried mushrooms. Put the dried mushrooms in a small pot, cover with water, and bring them to a boil. Reduce the heat and simmer the shiitakes for 2 minutes, then pull the pan off the heat, give the mushrooms a stir, cover the pot, and let them cool to room temperature. (Note: I prefer whole dried shiitakes but sometimes can find only sliced. Then I simply put them in a bowl, cover them with boiling water, and let them soak for 15 minutes.) Strain the mushrooms through a fine sieve. Strain the soaking liquid a second time through a sieve lined with a coffee filter. Reserve the strained broth and the rehydrated mushrooms separately.

Make the bacon broth by putting the bacon, ¼ cup soy sauce, ¼ cup sake, mirin, and chicken stock in a saucepan. Add ¼ cup of the mushroom broth and bring to a boil. Lower the heat and gently simmer until the bacon is cooked through and the broth is flavorful, about 30 minutes. Allow the stock to cool off the heat. Remove the bacon from the broth and chop it into pieces about the size of the chopped mushrooms. Reserve the bacon broth and chopped bacon separately.

To finish the filling, stem the rehydrated mushrooms (if necessary) and slice them. Heat a tablespoon or two of oil in a skillet over medium-high. Sauté the rehydrated mushrooms, stirring occasionally, until their edges begin to crisp, about 4 minutes. Remove the skillet from the heat and let the mushrooms cool, then chop them so they are the same size as the bacon and fresh mushrooms. Reserve them separately.

To finish the filling, put the chopped bacon in the skillet and cook it, stirring occasionally, over medium heat until it begins to brown, 1 to 2 minutes. Add both the roasted fresh and rehydrated mushrooms, and ¼ cup of the reserved bacon broth. Bring the liquid to a boil and cook, stirring until the pan is dry, about 1 minute. Take the pan off the heat and add 2 teaspoons of the shallot pickling liquid. Mince enough pickled shallots to yield 2 heaping tablespoons. Mix the minced shallots and scallions into the filling.

To make the miso mayonnaise, mix the mayonnaise with the miso and sriracha in a small bowl.

To form the buns, roll the dough out on a lightly floured piece of parchment into a rectangle about 10 × 12 inches, placing the longer sides at the top and bottom. Press the top edge down to thin it a bit (this makes it easier to seal the buns). Spread miso mayo all over the dough, except for a 1½-inch margin at the top edge. Evenly distribute the mushroom filling over the mayo. Starting at the bottom, roll the dough up into a tight cylinder. When you reach the top edge, press it into the cylinder to seal in the filling. Wrap parchment paper around the dough, put the wrapped dough on a baking sheet, seam-side down, and chill until it is firm enough to slice, at least 30 minutes in the refrigerator.

Slice the dough into 6 buns, each about 2 inches thick. Line a round or square baking dish large enough to hold the buns in a single layer with parchment paper. Place the buns, cut-sides up, about ½ inch apart in the baking pan. Press each bun down to flatten it slightly; at this stage, the buns can be wrapped and frozen for up to 2 days, then thawed and proofed before baking. Grease a piece of plastic wrap and loosely cover the buns. Set them aside to proof in a warm place until they rise and begin to look spongy, about 1 hour.

Meanwhile, make the glaze by combining the honey, 4 teaspoons soy sauce, ¼ cup of the reserved bacon stock, and the sriracha in a small saucepan. Bring to a boil, then adjust the heat and simmer until the color deepens and concentrates, about 3 minutes. Remove from the heat and keep warm at the back of the stove.

To finish the buns, preheat the oven to 350°F. Bake the buns for 10 minutes, then rotate the pan front to back and continue baking until they are golden brown, about 10 minutes longer. As soon as the buns come out of the oven, brush them with glaze. Wait 20 minutes, then glaze the warm buns a second time; let the glaze dry. Serve the buns warm or at room temperature with pickled cucumbers, if desired.

Potato Flambé Tart

Makes one 10-inch tart

This is a savory tart that I have served for breakfast and lunch and as an appetizer at dinner. For a crisp crust, I cook the tart in a preheated cast-iron skillet, but a heated baking sheet will also work. Note: This is a yeasted dough, so allow time for it to rise.

Crust:

½ recipe	**Cast-Iron Pizza Dough (page 177)**
Heaping ½ tsp	active dry yeast
166g	bread flour (5.9oz / about 1 cup + 2½ T)
1.5g	Diamond Crystal kosher salt (½ tsp)
2 T	extra-virgin olive oil

Topping:

25g	pancetta (1oz), cut into thin slivers
1 tsp	fresh thyme leaves
½ tsp	fresh rosemary leaves
2 T	crème fraîche, lightly beaten
100g	Yukon Gold or other all-purpose potatoes (3.5oz), scrubbed, sliced paper thin, and held in water until ready to use
1.5g	Diamond Crystal kosher salt (½ tsp)
0.6g	freshly ground black pepper (¼ tsp)
10g	Parmigiano-Reggiano (0.4oz / about 1¾ T), grated

To start the crust, follow the directions on page 177. While the dough proofs, preheat the oven to 500°F and put a 12-inch cast-iron skillet or a baking sheet in the oven to heat for at least 20 minutes.

To prepare the topping, bring a small pot of water to a boil over high heat. Blanch the pancetta, cooking it just until the water returns to a boil. Drain the pancetta and combine it in a bowl with the thyme and rosemary.

To assemble the tart, dry the soaked potatoes well. Roll or stretch the dough on a lightly floured surface into a round about 12 inches across. Transfer the dough to a lightly floured plate. Carefully take the hot skillet out of the oven and put it on top of the stove. Pour 2 tablespoons olive oil into the pan and quickly, but again carefully, slide the dough into the skillet. Spread crème fraîche over the crust, leaving a border around the edge, arrange the potatoes on the crème fraîche, and season with salt and pepper. Bake the tart until it begins to color, about 10 minutes. Remove the hot skillet from the oven again and evenly distribute the pancetta and herbs on top. Sprinkle everything with Parmigiano, return the tart to the oven, and bake until the crust is nicely brown and the cheese melted, about 10 minutes more. Allow the tart to cool in the pan for 3 to 5 minutes, transfer it to a wire rack to cool for about 10 minutes longer, then serve.

Spring Torta

Makes one 9-inch pie

This was my mother's answer to quiche, her go-to for a festive weekend lunch. She got the recipe from her sister Gilda, who brought it back with her from Rome, where she lived for a time. I make my version in a springform pan. A cake ring will work equally well, and a cake pan will suffice, though it may be difficult to unmold the torta. Choose your greens at the market. Dandelion greens are delicious; just be sure to chop the stems finely because they can be tough. Chard or spinach mixed with watercress, arugula, or lamb's-quarters are also very tasty.

Crust:

1 recipe	Crostata Dough (page 175), with the sugar reduced to 6g (1 ½ tsp; see Note on page 175)
143g	unsalted butter (5oz), chilled
210g	all-purpose flour (7.4oz / about 1½ cups)
12g	sugar (0.4oz / about 1 T)
3g	Diamond Crystal kosher salt (1 tsp)

Filling:

1 tsp	lemon zest
About 7.5g	Diamond Crystal kosher salt (2½ tsp), plus extra to taste
About 2.3g	freshly ground black pepper (1 tsp)
About 3 T	extra-virgin olive oil
4 cups	finely chopped spring greens, such as dandelion greens, chard, arugula, spinach, and/or watercress
⅔ cups	chopped fresh Italian parsley
6 T	chopped fresh basil
⅔ cups	thinly sliced scallions (green and white parts) (about 8)
1 T	minced garlic (about 3 medium cloves)
500g	ricotta cheese (1lb 1.5oz / about 2 cups), drained if wet
2	large eggs, lightly beaten
10g	Pecorino cheese (0.4oz / about 1¾ T), grated
75g	Parmigiano-Reggiano (2.6oz / about ¾ cup + 2 T), grated

To start the crust, prepare the dough as directed on page 175. Preheat the oven to 375°F. Roll the dough out on a lightly floured surface into a 12-inch round about ⅛ inch thick. Trim the dough to even the circle and fit it into a 9-inch springform pan. (The easiest approach: Slide the bottom of the pan under the dough, fold it loosely over the edges, drop the bottom into the pan, then unfold the edges and fit the dough into the pan and form the crust's edge.) Chill the dough in the freezer for 15 minutes or the refrigerator for at least 30 minutes.

To blind-bake the crust, line it with tinfoil and fill it with pie weights (beans or rice will work). Bake the crust until the dough looks set and the edges begin to color, about 20 minutes. Reduce the oven temperature to 350°F, remove the pie weights and foil, and continue cooking until the crust looks dry, about 10 minutes more. Allow the crust to cool completely.

To start the filling, in a large bowl, mix the lemon zest with 3 to 6 grams (1 to 2 teaspoons) of the salt,* ½ teaspoon of the pepper, and 1 tablespoon of the olive oil. Add the greens, parsley, and basil. Massage the oil mixture into the greens. Set the greens aside to wilt. If the greens are still dry, add up to an additional tablespoon of oil.

In a small saucepan, combine the scallions and 1 tablespoon of the olive oil over medium heat. Add a pinch of salt and cook, stirring occasionally, until the scallions soften, about 5 minutes. Add the garlic and cook until fragrant, 2 to 3 minutes. Stir the warm scallion mixture into the greens.

Preheat the oven to 350°F. In a separate bowl, combine the ricotta with the eggs, Pecorino, and 50 grams (1.8 ounces) of the Parmigiano (reserve the rest for topping the pie). Stir in the greens, then adjust the seasoning, adding about 1 teaspoon (3 grams) salt (depending on how heavily salted the greens are) and ½ teaspoon pepper. Spoon the filling evenly into the crust. Sprinkle the pie with the remaining 25 grams (0.8 ounces) Parmigiano and bake for 30 minutes, then rotate the torta front to back and continue baking until the filling is set, about 25 minutes more. Allow the torta to cool on a wire rack for at least 20 minutes, then serve warm or at room temperature.

---

* Dandelions are tough and bitter and require more salt to wilt, a full 6 grams (2 teaspoons), compared to tender greens (like arugula), which need only 3 grams (1 teaspoon) salt to soften them.

Squash Blossom Tart

Makes one 9-inch tart

This tart is a celebration of summer squash. Because the blossoms are so pretty, I wanted to feature them, but I also wanted a strong zucchini flavor, so I incorporate it three ways. I like this tart in a square pan, but a 9-inch round also works.

Tart shell:

½ recipe	Rough Puff Pastry (page 179), or 245g store-bought puff pastry, thawed if frozen
114g	all-purpose flour (4oz / about ¾ cup)
2.3g	Diamond Crystal kosher salt (¾ tsp)
114g	unsalted butter (4oz)

Squash puree:

2	medium garlic cloves, peeled and smashed
¼ cup	extra-virgin olive oil
2	medium zucchini
½ tsp	orange zest
2 T	orange juice
¼ cup	packed fresh basil leaves, roughly chopped
¼ cup	packed fresh Italian parsley leaves, roughly chopped
	Pinch of crushed red pepper flakes
About 2.3g	Diamond Crystal kosher salt (¾ tsp)
About 1.2g	freshly ground black pepper (½ tsp)

22g	Parmigiano-Reggiano (0.8oz / about ¼ cup), grated
11g	Pecorino cheese (0.4oz / about 2 T), grated

Zucchini topping:

About 3 T	extra-virgin olive oil, plus extra for drizzling
2	medium zucchini, sliced into ¼-inch thick rounds
About 1.5g	Diamond Crystal kosher salt (½ tsp)
About 0.6g	freshly ground black pepper (¼ tsp)
12 to 15	squash blossoms (depending on size)

Goat cheese cream and garnish:

115g	fresh goat cheese (4oz), room temperature
22g	Parmigiano-Reggiano (0.8oz / about ¼ cup), grated
11g	Pecorino cheese (0.4oz / about 2 T), grated, plus extra for sprinkling
0.6g	freshly ground black pepper (¼ tsp)
	Basil Oil (page 288) (optional)

To make the tart shell, make the dough according to the instructions on page 179. Preheat the oven to 425°F. On a lightly floured surface or piece of parchment, roll the dough out into an 11-inch square about ⅛ inch thick. Dock the dough, piercing it all over with a fork, then fit it to a 9-inch square tart pan with a removable bottom. (The easiest approach: Slide the rolled-out dough onto the bottom of the pan, loosely fold it over the edges, drop the bottom into the pan, then lift the edges up to fit the pan and form the crust's edge.) Trim the edges of the dough to even them (save the trimmings to make the Crisps on page 102). Chill the crust for 15 minutes in the freezer or at least 30 minutes in the refrigerator.

To blind-bake the crust, line the tart with tinfoil then fill it with pie weights (beans or rice work nicely). Bake the crust until the dough looks set and the edges begin to color, about 15 minutes, then remove the foil and weights, lower the temperature to 325°F, and bake the crust until it is golden and fully cooked, about 50 minutes more. Allow the crust to cool completely.

To start the squash puree, combine the garlic and ¼ cup oil in a skillet and cook over low heat until the garlic is soft and fragrant but not browned, about 15 minutes. Transfer the garlic and oil to a blender. Trim the zucchini by cutting off the ends, then cutting the squash lengthwise, away from their seedy cores. Discard the cores and roughly chop the squash. Add the chopped zucchini to the blender with the orange zest and juice, basil, parsley, red pepper flakes, 2.3 grams (¾ teaspoon) salt, and 1.2g (½ teaspoon) black pepper. Puree the mixture until it is smooth.

Spoon the puree back into the skillet and heat it over medium-high. When the puree bubbles, lower the heat and cook, stirring frequently, until the puree concentrates, darkens, and thickens, about 8 minutes. Stir in 22 grams (0.8 ounces) Parmigiano and 11 grams (0.4 ounces) Pecorino. Taste the puree and adjust the seasoning as necessary with salt and black pepper. Chill the puree for at least 20 minutes.

To prepare the zucchini topping, heat 3 tablespoons oil in the skillet over medium-high heat. Working in batches, cook the zucchini slices in a single layer. Season with salt and a little black pepper (more or less depending on the size of the batch) and sauté until the squash begins to color, about 4½ minutes. Flip the zucchini slices over, then immediately transfer them to a paper towel–lined plate to drain. Return the skillet to the heat and repeat, sautéing the remaining zucchini on one side.

Prepare the blossoms by carefully removing the pistil and stamen from each (you can use a paring knife, tweezers, or your fingers). Brush away any dirt inside the blossoms and set aside.

To make the goat cheese cream, in a bowl or the food processor, combine the softened goat cheese with 22 grams (0.8 ounces) Parmigiano and 11 grams (0.4 ounces) Pecorino. Season the cream with the black pepper and beat or process until smooth.

To finish the tart, preheat the oven to 350°F. Spread the goat cheese cream over the bottom of the tart shell. Spoon the squash puree evenly over the cream, then arrange the zucchini slices on the puree. Top the tart with the zucchini blossoms, arranged with the stems facing toward the rim. Sprinkle the blossoms with Pecorino.

Bake the tart until the filling is hot and the blossoms begin to soften, about 10 minutes. Drizzle the blossoms with olive oil, rotate the pan front to back, and continue baking until the blossoms are fully tender, about 15 minutes longer. Allow the tart to cool on a wire rack for at least 15 minutes, then serve warm or at room temperature, drizzled with basil oil, if desired.

Tomato Crostata

Makes one 10-inch crostata

Make this free-form tart when tomatoes are at their peak. I like to use several heirloom varieties, picking for both looks and taste. When I can't find marjoram, I substitute fresh oregano or basil leaves.

Crust:

1 recipe	Cheddar Crostata Dough (page 173)
88g	extra-sharp cheddar cheese (3.1oz / about 1¼ cups), grated
88g	unsalted butter (3.1oz), cut into ½-inch dice
210g	all-purpose flour (7.4oz / about 1½ cups)
1.5g	Diamond Crystal kosher salt (½ tsp)
1	large egg, beaten

Filling:

2 T	extra-virgin olive oil
114g	bacon (4oz), cut into slivers
14g	unsalted butter (0.5oz / about 1 T)
440g	leeks (1lb / 2 medium), cleaned, quartered, and sliced
About 3.7g	Diamond Crystal kosher salt (1¼ tsp), plus extra as needed
About 0.6g	freshly ground black pepper, plus extra as needed (¼ tsp)
1½ T	fresh marjoram leaves
600g	tomatoes (1lb 5oz / 3 medium-large), preferably heirloom, cored and sliced
1	large egg, lightly beaten
114g	extra-sharp cheddar cheese (4oz / about 1½ cups + 1 T), grated
	Sea salt and good-quality extra-virgin olive oil, for finishing

To prepare the crust, follow the instructions on page 173. Roll the dough out on lightly floured parchment into a 14-inch round. Put the parchment (and dough) on a baking sheet and chill it for 15 minutes in the freezer or at least 30 minutes in the refrigerator.

To start the filling, place the bacon and 1 tablespoon of the olive oil in a medium skillet and heat over medium-low. Gently cook the bacon until some of the fat has rendered and the meat begins to color, about 20 minutes. Drain the bacon on a paper towel–lined plate. Wipe out the skillet.

Melt the butter with the remaining tablespoon olive oil in the skillet over medium-low heat. Add the leeks, salt, pepper, and a tablespoon of water. Sweat the leeks, stirring occasionally, and cook (without browning) until they are tender, about 30 minutes. Add the chopped marjoram and additional salt and pepper to taste. Allow the leeks to cool.

To bake the tart, preheat the oven to 400°F. Trim the chilled dough, even the edges and brush a 2-inch border around the perimeter with the beaten egg. Scatter the grated cheddar over the dough, stopping short of the egg-washed border. Spread the leeks in an even layer over the cheese, then top with the bacon. Arrange the tomato slices so they overlap on the filling. Form the tart's sides by lifting a section of dough up around the filling, pleating it, and repeating to form a pastry rim. Brush the crust with beaten egg and bake the crostata for 15 minutes. Reduce the temperature to 350°F and continue baking until the crust is browned, about 35 minutes more. Transfer the crostata to a wire rack and allow it to settle for about 15 minutes. Serve the crostata warm or at room temperature, drizzled with good olive oil, sprinkled with sea salt, and garnished with marjoram leaves.

Cheddar Coins

Makes about 30 coins

Cheese coins (or pennies), in their many iterations, have long been favorite accompaniments to cold drinks in the South. Their considerable appeal led them to cross both the Atlantic Ocean and the Mason-Dixon Line. I use cheddar cheese and sesame seeds in my mostly traditional version. I also like to add a little fruity and slightly spicy Aleppo pepper; cayenne is a good alternate if you like heat, paprika works if you don't. These are best eaten the day they are made, but this dough freezes well, so make a log, then slice and bake as you need. (For more on saving dough, see page 95.)

3 T	sesame seeds
114g	all-purpose flour (4oz / about ¾ cup + 1 T)
1.5g	Diamond Crystal kosher salt (½ tsp)
½ tsp	Aleppo pepper, or a pinch of cayenne pepper or paprika
115g	extra-sharp cheddar cheese (4oz / about 1½ cups + 2 T), grated
56g	unsalted butter (2oz), room temperature
	Sea salt, such as Maldon (optional)

Toast the sesame seeds in a small skillet over medium-low heat, stirring occasionally, until they color and smell toasty, about 8 minutes, then transfer them to a bowl. When the sesame seeds are cool, add the flour, salt, and Aleppo pepper. In the bowl of a stand mixer and using the paddle attachment, combine the cheese and butter. Beat on low, then add the flour mixture, a third at a time, mixing to incorporate between additions. Add 1 tablespoon water and mix just until the dough is moist enough to hold together.

Turn the dough out onto a lightly floured surface. Knead it a little until it is smooth and then form it into a log about 1½ inches in diameter. Wrap the log in plastic and refrigerate for at least 1 hour, but overnight is fine.

Preheat the oven to 325°F and line a baking sheet with parchment paper. Slice the dough into very thin rounds—just the number you want in the short term; refrigerate or freeze the remaining dough. Put the coins on the prepared baking sheet and bake for 10 minutes, then rotate the pan front to back and continue baking until the coins are golden brown (check the bottoms), about 10 minutes more. Remove the pan from the oven and immediately sprinkle the coins with a little sea salt, if desired. Cool, then serve.

Chickpea Crackers

Makes about 7 dozen crackers

The topping here is inspired by Indian chat masala. Mango powder adds a tangy note, and black salt an unexpected mineral taste. Both are available at stores that feature Indian spices, such as Kalustyan's (kalustyans .com). Za'atar, a Middle Eastern spice mix that is becoming easier to find, and my Savory Mixed Seeds (page 290) also make excellent toppings for these crackers.

Crackers:

210g	all-purpose flour (7.4oz / about 1½ cups)
90g	chickpea flour (3.1oz / about ½ cup + 2 T)
4.5g	Diamond Crystal kosher salt (1½ tsp)
142g	unsalted butter (5oz), cut in a small dice and chilled
¾ cup	plain yogurt

Topping:

1½ T	cumin seeds
1½ T	coriander seeds
1½ tsp	black peppercorns
1½ T	dried mango powder
1 T	black salt
3g	Diamond Crystal kosher salt (1 tsp)

To start the crackers, combine the all-purpose and chickpea flours in a food processor. Add the kosher salt and pulse to mix. Add the butter and process until the mixture is the texture of fine meal, about 20 seconds. Add the yogurt and pulse until it is evenly incorporated, a minute or so more. Turn the dough out onto a lightly floured surface and knead it until it is smooth, then gather it into a ball. Wrap the dough in plastic, flatten it into a rectangle, and chill overnight.

To make the topping, toast the cumin and coriander seeds in a skillet over medium heat, stirring occasionally, until they smell toasty, about 10 minutes. Allow the spices to cool, then coarsely grind the cumin and coriander with the peppercorns in a spice grinder or mortar. Transfer the mixture to a bowl. Sift in the mango powder, then add the black and kosher salts.

Mix to combine. Stored in an airtight container, the topping mix will keep for several weeks.

To finish the crackers, preheat the oven to 325°F and line a baking sheet with parchment paper. Divide the dough into quarters. On a lightly floured surface or piece of parchment, roll the first portion of dough out as thinly as you can—you should be able to see through it. Transfer the parchment and dough to a baking sheet and chill it for 15 minutes. Sprinkle the surface of the dough with a quarter of the topping and cut the dough into 2-inch squares. Arrange the crackers on the prepared baking sheet and bake until the crackers are nicely browned, 15 to 20 minutes, rotating the pan midway from front to back. Repeat, rolling and baking the remaining dough. Cool the crackers. Serve at room temperature or store for up to a week in an airtight container.

Gouda Pizzelles

Makes about 40 pizzelles

Stroopwafels are Dutch caramel-filled crisps first made in the town of Gouda. They have always reminded me of Italian pizzelles. The last time I had my pizzelle iron out, I wondered if I could trade sugar for cheese and make a cocktail snack. I tried Gouda (in a nod to waffle cookie history). It was delicious and so is cheddar. As I mentioned in my recipe for sweet Pizzelles (page 109), I have an electric pizzelle maker, so I haven't tried any of the ingenious hacks I have read about on the internet—but if I didn't have an iron, I might.

230g	all-purpose flour (8.1oz / about 1½ cups + 2½ T)
1½ tsp	baking powder
3g	Diamond Crystal kosher salt (1 tsp)
¼ tsp	dry mustard
3	large eggs, lightly beaten
150g	aged Gouda cheese (5.3oz / about 1½ cups), grated
114g	unsalted butter (4oz), melted and cooled
	Cooking spray

Heat a pizzelle iron. Sift the flour with the baking powder, salt, and mustard into a bowl. In another bowl, combine the eggs with the cheese, then whisk in the melted butter. Using a wooden spoon, mix the wet ingredients into the dry to form a stiff batter.

Spray the pizzelle iron with cooking spray (you only need to do this before the first pizzelle). Spray a dinner spoon with cooking spray and drop a spoonful of batter onto the heated iron (I find it easier to get the batter off a dinner spoon than a measuring spoon). Lower the top of the iron and cook the wafer until it is golden, about 45 seconds. Remove the pizzelle and repeat, blotting any accumulated oil from the iron with a paper towel as necessary. Cool the pizzelles, then serve. Stored in an airtight container, pizzelles will keep for up to a week.

Gruyère and Onion Cocktail Biscuits

Makes about 50 cocktail biscuits

I have always loved *gougères,* but I have to say, I now prefer these flaky, flavorful bites with a glass of wine or champagne. At their best freshly baked, they can be rolled and cut early in the day, then refrigerated (or frozen) until baking time. They also freeze well after baking (in that case, reheat them in a cooler 350°F oven).

Onions:

2 T	extra-virgin olive oil
4	anchovy fillets, minced
½ tsp	crushed red pepper flakes
1	medium onion, peeled, halved, and sliced
3g	Diamond Crystal kosher salt (1 tsp)
½ cup + 1 T	heavy cream

Dough:

226g	all-purpose flour (8oz / about 1½ cups + 2 T)
1 T	baking powder
3.7g	Diamond Crystal kosher salt (1¼ tsp)
85g	unsalted butter (3oz), cut into ½-inch dice and frozen
½ tsp	freshly ground black pepper
71g	Gruyère cheese (2.5oz / about ¾ cup), grated, plus extra for sprinkling
14g	Parmigiano-Reggiano (0.5oz / about 2½ T), grated

To start the onions, combine the oil, anchovies, and red pepper flakes in a skillet set over medium-low heat. Add the onions and 3 grams (1 teaspoon) salt. Cook over medium-low heat, stirring occasionally and adjusting the heat as necessary, until the onions are soft and golden, about 45 minutes. Cool the onions then chop them. Put them in a bowl, mix in the cream, cover it, and chill for at least 15 minutes.

To start the dough, combine the flour, baking powder, and 3.7 grams (1¼ teaspoons) salt in a food processor. Pulse to mix. Add the frozen butter and process until the mixture is the texture of coarse meal, about 15 seconds. Transfer the mixture to a bowl and mix in the cheeses. Add the onion mixture and, using a fork, stir just until the onions are evenly distributed.

To finish the biscuits, preheat the oven to 400°F and line a baking sheet with parchment paper. Turn the dough out onto a lightly floured work surface and form it into a square about 8 × 8 inches. Cut the square into quarters with a sharp knife or bench scraper. Stack the quarters on top of each other. Using a rolling pin, gently flatten the layered dough and then roll it into a square ½ to ¾ inch thick. Trim the edges and cut out biscuits, each about 1 inch square. Reroll the trimmings and cut additional biscuits. Working in batches if necessary, arrange the biscuits you want to bake in the short term on the prepared baking sheet. Sprinkle them with additional Gruyère. (Freeze the biscuits remaining for later use.) Bake the biscuits for 7 minutes, rotate the pan front to back, and continue baking until the tops are golden, about 6 minutes more. Serve warm or room temperature.

Cheese Kiffles

Makes about 40 kiffles

Kiffles are an eastern European pastry typically made with a sweet filling. I was inspired to create two savory versions, this one with cheese and the Onion and Poppy Seed Kiffles on page 212. Both are great with a drink and can be formed and frozen, then cooked as needed. Note: The same dough-and-cheese mixture can also be used to make cheese straws; see Variation below.

Pastry:

1 recipe	**Cream Cheese Dough (page 174)**
140g	all-purpose flour (5oz / about 1 cup)
0.7g	Diamond Crystal kosher salt (¼ tsp)
114g	unsalted butter (4oz), diced and chilled
114g	cream cheese (4oz)

Filling:

53.2g	sesame seeds (2oz / about 6 T)
60g	extra-sharp cheddar cheese (2.1oz / about ¾ cup + 1½ T), grated
30g	Parmigiano-Reggiano (1oz / about 6 T), grated, plus extra for finishing
1 tsp	freshly ground black pepper
1 tsp	Aleppo pepper, or ¼ tsp paprika
2 T	sour cream
1	large egg, beaten

To start the pastry, prepare the cream cheese dough according to the instructions on page 174. Roll out half the dough on a lightly floured piece of parchment into a 10-inch square. Repeat with the remaining dough. Put the parchment (and dough) on a baking sheet. Chill the dough for at least 20 minutes.

To make the filling, arrange the sesame seeds in a single layer in a skillet and toast the seeds over medium-low heat, stirring occasionally, until they are golden, about 8 minutes. Put the seeds in a bowl and allow them to cool. Add the cheddar and Parmigiano and mix in the black and Aleppo peppers. Chill the cheese mixture for at least 15 minutes.

To form the kiffles, preheat the oven to 325°F and line a baking sheet with parchment paper. Transfer one square of dough to a lightly floured surface and trim it to even the edges (the trimmings can be re-rolled). Spread half of the sour cream over the dough, then top with half of the cheese filling. Using a sharp knife, cut the dough into 4 strips, each about 2½ × 10 inches. Cut each strip crosswise into squares. Fold a corner of each square over the filling, just past the center. Dab the dough with beaten egg, fold the opposing corner over, and press to seal. (Another way to form kiffles is to roll the dough into a round, cut it pizza-style into 20 wedges, and roll each into a tight spiral—see Grapefruit and Poppy Seed Rugelach, page 101.) Arrange the kiffles folded-side up on the lined baking sheet. Brush all the kiffles with egg and sprinkle with Parmigiano.

Bake the kiffles for 15 minutes, then rotate the pan front to back and continue baking until they are golden, about 15 minutes more. Allow the kiffles to cool on a wire rack. Repeat, forming and baking kiffles with the remaining dough. Serve kiffles at room temperature.

Variation: To make Cheese Straws, prepare the dough as described above but roll a half into a slightly thicker 8 × 8-inch square. Spread the dough with half of the sour cream and sprinkle with half of the chilled cheese mixture. Cut the dough in half, then cut each half crosswise into 4 × ½-inch strips (you'll wind up with 32 straws). Twist each strip and arrange them on parchment-lined baking sheets. Bake at 350°F until the straws are golden, rotating the pan front to back halfway through the bake; begin checking at 15 minutes. Repeat with the remaining dough and filling. Let cool and serve.

Onion and Poppy Seed Kiffles

Makes about 40 kiffles

Poppy seeds are available already ground at specialty stores. If you need to grind your own, I find that an electric spice grinder gets the job done nicely.

Pastry:

1 recipe	**Cream Cheese Dough (page 174)**
140g	all-purpose flour (5oz / about 1 cup)
0.7g	Diamond Crystal kosher salt (¼ tsp)
114g	unsalted butter (4oz), diced and chilled
114g	cream cheese (4oz)

Filling:

2	medium onions, peeled and diced
2 T	extra-virgin olive oil
3g	Diamond Crystal kosher salt (1 tsp) Pinch of freshly ground black pepper, plus extra as needed
27.2g	poppy seeds (1oz / about 3 T), ground, plus extra for finishing
1½ tsp	lemon zest
1 T	fresh thyme leaves
2 T	sour cream
1	large egg, lightly beaten Sea salt, such as Maldon, for finishing (optional)

To start the pastry, prepare the cream cheese dough according to the instructions on page 174. Roll out half the dough on a lightly floured piece of parchment into a 10-inch square. Repeat, rolling out the remaining dough. Put the parchment (and dough) on a baking sheet and chill for at least 20 minutes.

To prepare the filling, combine the onions and oil in a medium saucepan. Heat over medium, seasoning with 2.3 grams (¾ teaspoon) of the kosher salt and the pepper. Reduce the heat to low and slowly caramelize the onions, stirring them occasionally, until they are soft and golden, about 45 minutes. Add the ground poppy seeds, lemon zest, and thyme. Increase the heat a little and cook until the seeds soften slightly, about 7 minutes. Taste the mixture and add the remaining 0.7 grams (¼ teaspoon) kosher salt and more

pepper (if you like). Remove the pan from the heat and allow the onions to cool, then mix in the sour cream. (The onions can be cooked a day ahead and refrigerated.)

To make the kiffles, preheat the oven to 325°F and line a baking sheet with parchment paper. Transfer one sheet of dough to a lightly floured work surface and trim the dough to even the edges (the trimmings can be rerolled). Spread half the filling on the dough and cut the dough into 4 strips about 2½ × 10 inches each. Using a sharp knife, cut each strip crosswise to form squares. Fold a corner of each square over the filling, just past the center. Dab the dough with beaten egg and then fold the opposing corner over, pressing to seal the dough. (Another way to form kiffles is to roll the dough into a round, cut it pizza-style into 20 wedges, and roll each into a tight spiral—see Grapefruit and Poppy Seed Rugelach, page 101.) Arrange the kiffles folded-side up on the prepared baking sheet. Repeat with the remaining dough and filling. Brush the kiffles with egg and sprinkle with sea salt, if desired.

Bake the kiffles for 15 minutes, then rotate the pan front to back and continue baking until they are golden, about 15 minutes more. Allow the kiffles to cool on a wire rack. Repeat, forming and baking kiffles with the remaining dough. Serve at room temperature.

Pretzels

Makes 20 pretzels, or about 200 pretzel "pip-squeaks"

I really like pretzels, but until recently it had never occurred to me to make them. As soon as the idea hit, I realized I needed to do some research. I learned that traditional Bavarian pretzels are dipped in lye before baking—that is what gives them their distinctive, slightly mineral-y taste. That seemed a little much in my tiny kitchen, so I was happy to discover that Harold McGee suggests a method for concentrating the alkalis in baking soda in his book *On Food and Cooking*. He bakes the soda, then adds it to the pretzels' prebake water bath, successfully mimicking the effect of the acid. Start this dough a day ahead.

7g	active dry yeast (0.25oz)	6g	Diamond Crystal kosher salt (2 tsp)
1 T	molasses	5 T	baking soda
320g	bread flour (11.2oz / about 2 cups + 3½ T)	1	large egg, beaten
100g	rye flour (3.5oz / about 1 cup)	About 4 T	Savory Mixed Seeds (page 290) or sea salt, for finishing
½ cup	sparkling water		
28g	unsalted butter (1oz), diced, room temperature, plus extra for greasing		

Put ½ cup plus 1 teaspoon warm water in the bowl of a stand mixer. Sprinkle the yeast into the water and stir to dissolve it, then stir in the molasses. Set the mixture aside until the yeast activates and looks creamy, about 10 minutes. Add the bread and rye flours, sparkling water, diced butter, and kosher salt. Mix together with the paddle attachment, then switch to the dough hook and knead the dough until it is no longer sticky, 5 to 7 minutes. Grease a large bowl with butter. Transfer the dough to the greased bowl, turn it over to coat all sides, cover with plastic wrap, and refrigerate overnight.

Preheat the oven to 300°F. Line a rimmed baking sheet with tinfoil, then spread the baking powder in an even layer and bake for 1 hour. Cool the baking powder completely. (The roasted baking powder can be stored in an airtight container for weeks.)

Turn the dough out onto a lightly floured work surface. Flatten it into a square about 8 × 8 inches. Using a pastry cutter or sharp knife, cut the dough into 10 equal-size lengths each about ⅘ inch wide. Working one at a time and keeping the remaining dough covered with a damp cloth, use your hands to stretch and roll each dough length into a rope about 26 inches long.

Cut each rope in half, rolling the ends a little to taper them. Again, working one at a time, form each rope into a U shape, gently stretching as necessary to maintain the length. Lay the rope on the floured surface with the ends pointing toward you. Lift the ends, twist them together once, then separate them again as you draw them up and press firmly to attach them at the top of the pretzel loop knot. (For pip-squeaks, stretch the dough into fourteen 18-inch ropes and cut them into 1-inch bites.) Butter two baking sheets and two large pieces of plastic wrap. Put the pretzels on the baking sheets, cover them with the plastic wrap, and set them aside to rise at room temperature until they have increased in size by half, about

15 minutes (pip-squeaks will be sufficiently proofed in about 10 minutes).

Preheat the oven to 425°F. In a large pot, combine the roasted baking powder with 8 cups water and bring to a boil. Reduce the heat to maintain a simmer. Set up a rack (or line a baking sheet with towels). Working one (or two) at a time, drop a pretzel into the simmering water for 10 seconds, turn it over, cook for 10 seconds more, drain with a slotted spoon, and then dry the pretzels on the rack for at least 5 minutes.

Return the boiled pretzels to the buttered baking sheets. Brush them with beaten egg and sprinkle with mixed seeds or sea salt. Bake for 7 minutes, then rotate the pans front to back and bake until the pretzels brown, about 8 minutes more (cook pip-squeaks for about 10 minutes). Serve warm or at room temperature.

Pancetta Taralli

Makes about 40 taralli

Make this recipe with good pancetta. If only prepackaged is available, make Fennel Taralli (page 221) or Pecorino Taralli (page 222) instead. Traditionally, taralli are boiled before baking. The hot water turns the dough's surface starch into a gel, so it glistens after baking. I find it easier to brush mine with egg white instead, but both approaches work.

	Sponge:
2g	sugar (0.1oz / about ½ tsp)
½ tsp	active dry yeast
56g	all-purpose flour (2oz / about 6½ T)

	Taralli:
114g	pancetta (4oz), sliced ¼ inch thick
226g	all-purpose flour (8oz / 1½ cups + 2 T)

3.5g	freshly ground black pepper (1½ tsp) (omit if the pancetta is peppered)
0.7 to 2.3g	Diamond Crystal kosher salt (¼ to ¾ tsp) (depending on the saltiness of the pancetta)
¼ cup + 1 T	dry white wine
¼ cup	extra-virgin olive oil
1	large egg white, lightly beaten

To make the sponge, in a small bowl, dissolve the sugar in 3 tablespoons warm water, then mix in the yeast. Set the yeast aside until it is creamy and activates, about 10 minutes. Mix 56 grams (2 ounces) flour into the yeast a little at a time, stirring with a fork until combined. Cover the bowl with plastic wrap and set aside in a warm place until the sponge has doubled, about 1 hour.

To start the taralli, put the pancetta slices in a cold skillet and heat over low to medium-low. Slowly render the fat without crisping the pancetta, adjusting the burner if necessary, about 20 minutes. When the pancetta threatens to color, turn the slices over, cover the pan, remove it from the heat, and allow the pancetta to cool to room temperature. Strain the fat through a fine sieve and reserve it. Mince the pancetta and reserve it separately. Taste it to determine how much salt and pepper you'll need to add to the dough.

Measure 1 tablespoon of the reserved fat into a bowl and add the olive oil. In the bowl of a stand mixer, combine 226 grams (8 ounces) flour, the minced pancetta, pepper (if using), and salt. Using the paddle attachment on low speed, stream in the wine, then the fat/oil mixture. With the mixer running, add the sponge. Switch to the dough hook and knead until the dough is smooth and elastic. Grease a large bowl with olive oil. Form the dough into a ball, place it in the greased bowl, turn the dough over to coat it, cover the bowl with plastic, and set aside to rest in a warm place for 1 hour.

To shape the taralli, flatten the dough, pressing out any air. Cut the dough into strips about ¾ inch thick. Stretch the dough strips by rolling them with your hand on a lightly floured surface until they are about as thin as a pencil. (If your dough starts to fight back, let it rest for 5 minutes, then continue stretching it. I generally roll all the lengths until they are about ½ inch thick, let them rest, and find by the time I'm finished with the last lengths, the first are relaxed enough to continue rolling.) Cut each length into 4-inch segments. Shape the segments into rings, pressing the ends together. Line a baking sheet with parchment paper. Put the taralli on the baking sheet. Cover with plastic wrap and allow to proof until the taralli have risen and look puffy, about 1 hour.

Preheat the oven to 350°F. Brush the taralli with egg white and bake for 15 minutes, rotate the pan front to back, and continue baking until they are just golden, about 10 minutes more. Turn off the oven, leaving the taralli inside to dry for 30 minutes. Serve at room temperature. The taralli will keep at least a week stored in an airtight container.

Fennel Taralli

Makes about 40 taralli

I grew up eating taralli, the crisp, savory Italian pastries flavored with olive oil and usually wine. They are popular in southern Italy, and the bakeries on Allerton Avenue in the Bronx, where my grandmother shopped, carried several kinds, taralli with fennel always among them. Although I usually roast seeds before I use them, here I don't. Like the bakers in the Bronx (and in Italy), I prefer the more assertive flavor of raw fennel seeds in taralli.

Sponge:

2g	sugar (0.1oz / about ½ tsp)
½ tsp	active dry yeast
56g	all-purpose flour (2oz / about 6½ T)

Taralli:

226g	all-purpose flour (8oz / about 1½ cups + 2 T)

2 T	fennel seeds
3g	Diamond Crystal kosher salt (1 tsp)
¼ cup + 1 T	dry white wine
¼ cup + 1 T	extra-virgin olive oil, plus extra for greasing
1	large egg white, lightly beaten

To make the sponge, in a small bowl, dissolve the sugar in 3 tablespoons warm water, then mix in the yeast. Set the yeast aside until it is creamy and activates, about 10 minutes. Mix 56 grams (2 ounces) flour into the yeast a little at a time, stirring with a fork until combined. Cover the bowl with plastic wrap and set aside in a warm place until the sponge has doubled, about 1 hour.

To start the taralli, combine 226 grams (8 ounces) flour, the fennel seeds, and salt in the bowl of a stand mixer. Using the paddle attachment on low speed, stream in the wine and olive oil. With the mixer running, add the sponge. Switch to the dough hook and knead until the dough is smooth and elastic. Grease a large bowl with olive oil. Put the dough in the bowl, turn to coat it, cover the bowl with plastic wrap, and set aside to rest in a warm place for an hour.

To shape the taralli, flatten the dough, pressing out any air. Cut the dough into strips about ¾ inch thick.

Stretch the dough strips by rolling them with your hand on a lightly floured surface until they are about as thin as a pencil. (If your dough starts to fight back, let it rest for 5 minutes, then continue stretching it. I generally roll all the lengths until they are about ½ inch thick, let them rest, and find by the time I'm finished with the last lengths, the first are relaxed enough to continue rolling.) Cut each length into 4-inch segments. Shape the segments into rings, pressing the ends together. Line a baking sheet with parchment paper. Put the taralli on the baking sheet. Cover with plastic wrap and allow to proof until the taralli have risen and look puffy, about 1 hour.

Preheat the oven to 350°F. Brush the taralli with the egg white and bake for 15 minutes, then rotate the pan front to back and continue baking until the taralli are just golden, about 10 minutes more. Turn off the oven, leaving the taralli inside to dry for 30 minutes. Serve at room temperature. The taralli will keep at least a week in an airtight container.

Pecorino Taralli

Makes about 40 taralli

These are not as sharp tasting as you might expect given the amount of Pecorino and black pepper that goes into the dough. They are simply full of flavor and delicious.

Sponge:

2g	sugar (0.1oz / about ½ tsp)
½ tsp	active dry yeast
56g	all-purpose flour (2oz / about 6½ T)

Taralli:

226g	all-purpose flour (8oz / about 1½ cups + 2 T)
40g	Pecorino cheese (1.4oz / about 7 T), finely grated
3.5g	freshly ground black pepper (1½ tsp)
1.5g	Diamond Crystal kosher salt (½ tsp)
¼ cup + 1½ T	dry white wine
¼ cup + 1 T	extra-virgin olive oil, plus extra for greasing
1	large egg white, lightly beaten

To make the sponge, in a small bowl, dissolve the sugar in 3 tablespoons warm water, then mix in the yeast. Set the yeast aside until it is creamy and activates, about 10 minutes. Mix 56 grams (2 ounces) flour into the yeast a little at a time, stirring with a fork until combined. Cover the bowl with plastic wrap and set aside in a warm place until the sponge has doubled, about 1 hour.

To start the taralli, combine 226 grams (8 ounces) flour, the Pecorino, pepper, and salt in the bowl of a stand mixer. Using the paddle attachment on low speed, stream in the wine and olive oil. With the mixer still running, add the sponge a little at a time. Switch to the dough hook and knead until the dough is smooth and elastic. Grease a large bowl with olive oil. Form the dough into a ball, put it in the bowl, turn the dough over to coat, cover the bowl with plastic wrap, and set aside to rest in a warm place for 1 hour.

To shape the taralli, flatten the dough, pressing out any air. Cut the dough into strips about ¾ inch thick.

Stretch the dough strips by rolling them with your hand on a lightly floured surface until they are about as thin as a pencil. (If your dough starts to fight back, let it rest for 5 minutes, then continue stretching it. I generally roll all the lengths until they are about ½ inch thick, let them rest, and find by the time I'm finished with the last lengths, the first are relaxed enough to continue rolling.) Cut each length into 4-inch segments. Shape the segments into rings, pressing the ends together. Line a baking sheet with parchment paper. Put the taralli on the baking sheet. Cover with plastic wrap and allow to proof until the taralli have risen and look puffy, about 1 hour.

Preheat the oven to 350°F. Brush the taralli with egg white and bake for 15 minutes, rotate the pan front to back, and continue baking until they are just golden, about 10 minutes more. Turn off the oven, leaving the taralli inside to dry for 30 minutes. Serve at room temperature. The taralli will keep at least a week stored in an airtight container.

CHAPTER 6

Custards and
Semifreddos

About Eggs

This chapter owes a debt to the ingredients responsible for the most remarkable acrobatics in the dessert kitchen: sugar (which I have already discussed at some length on page 95) and eggs. Individually, and certainly together, these ingredients are capable of astonishing tricks. But as every cook knows, both need to be handled with care and attention. The recipes that follow all require a certain meticulousness. Tools help—an instant-read thermometer and a stand mixer—as does understanding, so let me share what I know about eggs.

I have tested the recipes with large eggs as defined by the USDA—meaning each in its shell weighs approximately 56.7 grams (2 ounces). To put things in perspective, extra-large eggs weigh about 63.8 grams (2¼ ounces) each, and medium eggs, 49.6 grams (1.7 ounces). If you keep chickens or buy eggs from a farmer, you may have to contend with size variations. To help you adjust, it is useful to know that, according to experiments conducted by *Cook's Illustrated* magazine, without the shell, a large egg weighs an average of 49 grams (1.7 ounces), the yolk weighs about 15 grams (0.5 ounces), and the white about 34 grams (1.2 ounces).

Experts assure us that refrigerated eggs are good for 4 to 5 weeks, measured from the time they are cleaned and packed. Check supermarket eggs for the federally required packing date, a three-digit number stamped on the carton (January 1 appears as 001 and December 31 as 365). Out of their shells, eggs are subject to contamination. In sealed containers, refrigerated yolks keep about 2 days, and whites, 4 days. Unless otherwise specified, I let eggs come to room temperature before I use them—it helps with emulsification in doughs and makes for voluminous meringues.

I freeze leftover egg whites. Thawed, they whip up beautifully. I use several types of meringues in the recipes in this book. Sweet Corn Puddings with Blueberries (page 241) include a French meringue—raw whites beaten with sugar—and I use a cooked Italian meringue in various ways, including to frost my White Cake with Plum Filling (page 81). All meringues require that the whites are cleanly separated from their yolks and that the bowl and whisk are free of residue. I often add cream of tartar (I specify when it's needed in a recipe) to help keep a meringue aloft. I always add the sugar very gradually while I whip.

Yolks do not freeze well. I use extras to make custards and their frozen relation, semifreddos. *Custard* is an umbrella term for a myriad of sweetened combinations of eggs and dairy (and sometimes starch) set by cooking them enough to coagulate the egg proteins. Some custards, like pastry creams, are heated on top of the stove, while stirring, until thick enough to *nap* (a term taken from the French that indicates a liquid is thickened sufficiently to lightly but evenly coat a spoon). Others, like Espresso Custard with Orange (page 231), are baked in a water bath in a warm oven (no hotter than 325°F). Eggs set at 165°F (yolks at 158°F). I check for doneness by eye. When the custards are cooked, the edges are semisolid but the middle still jiggles.

This chapter is focused on egg-filled custards but also includes panna cotta recipes. As is traditional, mine are egg-free and thickened with gelatin. Barely set, chilled, sweetened (flavored) cream tastes just a bit lighter to me than egg custard does. A great example: Yuzu Panna Cotta (page 236)—that is my idea of a perfect dessert.

Chocolate Mousse

Makes about 4 cups

Some recipes for chocolate mousse include butter and egg whites, but not mine. I use yolks, sugar, cream, and chocolate. I start by beating the yolks with sugar over simmering water. You want the sugar to dissolve and emulsify with the gently cooking egg. You need to keep the eggs moving—by whisking constantly—so the yolks don't scramble. It's not hard, but this process requires your full attention.

2½ cups	heavy cream, plus extra for serving	150g	sugar (5.3oz / about ¾ cup)
270g	extra bitter chocolate (9.5oz), chopped	6	large egg yolks

In a bowl, whip the cream until it holds soft peaks. Cover the bowl with plastic wrap and refrigerate.

Put the chocolate in a heatproof bowl. Set the bowl over a saucepan containing several inches of simmering water (take care that the bottom of the bowl doesn't touch the water). Melt the chocolate, stirring occasionally. Remove the bowl from the heat and reserve it in a warm place.

Put the sugar and egg yolks in the bowl of a stand mixer. Put several inches of water in a saucepan and bring it to a simmer. Set the mixer bowl over the simmering water (again make sure the bowl doesn't touch the water). Whisk the sugar and yolks together continuously and scrape the sides of the bowl often. (It is okay to briefly remove the bowl from the heat to scrape down the sides.) Cook the mixture until the yolks foam, become pale, increase in volume, and thicken enough so that, when lifted, the whisk leaves a ribbon trailing into the bowl, about 7 minutes.

Transfer the mixer bowl to the stand and, using the whisk attachment, whip the yolks on medium until the bowl returns to room temperature, about 5 minutes. Stir in the melted chocolate with a spatula, then pass the mixture through a fine sieve into a bowl; if it is too stiff, stir in 1 to 2 tablespoons of whipped cream.

Fold the whipped cream into the mousse and transfer it to a serving bowl (or individual cups). Cover the bowl with plastic wrap and chill for at least 2 hours and up to 2 days. Serve at room temperature topped with additional whipped cream.

Espresso Custard with Orange

Serves 8

Similar to a French pot de crème, this custard is full of eggs and yolks, which are partially cooked with hot cream, and then the custard is finished in a water bath in the oven. Silky and flavored with espresso and orange, this works well as an ending to a rich dinner.

2 cups	heavy cream	62g	sugar (2.2oz / 5 T)
2 cups	milk	2	large eggs
¼ cup	instant espresso powder	6	large egg yolks
	Zest of 2 oranges		

Preheat the oven to 325°F. In a heavy saucepan, combine the cream, milk, espresso powder, and orange zest with half of the sugar (31 grams / 1.1 ounce). Bring the mixture to a simmer over medium heat, stirring occasionally. Meanwhile, in a bowl, whisk the remaining 31 grams (1.1 ounce) sugar with the eggs and yolks.

Temper the eggs by whisking in a little of the hot cream mixture, then whisk continuously as you slowly stream in the rest. Strain the custard through a fine sieve into a bowl, then divide it evenly among eight 4-ounce ramekins.

Put the ramekins in a baking dish and add enough boiling water to come halfway up the sides of the ramekins. Cover the baking pan with foil, piercing it with a knife (so steam doesn't accumulate during baking). Bake the custards in the water bath until they have set at the edges but are still a bit jiggly in the center, about 35 minutes. Transfer the ramekins to a wire rack to cool, then cover each with plastic wrap and refrigerate overnight. Serve the custards in the ramekins topped with a dollop of whipped cream, if desired.

Coconut Custard

I make coconut milk for this custard, which I use as a filling for Coconut Layer Cake (page 72). I also like to eat this on its own. It is a great starting place for both winter and summer American-style layered parfaits.

80g	flaked unsweetened coconut (2.8oz / about 1 cup)		100g	sugar (3.5oz / about ½ cup)
1½ cups + 2 T	milk		0.7g	Diamond Crystal kosher salt (¼ tsp)
			3 T	cornstarch
4	large egg yolks		14g	unsalted butter (0.5oz), diced

Preheat the oven to 250°F and line a baking sheet with parchment paper. In a saucepan, combine the coconut flakes and 1¼ cups plus 2 tablespoons of the milk. Bring the mixture to a boil, then reduce the heat and simmer for 5 minutes. Remove the pan from the stove. Strain the mixture through a fine sieve into a bowl, pressing the coconut to extract as much liquid as possible and retaining the coconut and milk separately. Spread the coconut on the prepared baking sheet. Toast the coconut in the oven, turning it every 10 minutes so, until it is golden, about 30 minutes. Turn the oven off, crack the oven door, and allow the coconut to dry in the oven as it cools. Reserve the toasted coconut. (Stored in an airtight container, it will keep for weeks: I like it on yogurt and ice cream and use it to decorate cakes.)

In a bowl, whisk the yolks with the sugar, salt, cornstarch, and the remaining ¼ cup milk. Place the strained coconut milk in a saucepan and bring it to a boil over medium-high heat. Temper the yolks by whisking in a little of the hot coconut milk, then whisk continuously as you slowly stream in the rest. Return the egg/milk mixture to the saucepan over medium heat and cook, whisking constantly, until it thickens to pudding consistency, about 5 minutes. Simmer, still whisking, for 2 minutes longer to activate the cornstarch. Take the pot off the stove and whisk in the butter, a piece at a time, incorporating each before adding more. Transfer the custard to a bowl, cover it directly with plastic wrap (to prevent a skin from forming), and chill for at least 6 hours or overnight. Serve cold topped with the toasted coconut, if desired.

XVOO Lemon Cream

Makes about 2 cups

I replaced some of the butter traditionally used to make lemon curd with extra-virgin olive oil and got a custard that is so velvety smooth it tastes like cream—hence the recipe's name. I use this lots of ways, including as the star of my Lemon Tart (page 161) and as an occasional substitute for the Coconut Custard filling in the Coconut Layer Cake (page 72).

200g	sugar (7oz / about 1 cup)		1.5g	Diamond Crystal kosher salt (½ tsp)
	Zest of 4 lemons		142g	unsalted butter (5oz), diced, room temperature
4	large eggs			
¾ cup	freshly squeezed lemon juice		¾ cup	extra-virgin olive oil

In a nonreactive (stainless steel) saucepan, whisk the sugar with the lemon zest. Whisk in the eggs, one at a time, then whisk in the lemon juice and salt. Cook the custard mixture, whisking constantly, over medium heat until it thickens (the custard will be 180°F at this point). Immediately strain the lemon cream through a fine sieve into a blender. Allow the lemon cream to sit for 10 minutes, stirring it occasionally so it cools evenly. Turn the blender on high and incorporate the butter, adding it a piece at a time. When the butter is fully incorporated, begin slowly streaming in the olive oil with the blender still on high. Transfer the lemon cream to a container, cover it directly with plastic wrap (to prevent a skin from forming), and chill at least 6 hours or overnight. Serve cold.

Passion Fruit Custard

Makes about 2 cups

I begin this custard by reducing passion fruit juice to concentrate the flavor, then I add lemon juice to brighten the taste. Like the XVOO Lemon Cream (page 233), this not only makes a great cake filling but is the starting point for delicious parfaits.

1 cup	unsweetened passion fruit juice		1 T	cornstarch
1 T	freshly squeezed lemon juice		6	large eggs
200g	sugar (7oz / about 1 cup)		114g	unsalted butter (4oz), diced, room temperature
0.7g	Diamond Crystal kosher salt (¼ tsp)			

In a heavy-bottomed nonreactive (stainless steel) saucepan, bring the passion fruit juice to a boil. Adjust the heat and simmer until it has reduced to ½ cup. Stir the lemon juice into the passion fruit juice.

In a bowl, whisk the sugar with the salt and cornstarch. Whisk in the eggs, one at a time, then temper them by first whisking in a little of the warm passion fruit juice and slowly streaming in the rest while whisking continuously. Transfer the custard mixture to the saucepan and bring it to a simmer over medium heat, whisking constantly, until it thickens to pudding consistency, about 5 minutes. Whisk the custard over the heat for another minute or so, then remove the pot from the stove and whisk in the butter, several pieces at a time. Strain the custard through a fine sieve into a bowl. Cover the custard directly with plastic wrap (to prevent a skin from forming) and chill at least 6 hours or overnight. Serve cold.

Yuzu Panna Cotta

Makes six 4-ounce ramekins

Yuzu is a citrus fruit that is popular in Japan. It looks like a cross between a mandarin orange and a lemon. It is less acidic than the latter and tastes something like a tart, aromatic version of the former—delicious. Yuzu juice is available at Japanese groceries and online. I use buttermilk as well as cream in this recipe to underscore and smooth the bitter edges of the fruit's flavor. I suggest topping the custards with Blood Oranges in Caramel (page 273) or serving them with the Citrus Salad (page 269).

1½ tsp	gelatin		1¾ cups	buttermilk
1¼ cups	heavy cream		4 tsp	yuzu juice
84g	sugar (3oz / about 6½ T)			

Put 2 tablespoons plus 1 teaspoon cold water in a small bowl. Sprinkle the gelatin over the water, then set the gelatin aside to soften and bloom, about 5 minutes.

Warm the cream with the sugar in a small saucepan over medium heat, stirring occasionally, until the mixture steams and the sugar dissolves. Off the heat, whisk the softened gelatin into the cream until it is evenly dispersed. While whisking, stream in the buttermilk, then stir in the yuzu juice. Strain the custard through a fine sieve, then evenly divide it among six 4-ounce ramekins. Cover each with plastic wrap and chill overnight. To serve, unmold the panna cottas by running a knife around the edge of each and inverting them onto serving plates.

Chocolate Panna Cotta

Makes six 4-ounce ramekins

Although panna cotta translates from Italian to English as "cooked cream," you only heat the dairy enough to activate the gelatin, then you chill the custard, making this an ideal sweet to enjoy on hot summer days.

1½ tsp	gelatin
102g	milk chocolate (3.6oz), chopped
55g	extra bitter dark chocolate (2oz), chopped

1¼ cups + 2 T	heavy cream
¾ cup + 2 T	milk

Put 2 tablespoons cold water in a bowl, sprinkle the gelatin over the water, then set the gelatin aside to soften and bloom, about 5 minutes.

Combine the milk chocolate and dark chocolate in a bowl. Bring ¾ cup of the cream to a boil in a saucepan. Pour the hot cream over the chocolate, allow the chocolate to begin to melt, about 1 minute, then whisk until it is smooth. Reserve the ganache at room temperature.

Put the remaining ½ cup plus 2 tablespoons cream and the milk in the saucepan and bring them to a boil. Remove the pan from the heat, whisk in the bloomed gelatin. Whisk the hot cream mixture into the ganache. Strain the custard through a fine sieve, then evenly divide it among six 4-ounce ramekins. Cover and chill the panna cotta overnight. To serve, unmold the panna cottas by running a knife around the edge of each and inverting them onto serving plates.

Sweet Corn Puddings
with **Blueberries**

Makes six 6-ounce ramekins

This souffléed corn custard with blueberry compote hidden within is a showy dessert that is not difficult to pull off if you do a little logistical planning. The pastry cream and berry compote can be made up to a day ahead. The egg whites can be whipped and folded into the batter, and the puddings set up 2 hours before you plan to serve. That leaves only the baking for the last minute. The result is delicious and special. Note: Ears of corn vary in size; expect that you'll need about 3 medium ears, though I always buy an extra or two.

Corn base:

165g	fresh corn kernels (5.8oz / about ¾ cup + 1 T)
1 cup	milk
25g	sugar (0.9oz / about 2 T)
4 large	egg yolks
1 tsp	cornstarch
	Pinch of Diamond Crystal kosher salt

Blueberry compote:

10g	sugar (0.4oz / about 2½ tsp)
1 tsp	lemon zest
100g	fresh or frozen blueberries (3.5oz / about ½ cup + 2 T), stemmed if necessary

Pudding:

	Unsalted butter, softened, for greasing
5	large egg whites
37g	sugar (1.3oz / about 3 T), plus extra for the soufflé dishes
113g	fresh corn kernels (4oz / about ½ cup + 1½ T)
	Confectioners' sugar, for dusting

To start the corn base, combine 165 grams (5.8 ounces) corn kernels, the milk, and 12 grams (0.4 ounces) of the sugar in a saucepan and bring to a simmer over medium heat. Cook until the corn softens, about 5 minutes, then remove the pan from the heat. Puree the corn and the liquid in a blender until the mixture is smooth. Allow the mixture to come to room temperature, about 30 minutes. Press the puree through a fine sieve into a bowl. Measure 1 cup corn milk (if you are short, add a little milk). Discard the corn. (This can be done up to a day ahead.)

Put ¼ cup of the corn milk in a bowl and whisk it with the egg yolks, the cornstarch, and the remaining

13 grams (0.5 ounces) sugar. Put the remaining ¾ cup corn milk into a saucepan. Add a pinch of salt and heat the corn milk over medium until it scalds—steams but doesn't boil. Temper the yolk mixture by slowing whisking in a little of the hot corn milk, then gradually stream in the remainder, whisking constantly. Put the pastry-cream corn base back into the saucepan and cook it over medium heat, whisking constantly and scraping the sides as needed (it's okay to pull the pan off the heat to scrape down the sides). Simmer the custard until it thickens and begins to bubble, about 5 minutes, then whisk it over medium-low heat for an additional minute. Transfer the corn base to a bowl, let it cool a little, then cover it directly

with plastic wrap and chill it thoroughly, at least 3 hours or overnight.

To make the blueberry compote, mix 10 grams (0.6 ounces) sugar with the lemon zest in a saucepan. Add the blueberries and toss to combine. Cook over medium heat until the sugar dissolves and the berries begin to soften and pop, about 10 minutes. Transfer the compote to a bowl, cover it with plastic, and chill thoroughly, at least an hour or overnight.

To make the puddings, preheat the oven to 375°F. Prepare six 6-ounce ramekins by brushing each, the bottom and up the sides (to help guide the rise), with softened butter. Divide the berry compote evenly among them.

Shortly before serving, whip the egg whites in the bowl of a stand mixer using the whisk attachment until soft peaks form, then gradually beat in 37 grams (1.3 ounces) sugar. Once all the sugar has been added, continue beating until the whites stiffen and look shiny, about 4 minutes longer. In a bowl, combine the chilled corn base with 113 grams (4 ounces) corn kernels. Working by hand, whisk a third of the whites into the pudding base. Using a spatula, fold in the remaining whites in two additions. Spoon the pudding into the ramekins over the blueberry compote. Smooth the tops with an offset spatula and clean the rim of each ramekin by dampening your finger and running it around the edge (this prevents "sealing," which inhibits rising). Put the puddings on a baking sheet and bake until they are puffed and golden, about 17 minutes.

Dust the corn puddings with confectioners' sugar (at home I put the sugar in a fine sieve and shake it over the ramekins). Serve immediately with whipped crème fraîche, if desired.

Semifreddo: History and Technique

Italian scholars assert that Catherine de Medici brought gelato with her to France in the sixteenth century. Others suggest that frozen treats made their way north a hundred years later, when Francesco Procopio dei Coltelli moved to France and began serving gelato at Café Procope, the first café in Paris. The French certainly took to the sweet, and its popularity spread. So did gastronomic innovation, which by the nineteenh century led to the creation of the parfait. This combination of frozen custard, flavoring, and whipped cream (a more elegant and specific dessert than its American namesake) in turn inspired Italian chefs, and the semifreddo was born.

A French parfait is created by making an enhanced *pâte à bombe*—egg yolks whipped with sugar heated to the "firm ball stage," between 245°F and 250°F (see page 96 for more about cooking sugar), then lightened with whipped cream and meringue. A semifreddo can be made the same way, but need not be, and is sometimes made without any egg yolks. Italians believe that the method should depend on the qualities of the flavoring ingredient, with the focus on making a frozen dessert that leaves an impression of richness, creaminess, and airiness that never tastes icy. Getting the right balance of flavor, fat, and sugar is the only way to get the ideal half-frozen luscious mouthfeel.

Semifreddos are delicious, and in more good news, they don't need to be churned like ice cream, so there is no need for special equipment. I make semifreddo in a loaf or cake pan and build tiers of flavor, then add savor and texture with candied nuts and fruit, as in Banana and Espresso Semifreddo with Butterscotch and Macadamia Nuts (page 244) and my take on spumoni (see page 251). Both work as sophisticated endings to big-deal dinners and are truly scrumptious.

In the recipes that follow, I most often rely on a hybrid method: I make a custard, a relation of a *pâte à bombe*, but rather than cooking the yolks with sugar syrup, I stream in heated cream. I then fold in whipped cream. I landed here after a good bit of experimentation and owe thanks to Nancy Silverton, who pointed me in this direction. Learning further from her, I usually add melted white chocolate at the end. White chocolate has lots of sugar and fat and is generally magical. It makes semifreddo as creamy as can be. My method is exacting—you need a candy thermometer, preferably an instant-read—and you must allow for freezing time, but the sublime results are worth it.

I follow this scheme with my recipe for Squash Semifreddo Tart with Coconut and Pecans (page 248), although there I substitute cream of coconut for the white chocolate. The one recipe I have included that significantly diverges from this formula is the Black Raspberry and Chocolate Semifreddo (page 246), where I can use a different procedure because of the nature of my ingredients. I combine cooked berries, whipped yogurt, and cream with an Italian meringue (see page 85) stabilized with gelatin and then add dark chocolate for taste. But this is a summer dish, so I wanted to avoid time in the kitchen. Just for fun, I decided to see if store-bought marshmallow crème (aka Fluff) could replace the meringue; it worked like a charm. Make this on hot days when you want to impress without breaking a sweat.

Banana and Espresso Semifreddo with Butterscotch and Macadamia Nuts

Serves 6 to 8

Don't be put off by the number of ingredients in this dessert—a duet of semifreddos that I layer in a loaf pan, separating the banana semifreddo from the espresso semifreddo with a layer of butterscotch sauce and candied nuts. Do begin this at least a day ahead, because the bottom layer needs to freeze before you can continue, and the top layer needs to freeze before the parfait can be unmolded.

Butterscotch sauce:

⅓ cup	**Butterscotch Toffee Sauce (page 289)**	
152g	light brown sugar (5.4oz / about ⅔ cup)	
57g	unsalted butter (2oz)	
1¼ cups	heavy cream	
2 tsp	sherry vinegar	
1½ tsp	vanilla paste or pure vanilla extract	
3g	Diamond Crystal kosher salt (1 tsp)	

Sugared macadamia nuts:

¾ cup	**Sugared Macadamia Nuts (page 292)**
100g	macadamia nuts (7oz / about ¾ cup), roughly chopped
2 tsp	light corn syrup
1.5g	Diamond Crystal kosher salt (½ tsp)
20g	light brown sugar (0.7oz / about 1½ T)

Semifreddos:

2	medium bananas
½ tsp	freshly squeezed lemon juice
16g	dark brown sugar (0.6oz / about 1½ T)
126g	white chocolate (4.4g), chopped
2 cups	heavy cream
¼ cup + 2 T	milk
0.7g	Diamond Crystal kosher salt (¼ tsp)
9	large egg yolks
12g	sugar (0.4oz / about 1 T)
3 T	sour cream
½ tsp	vanilla paste or pure vanilla extract
1½ tsp	espresso powder

Prepare the butterscotch sauce as directed on page 289. Reserve ⅓ cup of the sauce at room temperature for the semifreddo and refrigerate the rest for future use. (Note: If the sauce breaks or separates, a whiz in the blender will bring it right back.)

Make the sugared macadamia nuts according to the instructions on page 292. Reserve ¾ cup. Store the rest in a sealed container for future use.

To start the banana semifreddo, preheat the oven to 375°F. Peel the bananas, slice them lengthwise, and arrange them cut-side down on a baking sheet. Roast the bananas until they are fully soft and have exuded their juices, about 30 minutes. Allow the bananas to cool, then puree them with the lemon juice and brown sugar in a blender or food processor. Transfer the puree to a bowl, cover it, and chill for at least 20 minutes.

To start the base for both semifreddos, put the white chocolate in a heatproof bowl. Set the bowl over a saucepan containing several inches of simmering water (take care that the bottom of the bowl doesn't touch the water). Melt the chocolate, stirring occasionally, then remove the bowl from the heat and reserve it in a warm place.

Combine 1¼ cups of the cream, the milk, and salt in a small saucepan and heat over medium-high until it scalds—steams but doesn't boil. Remove the pan from the heat but cover it to keep warm.

In the bowl of a stand mixer, beat the egg yolks with the white sugar on high speed until the mixture is pale yellow and the sugar fully dissolves, about 5 minutes. With the mixer running, temper the yolks by drizzling in a little of the reserved hot cream, then slowly stream in the remainder. Continue beating on medium speed until the yolks and cream are thoroughly combined. Transfer the base to a saucepan and wipe out the mixer bowl.

Cook the base, whisking continuously, over medium-high heat until it begins to bubble, pales, and thickens—like hollandaise—about 3 minutes. Remove the pan from the heat and whisk in the chocolate. Strain the base through a fine sieve back into the mixer bowl.

Whip the semifreddo base on high until it is fluffy, thickened, and cooled, about 12 minutes. Transfer the base to a bowl, cover it directly with plastic wrap, and chill it for at least 30 minutes.

Meanwhile, whip ½ cup of the heavy cream, 2 tablespoons of the sour cream, and the vanilla in a bowl until the cream holds soft peaks. (I prefer to whip a small amount like this by hand.) Cover the tangy whipped cream and chill it.

To start the espresso semifreddo, combine 1 ½ teaspoons espresso powder with the remaining ¼ cup heavy cream and 1 tablespoon sour cream in a bowl. Whisk until the cream holds soft peaks. Cover the espresso whipped cream and chill it.

To finish the banana semifreddo, line a 5 × 9-inch loaf pan with parchment paper. Spoon 2 cups of the chilled base into a bowl (reserve the rest for the espresso semifreddo). Whisk the banana puree into the base, whisk in a third of the tangy whipped cream, and then fold in the remainder in two additions. Transfer the banana semifreddo to the prepared loaf pan. Cover the semifreddo directly with parchment and freeze it until it is firm, at least 3 hours.

Pour room-temperature butterscotch sauce over the chilled banana semifreddo and top it with an even layer of sugared macadamia nuts (I spread them out with the back of a spoon). Return the semifreddo to the freezer until it is solid.

Complete the espresso semifreddo by whisking a third of the espresso whipped cream into the remaining base, then fold in the rest of the espresso whipped cream in two additions. Evenly spread the espresso semifreddo over the butterscotch and nuts, top directly with a piece of parchment, and freeze the semifreddo overnight.

To serve, unmold the semifreddo, slice, and serve with additional warmed butterscotch sauce, if desired.

Black Raspberry and Chocolate Semifreddo

Serves 8 to 10

This semifreddo doesn't contain egg yolks. The fruits' low moisture content and the marshmallow keep the finished dessert from becoming icy. You could make this with an Italian meringue (see page 85), but I don't. Instead I use Marshmallow Fluff, a commercially prepared marshmallow crème. I drain my own yogurt (because I find the consistency of pre-drained Greek-style yogurts varies), but, if you have some Greek yogurt on hand, use it.

Conserve:

453g	black raspberries (1lb / about 2¾ cups)
66g	sugar (2.3oz / about ⅓ cup)

Semifreddo:

1¾ cups	heavy cream
¾ cup	plain yogurt, drained in a cloth-lined fine sieve overnight, or ½ cup Greek yogurt
1 cup	marshmallow crème
160g	extra bitter chocolate (5.6oz / about 1 cup), chopped
	Coconut oil, for greasing

To make the black raspberry conserve, combine the berries and sugar in a saucepan and gently simmer over medium-low heat until the berries soften and form a thick compote, about 15 minutes. Remove the conserve from the heat and let it cool completely; this can be done up to 3 days in advance.

To make the semifreddo, whip the cream until it holds soft peaks. (I whip small amounts by hand; if you use a machine, mix only until the cream thickens, then finish the job manually to avoid overbeating.) Cover the bowl of cream and chill it. Put the drained yogurt into a large bowl. Whisk in the marshmallow crème, then the black raspberry conserve and chopped chocolate.

Fold one-third of the chilled whipped cream into the semifreddo base, then fold in the remainder in two additions. Brush an 8-inch cake pan with 2¼-inch sides with coconut oil (a 5 × 9-inch loaf pan or a 1½-quart terrine mold will also work). Spoon the semifreddo into the pan, cover it directly with parchment paper, and freeze it overnight. Slice and serve.

Squash Semifreddo Tart with Coconut and Pecans

Makes one 9-inch tart

I use coconut cream in this semifreddo (instead of white chocolate) for a smooth texture and to prevent iciness. Coconut cream (which is not the same as coconut milk) is usually stocked in groceries near the cocktail fixings.

Semifreddo:

600g	diced winter squash, such as sugar pumpkin or butternut (1lb 5oz / about 5 cups), or 1 cup canned pumpkin puree (not pumpkin pie filling)
210g	sugar (7.4oz / about 1 cup +1 T)
1	cinnamon stick
½ cup	coconut cream
6	large egg yolks
½ cup	heavy cream
1 tsp	light corn syrup
3	large egg whites
¼ tsp	cream of tartar

Crust:

50g	pecans (1.8oz / about ½ cup)
150g	shredded unsweetened coconut (5.3oz / about 2 cups)
6g	sugar (0.2oz / about 1½ tsp)
	Pinch of Diamond Crystal kosher salt
56g	unsalted butter (2oz), melted

To start the semifreddo, preheat the oven to 300°F. Put the squash in a large ovenproof skillet and add 60 grams (2.1 ounces) of the sugar and the cinnamon stick. Cover the pan (with a lid or tinfoil), and roast the squash until it softens, about 1 hour. Discard the cinnamon stick and mash the squash with a fork, then return the skillet to the oven, and roast uncovered, to allow the squash to dry out; start checking it after 15 minutes. When there is no more liquid visible in the pan, turn off the oven but leave the squash inside to continue to dry out for 30 minutes more (the puree needs to be concentrated to avoid icy semifreddo). Puree the squash in a blender or food processor, transfer the puree to a covered container, and chill it for at least 30 minutes.

To make the crust, raise the oven temperature to 325°F. Arrange the pecans in an even layer in an ovenproof skillet or on a baking sheet and roast until the nuts smell toasty, about 12 minutes. Remove the pecans from the oven and allow them to cool, then grind them in a food processor with the shredded coconut, 6 grams (0.2 ounces) sugar, and the salt. Drizzle in the melted butter and pulse to mix. Press the crust into a 9-inch high-sided tart or cake pan with a removable bottom. Bake the crust until it is set and darker, 8 to 10 minutes. Cool completely in the tart pan.

To continue the semifreddo, heat the coconut cream in a saucepan over medium-low until it reaches 248°F.

In the bowl of a stand mixer and using the whisk attachment, whip the yolks with the mixer on high. Very gradually stream in the hot coconut cream. Continue to whip on high until the mixture cools to room temperature, about 5 minutes. Transfer the yolk mixture to a bowl, cover directly with plastic wrap, and chill for at least 30 minutes.

Meanwhile, whip the heavy cream until it holds soft peaks (I prefer to whip small amounts of cream by hand). Cover the whipped cream with plastic wrap and chill it.

Next, make an Italian meringue by heating ¼ cup water in a small saucepan over medium. Add the remaining 150 grams (5.3 ounces) sugar and the corn syrup and cook until the sugar dissolves and the mixture reaches a temperature of 230°F. In the bowl of a stand mixer and using the whisk attachment, start whipping the egg whites with the cream of tartar. Continue to check the temperature of the syrup; when it reaches 248°F, with the mixer on high speed, very slowly stream the hot syrup into the whites. Whip until the meringue is stiff and glossy and the bowl cool to the touch, 5 to 10 minutes.

Fold a third of the meringue into the chilled whipped cream, then fold in the remainder in two additions. In a separate bowl, combine the coconut yolk mixture and squash puree. Whisk a little of the whipped cream/meringue into the squash mixture, then fold in the rest in two additions. Spoon the semifreddo into the crust, spreading it evenly and smoothing the top. Cover the tart with parchment and freeze it overnight.

To serve, unmold the tart, then top it with whipped cream and chopped pecans, if desired.

Spumoni with Meringue and Caramelized Oranges

Serves 6 to 8

This impressive, special occasion dessert is an undertaking, even without the meringue, but I like to add it because it is so glamorous. Recently I've been torching the meringue just before serving for a presentation that reminds me of Baked Alaska. In any event, I reduce active cooking time by making the base for the pistachio and olive oil semifreddos together (the orange base must be made separately), but always leave plenty of time. Each must freeze before the next is added. So I start a couple of days ahead of when I plan to serve. It's worth noting that once it's frosted with meringue, the spumoni can go back into the freezer, where it will hold overnight. Feel free to substitute good store-bought pistachio paste for homemade. Note: I've included separate recipes for each of the semifreddo layers; see pages 255, 256, and 258.

Pistachio paste and candied pistachios:

132g	shelled pistachios (4.7oz / about 1 cup)
1½ tsp	light corn syrup
12g	crystallized sugar, such as turbinado, Demerara, or Sugar In The Raw (0.4oz / about 1 T)
0.7g	Diamond Crystal kosher salt (¼ tsp)

Semifreddo base:

86g	white chocolate (3oz), chopped
1 ¼ cups	heavy cream
¼ cup	milk
1 T	honey
0.7g	Diamond Crystal kosher salt (¼ tsp)
2 T	sour cream
6	large egg yolks
8g	sugar (0.3oz / about 2 tsp)

Olive oil semifreddo:

¼ cup	extra-virgin olive oil

Orange semifreddo:

43g	white chocolate (1.5oz), chopped
½ cup + 2 T	heavy cream
2 T	milk
1½ tsp	honey
	Pinch of Diamond Crystal kosher salt
	Zest of 1 orange
1 T	sour cream
3	egg yolks
4g	sugar (0.1oz / about 1 tsp)
¼ cup	diced Candied Orange Rinds (page 275)
3	medium navel oranges
300g	sugar (10.6oz / about 1½ cups)
1 T	light corn syrup

Caramel:

1 recipe	Blood Orange Caramel (page 288) (see Note)
200g	sugar (7oz / about 1 cup)
1 tsp	light corn syrup
½ cup	blood orange or Cara Cara orange juice

Italian meringue and garnish:

4	egg whites
240g	sugar (8.5oz / 1 cup + 3 T)
1 tsp	light corn syrup
1½ tsp	orange flower water
2	blood or Cara Cara oranges, peeled, seeded, and sectioned (remove the pith from the suprêmes)
About 12g	chopped pistachios (0.4oz / 2 T)

To make the pistachio paste, bring a pot of water to a boil. Add the pistachios, take the pot off the heat, let the pistachios steep for 1 minute, then drain them. Gather the nuts in a kitchen towel and rub them so they shed their papery skins. Measure 50 grams (1.76 ounces) of the skinned pistachios, set them aside, and put the rest into a food processor. Add just enough hot water to make a paste, about 1 tablespoon, and puree until smooth. The paste can be wrapped in plastic and stored in the refrigerator for a week or frozen for months.

To make the candied pistachios, preheat the oven to 325°F and line a baking sheet with parchment paper. Put the reserved pistachios in a bowl, add 1½ teaspoons corn syrup, and mix well. Add the crystallized sugar and 0.7 grams (¼ teaspoon salt) and toss to coat. Spread the pistachios out in an even layer on the prepared baking sheet and roast until the nuts are lightly browned, about 15 minutes. Remove the nuts from the oven and allow them to cool. The candied pistachios will keep in an airtight container for up to 2 weeks.

To start the semifreddo base, put 86 grams (3 ounces) white chocolate in a heatproof bowl. Set the bowl over a saucepan containing several inches of simmering water (take care that the bottom of the bowl doesn't touch the water). Melt the chocolate, stirring occasionally, then remove the bowl from the heat and reserve it in a warm place.

Combine ¾ cup of the heavy cream, ¼ cup milk, the honey, and 0.7 grams (¼ teaspoon) salt in a small saucepan, heat over medium-high, and bring to a scald—steaming but not boiling. Remove the pan from the heat but keep the contents warm.

In the bowl of a stand mixer and using the whisk attachment, whip 6 egg yolks with 8 grams (0.3 ounces) sugar on high speed until the mixture is pale yellow and the sugar fully dissolves, about 5 minutes. With the mixer on medium-high, temper the yolks by drizzling in a little of the hot cream, then very slowly streaming in the remainder. Continue beating on medium speed until the yolks and cream are thoroughly combined. Transfer the base to a saucepan.

To finish the base, transfer it to a saucepan and cook it over medium to medium-high heat, whisking continuously, until it begins to bubble, pales, and thickens—like hollandaise—about 3 minutes. Immediately remove the pan from the heat and whisk in the melted chocolate. Strain the base through a fine sieve into a bowl. Transfer half to the mixer bowl and keep the remainder warm by covering the bowl.

To make the pistachio base, whisk 2 tablespoons of the pistachio paste into the base in the mixer. Whip on high with the whisk attachment until it is fluffy, thicker, and no longer warm, about 5 minutes. Transfer the mixture to a container, cover it directly with plastic wrap, and chill it for at least 30 minutes. Wipe out the mixer bowl.

To make the olive oil semifreddo, put the remaining base in the mixer bowl. Whip it on high speed. When the base begins to pale and thicken, gradually stream in the olive oil. Whip until the olive oil semifreddo has cooled to room temperature, about 5 minutes, then transfer it to a container, cover it directly with plastic wrap, and chill for at least 6 hours.

Make the tangy whipped cream by whipping the remaining ½ cup heavy cream with 2 tablespoons sour cream until it holds soft peaks. (I prefer to whip a small amount like this by hand.) Cover and chill for at least 20 minutes.

To finish the pistachio semifreddo, line a 5 × 9-inch loaf pan with parchment paper. Measure out half of the tangy whipped cream, leaving the remainder in the refrigerator for the olive oil semifreddo. Whisk a little of the measured whipped cream into the pistachio semifreddo base, then fold in the rest (of this half portion) in two additions. Spoon the pistachio semifreddo into the prepared pan. Cover the semifreddo directly with parchment and freeze until it firms, at least 3 hours. Top the semifreddo with the sugared pistachios, re-cover with parchment, and return it to the freezer until it is frozen, at least 3 more hours.

Once the pistachio semifreddo is fully frozen, finish the olive oil layer. Whisk a little of the reserved tangy whipped cream into the olive oil semifreddo, then fold in the rest, half at a time. Spoon the olive oil semifreddo evenly over the sugared nuts, then re-cover the semifreddo with parchment and return it to the freezer until it is solid, at least 4 hours.

To start the orange semifreddo, put 43 grams (1.5 ounces) white chocolate in a heatproof bowl. Set the bowl over a saucepan containing several inches of steaming water over low heat (again, don't allow the bowl to touch the water). Melt the chocolate, stirring occasionally, then remove the bowl from the heat and hold it in a warm place.

Combine 6 tablespoons of the heavy cream, 2 tablespoons milk, 1 ½ teaspoons honey, and a pinch of salt in a small saucepan. Stir in the orange zest and bring to a scald over medium-high heat, then remove the pan from the heat but cover and keep it warm.

In the bowl of a stand mixer, beat 3 egg yolks with 4 grams (0.1 ounces) sugar on high speed until the mixture is pale yellow and the sugar fully dissolves, about 5 minutes. With the mixer on medium-high, temper the yolks by drizzling in a little of the warm cream, then slowly stream in the rest. Continue beating on medium-high until the yolks and cream are combined.

Put the orange base into a saucepan. Whisking continuously, cook it over medium-high heat until it begins to bubble and thicken, about 3 minutes. Remove the pan from the heat and whisk in the melted chocolate. Strain the base through a fine sieve into the mixer bowl and whip it on high until it is fluffy and cools to room temperature, about 5 minutes. Transfer the semifreddo to a bowl, cover it directly with plastic wrap, and chill it for at least 30 minutes.

Meanwhile, make the tangy whipped cream by whipping the remaining ¼ cup heavy cream with 1 tablespoon sour cream in a small bowl until it holds soft peaks. Cover the bowl and chill.

Whisk a third of the tangy whipped cream into the orange base, then fold in the remainder in two additions.

To finish assembling the spumoni, arrange the candied orange rinds on top of the olive oil semifreddo. Spoon the orange semifreddo on top, cover it directly with parchment, and freeze until it is solid.

To make the orange caramel, follow the instructions on page 288. (The caramel can be made ahead of time and kept in a covered container in the refrigerator, but warm it to room temperature before using.)

To make the Italian meringue, put 5 tablespoons water in a small saucepan. Add 240 grams (8.5 ounces) sugar and 1 ½ teaspoons corn syrup and bring to a simmer over medium-high heat without stirring. Meanwhile, put the egg whites in the bowl of a stand mixer. When the sugar mixture reaches 230°F, begin whipping the whites at high speed with the whisk attachment. When the sugar syrup reaches 248°F, begin streaming it very gradually into the whipping whites. Beat the whites until they are shiny and stiff and the mixer bowl no longer feels warm, about 5 minutes. Fold the orange flower water into the meringue, then spoon it into a piping bag.

Unmold the spumoni, turning it out onto a serving platter. Pipe meringue on the sides, top, and the ends of the semifreddo (at this point the spumoni can be returned to the freezer).

Immediately before serving, brown the meringue with a handheld torch, if desired. Slice the spumoni, drizzle each serving with caramel, and garnish with oranges and pistachios.

Olive Oil Semifreddo

This is an elegant, mildly flavored semifreddo that I like to serve with fresh or roasted figs.

86g	white chocolate (3oz), chopped		½ cup	extra-virgin olive oil
1¼ cups	heavy cream		2 T	sour cream
¼ cup	milk		6	large egg yolks
1 T	honey		8g	sugar (0.3oz / about 2 tsp)
0.7g	Diamond Crystal kosher salt (¼ tsp)			

To start the semifreddo base, put the chocolate in a heatproof bowl. Set the bowl over a saucepan containing several inches of simmering water (take care that the bottom of the bowl doesn't touch the water). Melt the chocolate, stirring occasionally, then remove the bowl from the heat and reserve it in a warm place.

Combine ¾ cup of the cream, the milk, honey, and salt in a small saucepan and bring to a scald—steaming but not boiling—over medium-high heat. Remove the pan from the heat but cover it to keep warm.

Meanwhile, make the tangy whipped cream. Whip the remaining ½ cup cream with the sour cream in a bowl until it holds soft peaks. (If you use a mixer, finish whipping the cream manually to avoid overbeating.) Cover the bowl with plastic wrap and chill.

In the bowl of a stand mixer, whip the egg yolks with the sugar until the mixture is pale yellow and the sugar dissolves, about 5 minutes on high. With the mixer running, temper the yolks by drizzling in a little of the reserved hot cream, then slowly stream in the rest. Continue whipping on medium-high until the yolks and cream are thoroughly combined. Transfer the semifreddo base to a saucepan.

Whisking continuously, cook the base over medium-high heat until it bubbles, pales, and thickens—like hollandaise—about 3 minutes. Immediately remove the pan from the heat and whisk in the melted chocolate. Strain the base through a fine sieve back into the mixer bowl.

Whip the semifreddo on high speed until it is fluffy and thicker, then gradually stream in the olive oil, continuing to whip until it is mousse-like and cools to room temperature, about 12 minutes. Transfer the semifreddo base to a bowl, cover it directly with plastic, and chill for at least 30 minutes.

Whisk a third of the tangy whipped cream into the cold base, then fold in the remainder in two additions. Spoon the semifreddo into a parchment-lined 5 × 9-inch loaf pan, cover it directly with parchment, and freeze until it is solid. Unmold, slice, and serve.

Orange Semifreddo

Serves 6

Candied Orange Rinds (page 275) make a nice garnish for this semifreddo, as do Blood Oranges in Caramel (page 273) or Citrus Salad (page 269), but it is also good on its own or simply garnished with some whipped cream.

86g	white chocolate (3oz), chopped		2 T	sour cream
1¼ cups	heavy cream		6	large egg yolks
¼ cup	milk		8g	sugar (0.3oz / about 2 tsp)
1 T	honey		½ cup	Candied Orange Rinds (page 275)
0.7g	Diamond Crystal kosher salt (¼ tsp)			(optional)
	Zest of 2 oranges			

To start the semifreddo base, put the chocolate in a heatproof bowl. Set the bowl over a saucepan containing several inches of simmering water (take care that the bottom of the bowl doesn't touch the water). Melt the chocolate, stirring occasionally, then remove the bowl from the heat and reserve it in a warm place.

Combine ¾ cup of the cream, the milk, honey, and salt in a small saucepan and heat over medium-high. Add the orange zest and bring to a scald—steaming but not boiling. Remove the pan from the heat but cover to keep it warm.

Meanwhile, make the tangy whipped cream. Whip the remaining ½ cup cream with the sour cream in a bowl until it holds soft peaks. (If you use a mixer, finish whipping manually to avoid overbeating.) Cover the bowl with plastic wrap and chill the cream.

In the bowl of a stand mixer, beat the egg yolks with the sugar until the mixture is pale yellow and the sugar fully dissolves, about 5 minutes on high speed. With the mixer running, temper the yolks by drizzling in a little of the hot cream, then slowly stream in the rest. Continue beating on medium-high speed until the yolks and cream are thoroughly combined, then transfer the semifreddo base to a saucepan.

Whisking continuously, cook the base over medium-high heat until it begins to bubble, pales, and thickens—like hollandaise—about 3 minutes. Immediately remove the pan from the heat and whisk in the melted chocolate. Strain the base through a fine sieve back into the mixer bowl.

Whip the semifreddo on high speed until is fluffy, thicker, and cooled to room temperature, about 6 minutes. Transfer it to a bowl. Cover it directly with plastic wrap and chill at least 30 minutes.

Whisk a third of the tangy whipped cream into the semifreddo, then fold in the remainder in two additions. Spoon the semifreddo into a parchment-lined 5 × 9-inch loaf pan, cover it directly with parchment, and freeze until solid.

Unmold, slice, and serve the semifreddo garnished with candied orange rinds, if desired.

Pistachio Semifreddo

Serves 6

The quality of the pistachio paste is important for this dessert, that's why I make my own. It's easy enough to do, particularly when, as here, I am making candied pistachios, but feel free to substitute good store-bought paste—I've had some nice ones imported from Sicily.

Pistachio paste and candied pistachios:

114g	shelled pistachios (4oz / about ½ cup + 6½ T)
1½ tsp	light corn syrup
0.7g	Diamond Crystal kosher salt (¼ tsp)
12g	sugar (0.4oz / 1 T)

Semifreddo:

86g	white chocolate (3oz), chopped
1¼ cups	heavy cream
¼ cup	milk
1 T	honey
0.7g	Diamond Crystal kosher salt (¼ tsp)
2 T	sour cream
6	large egg yolks
8g	sugar (0.3oz / about 2 tsp)

To make the pistachio paste, bring a pot of water to a boil and add the pistachios. Take the pot off the heat and let the pistachios steep for 1 minute, then drain them. Gather the nuts in a kitchen towel and rub so they shed their papery skins. Set 50 grams (1.8 ounces) aside to be candied. Put the remaining 114 grams (2.2 ounces) pistachios in a food processor. Process with enough hot water to make a paste, about 1 tablespoon. (The paste can be wrapped in plastic and refrigerated for a week or frozen for months.)

To candy the pistachios, preheat the oven to 325°F and line a baking sheet with parchment paper. Put the reserved 50 grams (1.8 ounces) pistachios in a bowl. Add the corn syrup and mix well. Add 0.7 grams (¼ teaspoon) salt and 12 grams (0.4 ounces) sugar and toss to thoroughly coat the nuts. Arrange the pistachios in a single layer on the prepared baking sheet. Bake until the nuts are light brown, about 15 minutes. Allow the nuts to cool.

To start the semifreddo, put the white chocolate in a heatproof bowl. Set the bowl over a saucepan containing several inches of simmering water (take care that the bottom of the bowl doesn't touch the water). Melt the chocolate, stirring occasionally, then remove the bowl from the heat and reserve it in a warm place.

Combine ¾ cup of the cream, the milk, honey, and 0.7 grams (¼ teaspoon) salt in a saucepan and bring to a scald—steaming but not boiling—over medium-high heat, stirring occasionally. Remove from the heat but keep warm.

Make the tangy whipped cream by whipping the remaining ½ cup cream with the sour cream in a bowl until it holds soft peaks. (If you use a mixer, finish whipping manually to avoid overbeating.) Cover the bowl with plastic wrap and chill the cream.

In the bowl of a stand mixer, beat the yolks with the sugar until the mixture is pale yellow and the sugar fully dissolves, about 5 minutes on high speed. With the mixer running, temper the yolks by drizzling in a little of the hot cream, then slowly stream in the rest. Continue beating on medium-high until the yolks and cream are thoroughly combined. Transfer the semifreddo base to a saucepan.

Whisking continuously, cook the base over medium-high heat until it begins to bubble, pales, and thickens—like hollandaise—about 3 minutes. Remove the pan from the heat and whisk in the melted chocolate. Strain the base through a fine sieve back into the mixer bowl. Stir in ¼ cup of the pistachio paste.

Whip the semifreddo base on high speed until it is fluffy, thicker, and cooled to room temperature, about 12 minutes. Transfer the semifreddo to a bowl, cover it directly with plastic wrap, and chill for at least 30 minutes.

Whisk a third of the tangy whipped cream into the semifreddo, then fold in the remainder in two additions. Spoon the semifreddo into a parchment-lined 5 × 9-inch loaf pan. Cover it directly with parchment and freeze until it is solid. To serve, unmold, slice, and top with sugared pistachios.

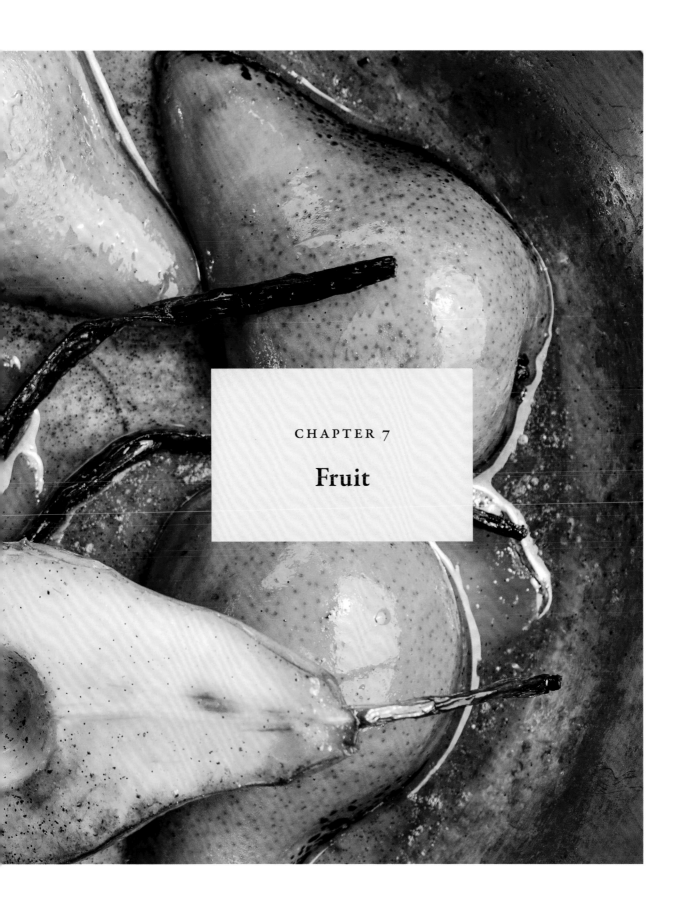

CHAPTER 7

Fruit

Cooking in Season

From my first menus onward, fruit served as a culinary guide through the year and a tool in my efforts to balance flavors and add excitement to my desserts. Chocolate or almonds might at times claim the spotlight, but fruit invariably made it onto the plate and was key to the pleasure of eating. Short-seasoned and highly perishable varieties—rhubarb, sour cherries, figs, and Concord grapes—have always defined the boundaries and pushed my mind into creative gear. My love of fruit is evident throughout the pages of this book. Here though, I want to focus on cooked fruit preparations in a specific fashion, in the multifaceted way I learned to as a pastry cook. Looking at fruit through that lens, I think, is equally useful when I am baking. In both instances, my relationship to this family of ingredients is complex; sometimes fruit is the star, while other times it's a supporting player or a member of the chorus.

Rather than organize this chapter seasonally, I've arranged it like the credits of a movie with the leading ladies first, the extras toward the end, and then I finish with a few special appearances. I begin with the divas. I let them perform without undue adornment. The Roasted Peaches with Caramel and Cherries (page 265) and the Roasted Pears with Maple and Goat Cheese Cream (page 266) are simple but complete dishes. These are confident plates I make for people who appreciate the allure of peak season tastes.

Next are several fruit preparations that I use alternately as the starting place for more layered dishes and include in ensembles. Many of these recipes extend the life of seasonal produce, and all are suited to mixing and matching. Poaching quince, for example, not only produces a necessary component of the Quince Goat Cheese Cake (page 64), but it turns the fruit into an ingredient which will keep for weeks in my refrigerator. Not limited to big productions, the poached quince is delicious served simply with candied walnuts and goat cheese cream (see Roasted Pears with Maple and Goat Cheese Cream on page 266). The Citrus Salad (page 269), a part of this subset of dishes, is more than a garnish; it is an accompaniment to cake or custard that elevates the finished plate. Like the poached quince, this preparation works as a featured performer. I need only add a scoop of sorbet for a satisfyingly bright sweet. Focusing on the Citrus Salad for another minute, this dish makes clear that, though I eat fruit seasonally, I don't limit myself to eating locally.

I lean heavily on tropical and semitropical fruit in the winter, but when local fruit fits the bill, I prefer it. Both types appear in the next group of recipes, which I think of as the supporting cast. They work as garnishes or players in other dishes and include preserves. Apple Butter (page 278) and Wintertime Apricot Jam (page 280) are recipes I make in bulk to use as fillings as well as to eat on toast for breakfast. I always have jars of candied citrus rinds (see pages 275–77) in my pantry in the cooler months. They are pretty, useful, and delicious.

Finally, I have included both a savory conserve and a quick pickle in this chapter. Both are made with fruit—eggplant, peppers, and tomatoes on the one hand, and cucumbers on the other (yes, botanically speaking, these are all fruits). I am drawn to the line between sweet and savory. Regardless of which side I wind up on, it is fruit that always leads the way.

Roasted Peaches with Caramel and Cherries

On Long Island, there are years when cherries and peaches are not ripe at the same time—when they are, I celebrate. For this dessert, choose peaches that are still a little firm. As far as the cherries go, I pit them by slicing off half, then cutting the remaining fruit from the pit in quarters. Not only is this method easiest, but I like the way the mix of cherry halves and quarters looks together. Note: The recipe for Sugared Almonds makes more than you need for this recipe, but I always make the whole batch and save the extra.

⅓ cup	**Sugared Almonds (page 291)**
100g	sliced almonds (3.5oz / about 1 cup + 1½ T)
2 tsp	light corn syrup
1.5g	Diamond Crystal kosher salt (½ tsp)
30g	crystallized sugar, such as turbinado, Demerara, or Sugar In The Raw (1oz / about 2 T)

100g	**sugar (3.5oz / about 1 cup + 1½ T)**
3	**peaches, pitted and halved**
¼ cup	**bourbon**
14g	**unsalted butter (0.5oz)**
18	**cherries**
½ cup	**sour cream, beaten slightly**

Prepare the sugared almonds according to the directions on page 291. Reserve ⅓ cup and set the rest aside for another use.

To make the caramel, preheat the oven to 350°F. Put a skillet large enough to accommodate 6 peach halves on a burner over medium heat. Sprinkle the sugar in an even layer in the pan. Leave the skillet on the heat undisturbed until the sugar melts and turns a light amber, about 12 minutes.

Arrange the peaches, cut-side down, in the caramel and put the pan in the oven. Bake until the cut sides (in the caramel) are golden and the peach halves are softer (I test by inserting the tip of a paring knife), about 15 minutes. Remove the peaches from the oven and let them cool slightly in the pan. When you can comfortably touch the fruit, peel away the loosened skins and discard them. (The recipe can be prepared up to this point several hours ahead of time. In that case, pop the peaches in the oven to heat them up for 10 to 15 minutes before serving.)

To finish the dish, using a spatula, lift the warm peach halves out of the caramel and put each in a bowl, cut-side up. Return the skillet to the stove and reheat the caramel over medium-low. When it starts to bubble, carefully add the bourbon. Swirl it as it mixes with the sauce in the pan and simmer until the mixture is integrated and viscous, 3 to 5 minutes. Remove the skillet from the heat and add the butter, swirling it until it melts. Add the cherries and swirl them in the sauce, letting them soften slightly as the sauce cools to warm (rather than scalding), about 3 minutes.

To serve, spoon the cherries and sauce over each peach half, then top with sugared almonds and a spoonful of sour cream.

Roasted Pears with Maple and Goat Cheese Cream

Serves 4

Both sweetened and unsweetened whipped cream have a place in my heart, but I especially love cream whipped with something that has a slight acidic bite, like yogurt or, in this case, goat cheese. It adds another dimension and becomes the perfect accompaniment to these roasted pears. I usually serve this garnished with Maple Sugared Pecans.

Goat cheese cream:

114g	fresh goat cheese (4oz), room temperature
¾ cup	heavy cream
16g	confectioners' sugar (0.6oz / about 2 T)
1½ tsp	vanilla paste or pure vanilla extract

Pears:

57g	unsalted butter (2oz)
2	Bosc pears, halved and cored
¼ cup	maple syrup
½ tsp	peeled and freshly grated ginger
0.7g	Diamond Crystal kosher salt (¼ tsp)
¼	vanilla bean, split
2 tsp	bourbon
½ cup	Maple Sugared Pecans (page 293), for garnish (optional)

Preheat the oven to 400°F.

To make the goat cheese cream, combine the goat cheese, cream, confectioners' sugar, and vanilla in the bowl of a stand mixer. Mix on low just to combine, then increase the speed to high and whip until the cream holds firm peaks. Transfer the cream to a bowl, cover with plastic wrap, and refrigerate until ready to use. (The cream can be whipped up to 2 hours in advance.)

To start the pears, melt the butter over medium-low heat in a skillet large enough to hold the pear halves in a single layer. Continue to cook the butter until it smells nutty and begins to brown, about 10 minutes. Meanwhile, combine the syrup, ginger, and salt in a measuring cup and add the vanilla bean.

Add the pears to the butter, cut-sides down. Increase the heat a little and cook until the pears begin to brown, about 5 minutes. Pour the syrup mixture into the pan, bring it to a simmer, then transfer the skillet to the oven. Cook the pears until they are just tender (I test by inserting the tip of a paring knife), about 5 minutes. Remove the skillet from the oven and allow the pears to cool in the sauce for 15 minutes.

To finish the dish, transfer the pears to a serving bowl or individual plates. Bring the sauce to a simmer over medium-high heat, then carefully add the bourbon off the heat. Return the sauce to the burner, swirl the pan to incorporate the bourbon, let the sauce bubble for a minute or so, then strain it over the pears.

Serve the pears topped with the goat cheese cream and sugared pecans (if desired).

Roasted Figs with Sugared Pistachios

Serves 4

Figs are one of my favorite fruits to cook with. They are naturally sweet and jammy but have a depth of flavor that draws me. Their dry texture also appeals. For this recipe, my first choice would be Black Mission figs, but honestly any variety will work—just make sure they are pristine because they are taking center stage.

⅓ cup	Sugared Pistachios (page 294)	100g	sugar (3.5oz /about ¾ cup)
100g	shelled pistachios (3.5oz / about ¾ cup), roughly chopped	8	fresh figs, trimmed and halved
2 tsp	light corn syrup	¼ cup	freshly squeezed orange juice
3g	Diamond Crystal kosher salt (1 tsp)	1 T	Grand Marnier or other orange liqueur
30g	crystallized sugar, such as turbinado, Demerara, or Sugar In The Raw (1oz / about 2 T)	14g	unsalted butter (0.5oz)
		About ¾ cup	crème fraîche, beaten slightly

Prepare the sugared pistachios according to the directions on page 294. Reserve ⅓ cup and set the rest aside for another use.

To make the caramel and cook the figs, preheat the oven to 350°F. Heat a skillet large enough to accommodate the figs in a single layer over medium heat. Sprinkle the sugar in an even layer into the pan. Leave the skillet on the heat undisturbed until the sugar melts and turns a light amber, about 12 minutes.

Arrange the figs, cut-side down, in the caramel and put the pan in the oven. Bake the figs until the cut sides are golden (check by lifting a fig up), about 10 minutes. Remove the figs from the oven and let them cool slightly in the pan. Using a spatula, lift the warm fig halves out of the caramel and arrange them in four bowls, cut-sides up. Return the skillet to the burner and reheat the caramel over medium-low. When the caramel bubbles, carefully add the orange juice and Grand Marnier. Swirl the sauce as it reduces, cooking it until it is nicely viscous, 3 to 5 minutes. Remove the skillet from the heat and add the butter, swirling it until it melts.

To serve, spoon the sauce over the figs. Top with crème fraîche and sugared pistachios.

Poached Quince

Makes 2

Quince can be a little hard to find—look at farmers' markets (in the Northeast, they are available in October and November). Unlike apples, they must be cooked to tame their astringency. Poached in white wine, quince turn a pretty rose color and make a beautiful and tasty accompaniment to cake and a great cheesecake topping (see Quince Goat Cheese Cake, page 64). Poached quince is also nice served more simply, in a bowl with whipped crème fraîche. Because they keep well, I always make at least a double batch.

2	medium quince		1	clove stuck into a piece of orange peel
300g	sugar (10.6oz / about 1½ cups)		½	cinnamon stick
1 cup	white wine		1	whole star anise

Trim both ends of the quince, then peel, quarter, and core them. Put 3 cups water in a saucepan large enough to hold the quince in a single layer. Add the sugar, wine, clove-studded orange peel, cinnamon, and star anise. Add the quince, cover them with a circle of parchment paper, and put a plate on top to weight the quince and keep them submerged. Bring the liquid to a boil, then reduce the heat to medium-low and simmer until the quince is tender, about 2 hours. Allow the quince to cool in the liquid, then transfer the quince and the poaching liquid to a container, cover, and refrigerate until ready to use. The quince will keep for several weeks.

Citrus Salad

Serves 6 to 8 as a garnish

This salad is a favorite of mine. I eat it all winter long—it tastes so lively, it's what I want in February. I have served it many ways, including with Yuzu Panna Cotta (page 236), Cornmeal and Olive Oil Cake (page 69), and Fennel Tea Cake with Pernod Whipped Cream (page 71). If you can't find kumquats, try substituting Poached Grapefruit with Fennel (page 272).

½ cup	**Candied Kumquats (page 271) plus ⅓ cup poaching liquid**
350g	kumquats (12.3oz)
400g	sugar (7oz / about 2 cups)
1 T	corn syrup

3	**large fresh shiso* or mint sprigs**
6	**blood oranges**
3	**navel oranges**

Candy the kumquats according to the instructions on page 271. Set aside ½ cup in a large bowl plus ⅓ cup of the poaching liquid in a separate bowl. Reserve the rest of each for another purpose.

Combine the kumquat poaching liquid and shiso in a saucepan and bring the mixture to a simmer over medium heat, muddling the herbs by pressing them against the side of the pan with a wooden spoon. Pull the pan off the heat and allow the syrup to cool almost to room temperature.

Meanwhile, peel, section, and seed the blood and navel oranges, removing the white membrane from each suprême. Add the orange sections to the bowl of kumquats. Strain the minted syrup over the fruit and toss to combine.

---

* Shiso, also known as perillo, is a member of the mint (Lamiaceae) family. It is native to China and popular in Japan. Shiso is available at Japanese groceries and farmers' markets, and it is easy to grow.

Poached Rhubarb

I like to poach rhubarb in dry rosé. The wine's slight fruitiness brings out this tart vegetable's best qualities. Rather than cook it on the stovetop, I prefer to oven-poach rhubarb—it works perfectly every time. A terrific accompaniment to cake or a custard, poached rhubarb keeps for weeks refrigerated in the poaching liquid.

1½ cups	rosé wine (375g / 13.2oz)
375g	sugar (13.2oz / about 1¾ cups + 2 T)
1	vanilla bean
2-in piece	ginger, peeled
4 cups	diced (1-inch dice) rhubarb

Preheat the oven to 350°F. In a saucepan, bring the wine to a boil, then decrease the heat and simmer the wine until it reduces slightly, about 10 minutes. Add the sugar and continue to simmer until it dissolves. Split the vanilla bean lengthwise, scrape the seeds into the wine, and add the pod. Bruise the ginger with the flat of a knife and add it to the saucepan.

Arrange the rhubarb in a single layer in a shallow, nonreactive ovenproof baking dish or pan (Pyrex or ceramic). Bring the wine back to a boil and pour it over the rhubarb. Cover the pan with tinfoil and make four slits in the foil to allow steam to escape. Oven-poach the rhubarb for 10 minutes. Remove the pan from the oven, discard the foil, and allow the rhubarb to cool completely. Store the rhubarb in the poaching liquid in the refrigerator. It will keep for at least 2 weeks.

Candied Kumquats

Makes about 2 cups

Experts disagree about whether kumquats are members of the citrus family. Regardless of their botanical classification, these orange beauties with thin, edible skins are a tasty winter treat. They are the star of the tatin on page 163 and an ingredient in Citrus Salad (page 269). They also make a terrific garnish I like to serve with cake.

350g	kumquats (12.3oz), scrubbed, halved crosswise, and seeded

400g	sugar (14.1oz / about 2 cups)
1 T	light corn syrup

Slice the kumquats into rounds. Put 2 cups water in a saucepan. Add the sugar and corn syrup and bring the mixture to a simmer over medium heat, stirring occasionally, so the sugar dissolves. Add the kumquats, reduce the heat, and gently simmer over medium-low until the rinds are translucent, about 10 minutes. Remove the kumquats from the heat and allow them to cool in the syrup. Store them in an airtight container in their liquid in the refrigerator. They will keep for at least a month.

Poached Grapefruit with Fennel

Slowly poaching grapefruit slices in simple syrup produces a lovely sweet/tart garnish. Cut in quarters, the fruit slices are also nice added to Citrus Salad (page 269) either instead of, or in addition to, Candied Kumquats (page 271).

1 T	fennel seeds
400g	sugar (14.1oz / about 2 cups)
1 T	light corn syrup

1	small grapefruit
1 T	Pernod

Preheat the oven to 325°F. Roast the fennel seeds in a small ovenproof skillet until they smell toasty, about 12 minutes. Remove the seeds from the oven and allow them to cool slightly, then bruise the seeds by pressing them with the flat of a knife. Transfer the roasted fennel seeds to a small saucepan. Add 2 cups water, then add the sugar and corn syrup and bring the mixture to a boil, stirring occasionally so the sugar dissolves.

Meanwhile, scrub the grapefruit and trim both ends. Thinly slice the grapefruit, cutting it crosswise through the rind into rounds about 1 inch thick. Arrange the slices in a nonreactive baking dish (ceramic or Pyrex). Pour the fennel/sugar syrup over the grapefruit and add the Pernod.

Poach the grapefruit in the oven until the slices are translucent, about 1 hour. Allow the grapefruit to cool in the syrup, then transfer the grapefruit and syrup to a container, cover, and refrigerate. The grapefruit slices will keep for at least a month.

Blood Oranges in Caramel

Like the Poached Grapefruit with Fennel (facing page), this recipe involves oven-poaching citrus, this time oranges. The caramel-poached oranges are a nice way to add another flavor and texture note to cakes and custards.

1 tsp	fennel seeds		1 T	light corn syrup
300g	sugar (10.6oz / about 1½ cups)		2	blood oranges

Preheat the oven to 325°F. Roast the fennel seeds in a small ovenproof skillet until they smell toasty, about 12 minutes. Remove the seeds from the oven (do not turn it off) and allow them to cool slightly, then bruise the seeds by pressing them with the flat of a knife. Transfer the roasted fennel seeds to a small saucepan. Add 1 cup water, then the sugar and corn syrup and bring the mixture to a boil, stirring occasionally, and cook until the sugar dissolves and the liquid simmers and begins to turn amber.

Meanwhile, scrub the oranges and trim both ends. Thinly slice the oranges, cutting them crosswise through the rind into rounds. Put the slices in a glass pie plate. Pour the sugar syrup evenly over the oranges.

Poach the oranges in the oven until the slices are translucent, about 1 hour. Remove from the oven and allow the orange slices to cool in the syrup. Transfer the oranges and syrup to an airtight container, cover, and refrigerate. The oranges will keep for at least a month.

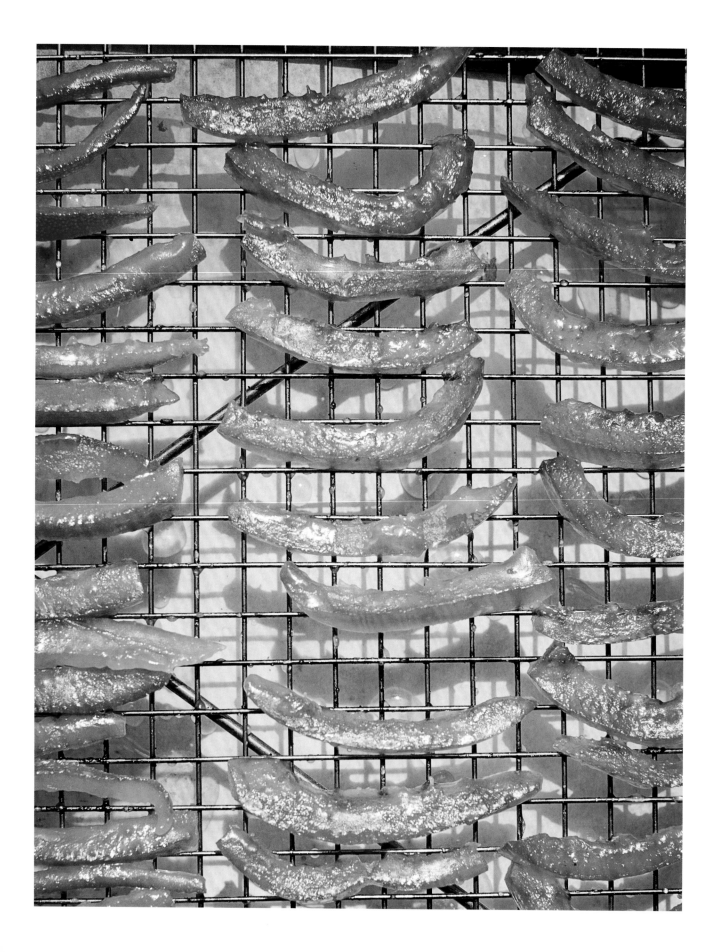

Candied Orange Rinds

Makes about 2 cups

Candied orange rinds are an ingredient in Strawberry Cassata Cake (page 59), Spumoni with Meringue and Caramelized Oranges (page 251), Orange Semifreddo (page 256), and Pastiera (page 167). They are also tasty as is, delicious rolled in sugar, and wonderful dipped in tempered chocolate (see Variation below).

3	medium navel oranges	1 T	light corn syrup
300g	sugar (10.6oz / about 1½ cups), plus extra (optional) for finishing		

Cut the ends off the oranges. Score each orange's rind lengthwise with a paring knife six times, then peel the oranges, keeping the six segments intact if possible; reserve the fruit for another purpose. Slice the peels into lengths about ¼ inch thick.

Put the orange rinds in a pot and cover with water. Bring the water to a boil over high heat. Strain off the water, then add enough water to cover the peels again; repeat boiling and straining twice more.

Once the rinds have been blanched and drained three times, put ¾ cup water in a saucepan. Add the sugar and corn syrup and bring the mixture to a boil. Add the blanched rinds and reduce the heat to low. Simmer the rinds until the syrup thickens and reaches a temperature of 230°F; begin checking after about 45 minutes (the time will vary depending on your choice of pot).

Strain the rinds, reserving the syrup to drizzle on cakes or to sweeten drinks or yogurt. Arrange the rinds on a wire rack set over a baking sheet to dry overnight. Serve the rinds as is or roll them in sugar (about 100 grams / 3.5 ounces / ½ cup). Stored in an airtight container, they will last at least a month.

Variation: To make Chocolate Orange Rinds, follow the recipe above, allowing the candied rinds to dry on a wire rack overnight. The next day, dip the rinds in Tempered Chocolate (page 111), then return the rinds to the rack to allow the chocolate to set before serving or storing.

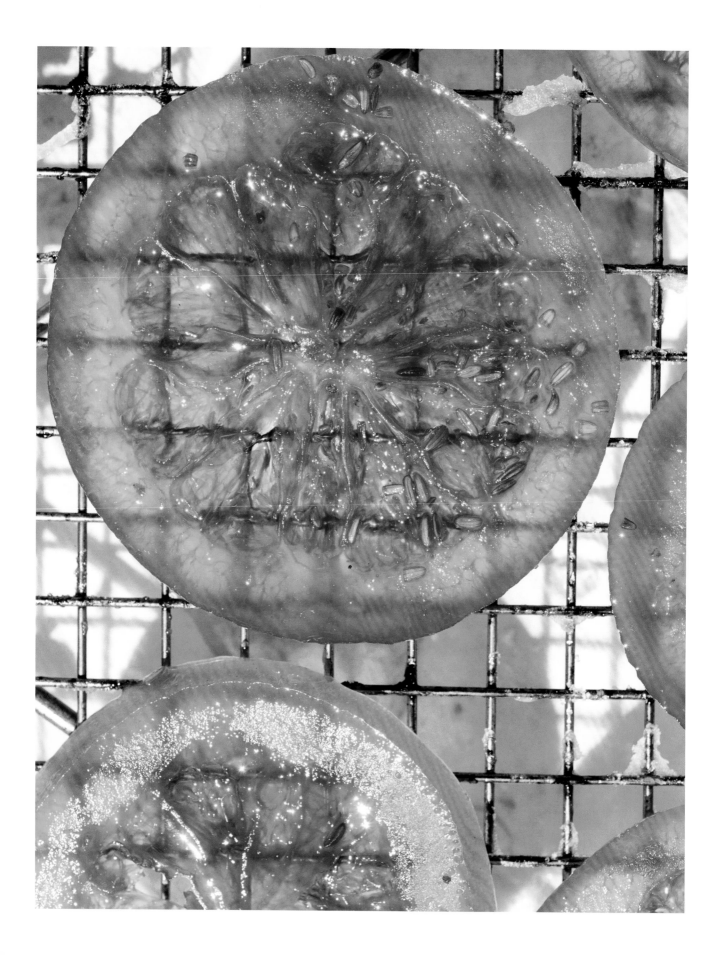

Candied Grapefruit Rinds

Makes about 2 cups

I use these rinds with their syrup to garnish cakes and as the starting place for Grapefruit Conserve (page 279), but like Candied Orange Rinds (page 275), these are also a yummy snack dipped in chocolate (see Tempered Chocolate, page 111) or simply rolled in sugar.

2	grapefruits, preferably pink
300g	sugar (10.6oz / about 1½ cups), plus extra for finishing (optional)

1 T	light corn syrup

Cut the ends off the grapefruit. Score each grapefruit's rind lengthwise with a paring knife six times. Peel the grapefruits, keeping the six segments intact if possible; reserve the fruit for another purpose. Expect about ¼ inch of pith on the peels; if there is more, trim it down. Slice the peels into ¼-inch-wide lengths.

Put the grapefruit rinds in a pot and cover with water. Bring to a boil over high heat. Strain off the water. Add enough fresh water to cover the peels again; repeat boiling and straining twice more.

Once the rinds have been blanched and drained three times, put ¾ cup water in a small saucepan. Add the sugar and corn syrup and bring to a boil over high heat. Add the rinds and reduce the heat to low. Simmer until the syrup thickens and reaches a temperature of 230°F; begin checking after about 45 minutes (the time will vary depending on your choice of pot).

Strain the rinds, reserving the syrup separately. Keep the syrup in a covered container in the refrigerator to use as a sweetener in drinks and as a drizzle on cakes (see Fennel Tea Cake with Pernod Whipped Cream on page 71). Arrange the rinds on a wire rack set over a baking sheet to dry overnight. To serve, roll them in sugar, dip them in Tempered Chocolate (page 111) and chopped pistachios if you like, or reserve them as is to make preserves or to use as a garnish.

Apple Butter

Makes about 1 quart

I use apple butter—concentrated applesauce that I flavor with brown sugar, apple cider, and cider vinegar—as the base layer of Apple Tartlets (page 155), but whenever I make it, I cook extra because, happily, apple butter keeps for weeks in the refrigerator. Incidentally, apple peels and seeds have lots of pectin, so I cook them in my butter (then strain them out before serving or storing).

1125g	unpeeled apples (2½ lb), a mixture works but avoid Macintosh (they cook too quickly)
230g	light brown sugar (8.1oz / about 1 cup)
1 cup	apple cider
2 T	apple cider vinegar
1	cinnamon stick
4	whole cloves
	Peel of ½ orange
1	vanilla bean, split lengthwise

Preheat the oven to 300°F. Coarsely chop the apples (including the cores) and put them in a Dutch oven. Add the sugar, cider, cider vinegar, and cinnamon. Stick the cloves into the orange peel and add it to the pot. Scrape in the vanilla seeds and add the pod. Cover the pot and cook for 1½ hours. Remove the lid and continue baking until the apples are very soft, checking every 30 minutes or so and mashing the apples with a spoon when you are able. Cook the mixture until the apple butter looks like darker, thicker applesauce, another 2 to 3 hours.

Allow the apple butter to cool slightly, then pass it through a medium to fine sieve into a bowl. Store the apple butter in a covered container in the refrigerator for up to a month.

Grapefruit Conserve

Makes about 1⅔ cups

An ingredient in Grapefruit and Poppy Seed Rugelach (page 101), this marmalade-like preserve is easy to make and will last in the refrigerator for months. Although in theory you could make this without a candy thermometer, I always use one when I make preserves.

½ cup	minced **Candied Grapefruit Rinds** (page 277)
½	grapefruit, preferably pink
150g	sugar (5.3oz / about ¾ cup)
1½ tsp	light corn syrup

2	medium pink grapefruits, peeled
About 200g	sugar (7oz / about 1 cup)
1 tsp	freshly squeezed lemon juice

Make the candied grapefruit rinds according to the instructions on page 277. Mince and reserve ½ cup for this recipe. Save the remaining candied rind and grapefruit poaching liquid for another purpose.

Section and seed the grapefruits, removing the tough white membrane. Roughly chop the sections. Squeeze the juice from the grapefruit core into a bowl. Weigh the chopped fresh grapefruit. Add the fruit to the juice in the bowl, then add enough sugar to equal half the weight of the chopped fruit. Set the mixture aside to macerate at room temperature for 1 hour.

Put the grapefruit mixture in a wide, deep nonreactive pot (stainless steel works); the conserve will bubble up as it cooks so don't fill the pot more than halfway. Bring the conserve to a boil, then lower the heat to medium-low. Simmer the conserve until it jells (reduces, darkens slightly, and becomes viscous) and hits a temperature of 220°F, about 1 hour. Allow the conserve to cool a bit, then stir in the lemon juice and minced candied rind. Spoon the conserve into jars and refrigerate. Stored in the refrigerator the conserve will be good for several months.

Variation: To make Orange Conserve, substitute 4 medium oranges for the grapefruit and ½ cup Candied Orange Rinds (page 275) for the grapefruit rind in the recipe. Add the zest of 1 lemon to the pot along with the macerated fruit segments and sugar and proceed as above.

Wintertime Apricot Jam

Makes 3 cups

Making jam from dried apricots gives the finished preserve a powerful flavor I really like. Honey adds some warmth as it smooths out the taste, and grapefruit juice and zest add vibrancy.

260g	dried pitted apricots (2.1oz / about 1⅓ cups)		1½ cups	grapefruit juice
2 tsp	grapefruit zest		½ cup	honey

Put the apricots in a large heatproof bowl. Bring 4 cups water to a boil, pour it over the apricots, and set them aside to soften for about 1 hour. (Alternatively, cover the fruit with 4 cups room-temperature water and soak overnight.)

Strain the apricots, reserving the soaking liquid. Chop the apricots and put them in a saucepan with the grapefruit zest and juice, honey, and the reserved soaking liquid. Bring the mixture to a boil, then reduce the heat to medium-low and cook at a gentle simmer, stirring frequently to prevent the fruit from sticking to the pan. Once the fruit has fully softened, about 20 minutes, mash it with a fork or wooden spoon. Continue gently simmering the jam, stirring more frequently, until the jam is nicely thick, 10 to 20 minutes more.

Allow the jam to cool. Transfer it to a container and store in the refrigerator; it will keep for several months.

Eggplant Caponata

Makes about 8 cups

Eggplant is a fruit, though it is generally pushed in a savory direction. That is certainly the case in this recipe for my absolute favorite piquant conserve. I celebrate it in the Eggplant Caponata Tart (page 187), where I use a half batch—the amounts below in brackets indicate the required quantities. Truthfully, I am quite happy eating this in a bowl with a spoon, maybe with some bread or crackers. So while in theory, this lasts a week or more in the refrigerator—in my house, a batch this size is gone in days.

2	red and/or yellow bell peppers [1]		2	garlic cloves, peeled and sliced [1 clove]
About ¾ cup	extra-virgin olive oil [⅓ cup], plus extra as needed		¼ tsp	crushed red pepper flakes, or to taste [pinch]
About 900g	Italian eggplant (2lb), trimmed and cut in 1½-inch dice [450g / 1lb]		24g	sugar (0.8oz / about 2 T) [12g / 0.4oz / about 1 T]
About 9g	Diamond Crystal kosher salt (1 T) [4.5g / 1½ tsp]		1 T	tomato paste [1½ tsp]
About 2.3g	freshly ground black pepper (1 tsp) [1.2g / ½ tsp]		½ cup	red wine vinegar [¼ cup]
1	large onion, peeled and diced [1 small]		¼ cup	dry white wine [2 T]
6	celery ribs, sliced on a diagonal [3 ribs]		1 cup	green olives, such as Cerignola, halved, pitted, and chopped [½ cup]
			¼ cup	capers, rinsed and drained [2 T]
			¼ cup	chopped fresh parsley [2 T]
			2 T	chopped fresh basil [1 T]

Char the bell peppers over an open flame (or roast them in a preheated 350°F oven until the skin wrinkles, about 30 minutes). Put them in an airtight container until they are cool enough to handle, then peel, seed, and dice them.

Heat about 1 ½ inches of oil in a large skillet over medium heat. Working in batches to avoid overcrowding the pan, fry the eggplant until it is golden, about 4 minutes, then flip each piece and continue frying about a minute or so on each of the remaining sides. Transfer the eggplant to a paper towel–lined plate to drain, seasoning each batch with salt and black pepper while it is still warm. Repeat with the remaining eggplant, adding more oil to the skillet if necessary. When all the eggplant is cooked, set it aside and pour off all but a skim of the oil. Add the onions, season them lightly with salt and black pepper, and cook over medium heat, stirring occasionally, until they soften, about 10 minutes. Add the celery and garlic and cook, stirring more frequently, until the celery is tender, about 7 minutes. Stir in the red pepper flakes and sugar. When the sugar dissolves, add the tomato paste, stirring to make sure it is evenly distributed. Cook until the tomato paste caramelizes a little, about 5 minutes, then stir in the vinegar and wine.

(recipe continues)

Return the eggplant to the skillet. Bring the liquid in the pan to a simmer, then adjust the heat so it bubbles gently. Cook the caponata until the eggplant is soft, about 25 minutes. Stir in the olives, capers, and diced roasted pepper. Let the caponata bubble another few minutes, then stir in the parsley and basil. Set the caponata aside to cool. Taste it, adjust the seasoning with salt and black pepper if needed, and refrigerate until you are ready to use.

Quick-Pickled Cucumbers

Makes about 1 cup

I add these pickles to sandwiches and salads and serve them with Shiitake Sticky Buns (page 193). They are best eaten within a couple of days.

¼ cup	rice vinegar
25g	sugar (0.9oz / about 2 T)
3g	Diamond Crystal kosher salt (1 tsp)
1½ tsp	coriander seeds

2	Persian cucumbers, or 1 smallish English cucumber, unpeeled and scrubbed

Combine the vinegar, sugar, salt, and coriander in a small saucepan. Add ½ cup water and bring to a boil, then remove from the heat. Allow the pickling liquid to cool to room temperature. Meanwhile, slice the cucumbers crosswise about ¼ inch thick. Combine the cucumbers and pickling liquid in a bowl or container. Mix gently but well, then set the cucumbers aside for at least 2 hours at room temperature or overnight in the refrigerator. Once they are pickled, keep the cucumbers in the refrigerator.

CHAPTER 8

Pantry

Be Prepared

All chefs stock their storerooms (which generally include sections of the refrigerator and freezer) with ingredients they have created that add flavor, savor, and point of view to their food. Pastry chefs do the same. Cooking at home, I found this approach is perhaps even more helpful. Having pie and tart doughs and crumbles ready to go in my freezer, poached fruit and preserves in my refrigerator, and sugared nuts in my pantry sets me up to put together great things to eat. Most simply, I can top ice cream with toasted Oat Crumble (page 298), Brown Butter Pecan Crumble (page 296), or with a sprinkling of one or another sugared nuts for dessert. Add Butterscotch Toffee Sauce (page 289), and I have the makings of an old-fashioned soda fountain–style sundae. Freshly picked berries become a berry-crisp by doing little more than firing up my oven, tossing them with sugar—a measure equal to about 20 percent of their weight—then reaching into the freezer for the crumble that suits. On a more involved note, if I have Chocolate Crumble (page 298) and Candied Orange Rinds (page 275) in reserve, making Chocolate Babka Buns (page 31) becomes a straightforward matter of preparing the yeasted dough.

Working this way puts interesting food within everyday reach. Throughout these pages, I have urged making larger batches of things that keep well. Consistent with that approach, in this last chapter, I want to share a few more recipes for things I keep on hand to elevate my cooking.

Basil Oil

Makes about ½ cup

This herbaceous oil is a summertime go-to. It is pretty and delicious drizzled over tomatoes and/or fresh mozzarella. It is also my final dressing for the Eggplant Caponata Tart (page 187).

	Diamond Crystal kosher salt	½ cup	canola or other neutral-tasting oil
24g	basil leaves with stems (0.8oz), both chopped but kept separate		

Bring a small pot of heavily salted water to a boil over high heat. Add the basil stems. When the water returns to a boil, add the leaves and blanch, cooking just until the water returns to a boil and the leaves are bright green. Drain the basil, then shock the leaves and stems in ice water to preserve the color. Dry the basil thoroughly with paper towels and put it all in a blender with the oil. Puree until smooth, then set the mixture aside for an hour to allow the flavor to deepen. Use the oil as is or strain it through a fine sieve. Store in an airtight container in the refrigerator for up to 3 days.

Blood Orange Caramel

Makes 1 cup

I warm orange segments in this bittersweet caramel to use as a garnish for Spumoni with Meringue and Caramelized Oranges (page 251). On its own, the caramel is a tasty ice cream topping.

200g	sugar (7oz / about 1 cup)	½ cup	blood orange juice
1 tsp	light corn syrup		

Put ½ cup water in a small deep saucepan. Add the sugar and corn syrup and heat over medium-high until the sugar dissolves and turns a deep amber, about 20 minutes. Remove the pan from the heat and carefully add the blood orange juice to stop the cooking (the mixture will bubble up and then seize). Return the pan to the stove over very low heat and whisk the caramel until it is completely smooth; set it aside to cool. Stored in an airtight container in the refrigerator, the caramel will keep several weeks. Bring it to room temperature before using.

Butterscotch Toffee Sauce

Makes 1 cup

This butterscotch sauce is great on ice cream. It is also an ingredient in Banana and Espresso Semifreddo with Butterscotch and Macadamia Nuts (page 244). If you find the sauce has separated in the refrigerator, a whiz in the blender will bring it back.

152g	light brown sugar (5.4oz / about ½ cup + 3 T)	2 tsp	sherry vinegar
57g	unsalted butter (2oz)	1½ tsp	vanilla paste or pure vanilla extract
1¼ cups	heavy cream	3g	Diamond Crystal kosher salt (1 tsp)

Combine the brown sugar, butter, and cream in a saucepan and bring to a boil. Reduce the heat and simmer until the mixture reaches 225°F.

Meanwhile, combine the vinegar, vanilla, and salt in a small bowl. Remove the pan from the heat and whisk in the vinegar mixture. Allow the sauce to cool until it is just warm. Serve warm or at room temperature. Stored in an airtight container and refrigerated, the sauce will keep for at least a month.

Honey Butter

Makes about ½ cup

I add a little lime zest to the honey butter I like to serve with Chipotle Cornbread (page 25) to jazz it up. Orange zest would be a nice alternative.

114g	unsalted butter (4oz), room temperature	½ tsp	lime zest
		¼ cup	honey

Combine the butter, zest, and honey in a bowl and mix well. Roll the honey butter into a log in parchment paper (I use the same technique to make tight dough logs on page 95). Refrigerate until ready to serve or for up to a week.

Savory Mixed Seeds

Makes 7 tablespoons

This seed mixture is tasty with cream cheese on toast. I also use it to top Pretzels (page 215) and Chickpea Crackers (page 206) and sprinkle it on slices of vine-ripened tomatoes.

36g   sesame seeds (1.3oz / about ¼ cup)

13g   caraway seeds (0.5oz / about 2 T)

9g   poppy seeds (0.3oz / about 1 T)

Preheat the oven to 350°F and line a rimmed baking sheet with parchment paper. Arrange the sesame and caraway seeds in a single layer on the prepared baking sheet and roast them until the sesame seeds are golden, about 5 minutes. Remove the seeds from the oven and allow them to cool. Mix in the poppy seeds and store the mixture in an airtight container. The seeds will stay fresh for at least a week.

SUGARED NUTS AND SEEDS

Nuts and seeds are very nutritious. They have been important foods worldwide for a very long time. Coated with sugar (or maple syrup or molasses) and then toasted, nuts and seeds add sweet flavor and texture to a dish. As a pastry chef, I used them daily. At home, I find I reach for them almost as often to spoon on ice cream or fresh fruit. I also use them to garnish cakes and as ingredients in more involved recipes.

Sugared Almonds

Makes about 1 cup

100g	sliced almonds (3.5oz / about 1 cup + 1½ T)	30g	crystallized sugar, such as turbinado, Demerara, or Sugar In The Raw (1oz / about 2 T)
2 tsp	light corn syrup		
1.5g	Diamond Crystal kosher salt (½ tsp)		

Preheat the oven to 325°F and line a rimmed baking sheet with parchment paper. Put the almonds in a bowl. Add the corn syrup and mix well (I use my hands). Add the salt and crystallized sugar and toss to coat. Arrange the almonds in a single layer on the prepared baking sheet and bake until they are golden, about 15 minutes. Cool them and then store them in an airtight container. They will keep for at least 2 weeks.

Sugared Hazelnuts

Makes about ¾ cup

100g	hazelnuts (3.5oz / about ¾ cup), roughly chopped
2 tsp	light corn syrup
1.5g	Diamond Crystal kosher salt (½ tsp)
20g	light brown sugar (0.7oz / about 1½ T)

Preheat the oven to 325°F and line a rimmed baking sheet with parchment paper. Put the nuts in a bowl. Add the corn syrup and mix well (I use my hands). Add the salt and brown sugar and toss to coat. Arrange the nuts in a single layer on the prepared baking sheet and bake until they are golden and smell toasty, about 15 minutes. Cool them and then store them in an airtight container. They will keep for at least 2 weeks.

Sugared Macadamia Nuts

Makes about ¾ cup

100g	macadamia nuts (7oz / about ¾ cup), roughly chopped
2 tsp	light corn syrup
1.5g	Diamond Crystal kosher salt (½ tsp)
20g	light brown sugar (0.7oz / about 1½ T)

Preheat the oven to 325°F and line a rimmed baking sheet with parchment paper. Put the nuts in a bowl. Add the corn syrup and mix well (I use my hands). Add the salt and brown sugar and toss to coat. Arrange the nuts in a single layer on the prepared baking sheet and bake until they are golden and smell toasty, about 15 minutes. Cool the nuts and then store them in an airtight container. They will keep for at least 2 weeks.

Maple Sugared Pecans

Makes about 1 cup

100g	pecan halves (3.5oz / about 1 cup), roughly chopped	1.5g	Diamond Crystal kosher salt (½ tsp)
1 T	maple syrup	25g	maple sugar (0.9oz / about 2 T)

Preheat the oven to 325° and line a rimmed baking sheet with parchment paper. Put the pecans in a bowl. Add the corn syrup and mix well (I use my hands). Add the salt and maple sugar and toss to coat. Arrange the nuts in a single layer on the prepared baking sheet and bake until they smell toasty, about 15 minutes. Cool them and then store in an airtight container. They will keep for at least 2 weeks.

Molasses Pecans

Makes about 1¼ cups

120g	pecans (4.2oz / about 1 cup + 3 T), roughly chopped	5g	crystallized sugar, such as turbinado, Demerara, or Sugar In The Raw (0.2oz / about 1 tsp)
1 T	molasses		
1.5g	Diamond Crystal kosher salt (½ tsp)		
7g	light brown sugar (0.2oz / about 1½ tsp)		

Preheat the oven to 325°F and line a rimmed baking sheet with parchment paper. Put the pecans in a bowl. Add the molasses (I coat my measuring spoon with neutral oil before dipping it into the molasses to prevent it from sticking) and mix well (I use my hands). Add the salt and brown and crystallized sugars and toss to coat. Arrange the pecans in a single layer on the prepared baking sheet and bake until they smell toasty, about 15 minutes. Cool them and then store them in an airtight container. They will keep for at least 2 weeks.

Sugared Pine Nuts

Makes ¾ cup

100g	pine nuts (7oz / about ¾ cup)
2 tsp	light corn syrup
1.5g	Diamond Crystal kosher salt (½ tsp)
20g	light brown sugar (0.7oz / about 1½ T)

Preheat the oven to 325°F and line a rimmed baking sheet with parchment paper. Combine the pine nuts and corn syrup in a bowl. Mix well (I use my hands). Add the salt and brown sugar and toss to coat. Arrange the pine nuts in a single layer on the prepared baking sheet and bake until they are golden, about 10 minutes. Cool the pine nuts and then store them in an airtight container. They will keep for at least a week.

Sugared Pistachios

Makes about ¾ cup

100g	pistachios (7oz / about ¾ cup), roughly chopped
2 tsp	light corn syrup
1.5g	Diamond Crystal kosher salt (½ tsp)
30g	crystallized sugar, such as turbinado, Demerara, or Sugar In The Raw (1oz / about 2 T)

Preheat the oven to 325°F and line a baking sheet with parchment paper. Put the nuts in a bowl. Add the corn syrup and mix well (I use my hands). Add the salt and crystallized sugar and toss to coat. Arrange the pistachios in a single layer on the prepared baking sheet and bake until they are golden and smell toasty, about 15 minutes. Cool them and then store them in an airtight container. They will keep for at least 2 weeks.

Sugared Pumpkin Seeds

Makes about ¾ cup

100g	pumpkin seeds (3.5oz / about ¾ cup 1 T)
3 tsp	light corn syrup
1.5g	Diamond Crystal kosher salt (½ tsp)
30g	crystallized sugar, such as turbinado, Demerara, or Sugar In The Raw (1oz / about 2 T)

Preheat the oven to 325°F and line a rimmed baking sheet with parchment paper. Put the seeds in a bowl. Add the corn syrup and mix well (I use my hands). Add the salt and crystallized sugar and toss to coat. Arrange the seeds in a single layer on the prepared baking sheet and bake until they are lightly browned, about 15 minutes. Cool them and then store them in an airtight container. They will keep for at least 2 weeks.

Maple Sugared Walnuts

Makes about ¾ cup

100g	walnuts (3.5oz / about ¾ cup + 1 T), roughly chopped
1 T	maple syrup
1.5g	Diamond Crystal kosher salt (½ tsp)
25g	maple sugar (0.9oz / about 2 T)

Preheat the oven to 325°F and line a rimmed baking sheet with parchment paper. Put the walnuts in a bowl. Add the corn syrup and mix well (I use my hands). Add the salt and maple sugar and toss to coat. Arrange the nuts in a single layer on the prepared baking sheet and bake until they smell toasty, about 15 minutes. Allow the nuts to cool and then store them in an airtight container. They will keep for at least 2 weeks.

A Trio of Crumbles

Agood fruit crumble is as satisfying as it is simple to make. Things get even easier if you do as I do and make large batches, then bag and keep them in the freezer ready to go. I use toasted crumbs not only as a topping for baked and fresh fruit, but also to finish crostatas, on ice cream, and stirred into yogurt for breakfast. The three that follow are my favorites. Use them as is but also feel free to play with the recipes. Just be sure to keep the proportion of butter to the dry ingredients about the same so your crumble is crumbly.

Brown Butter Pecan Crumble

Makes 3 cups

142g	unsalted butter (5.2oz)	180g	all-purpose flour (6.3oz / about 1¼ cups)
45g	pecans (1.6oz / about 6 T), chopped	⅛ tsp	ground cardamom
110g	light brown sugar (3.9oz / about ½ cup)	¼ tsp	ground cinnamon
50g	sugar (1.8oz / about ¼ cup)	0.7g	Diamond Crystal kosher salt (¼ tsp)

Melt the butter in a skillet and continue cooking over medium-low heat until it browns, about 25 minutes. Remove the butter from the heat and let it cool. Meanwhile, preheat the oven to 325°F. Roast the chopped pecans in an ovenproof skillet until they smell toasty, about 12 minutes. Remove the nuts from the oven and put them in a bowl. Add the brown and white sugars, the flour, cardamom, cinnamon, and salt. Mix well with a fork, then drizzle in the browned butter, stirring to mix it in evenly. Use according to the recipe instructions or store the crumble in a sealed plastic bag in the freezer; it will keep for 3 months or more. (To use on its own, crumble the mixture onto a baking sheet and bake at 350°F until the crumbs are toasted, about 25 minutes.)

Oat Crumble

Makes about 2½ cups

100g	sugar (3.5oz / about ½ cup)
110g	light brown sugar (3.9oz / about ½ cup)
105g	all-purpose flour (3.7oz / about ¾ cup)
80g	rolled oats (2.8oz / about ¾ cup 2 T)
½ tsp	ground cinnamon
0.7g	Diamond Crystal kosher salt (¼ tsp)
132g	unsalted butter (4.6oz), melted and cooled

Combine the white and brown sugars, flour, oats, cinnamon, and salt in a bowl and mix. Stir in the melted butter with a fork. Use according to the recipe instructions or store the crumble in a sealed plastic bag in the freezer; it will keep for 3 months or more. (To use on its own, crumble the mixture onto a baking sheet and bake at 350°F until the oats are toasted and golden, about 25 minutes.)

Chocolate Crumble

Makes about 3 cups

114g	unsalted butter (4oz)
1 tsp	orange zest
147g	all-purpose flour (5.2oz / about 1 cup + 1 T)
75g	sugar (2.6oz / about 6 T)
75g	light brown sugar (2.6oz / about 5½ T)
0.7g	Diamond Crystal kosher salt (¼ tsp)
½ tsp	ground cinnamon
¼ tsp	baking soda
47g	Dutch-processed cocoa powder (1.7oz / about ½ cup)

Combine the butter and orange zest in a skillet and heat over low until the butter melts; set aside to cool. In a bowl, whisk the flour with the white and brown sugars, salt, cinnamon, baking soda, and cocoa powder. Switch to a fork and stir together, then drizzle in the butter, stirring to mix it in evenly. Use according to the recipe instructions or store the crumble in a sealed plastic bag in the freezer; it will keep for 3 months or more. (To use on its own, crumble the mixture onto a baking sheet and bake at 350°F until the crumbs are toasted, about 15 minutes.)

ACKNOWLEDGMENTS

The recipes I have shared are the product of working at home, mostly alone, but this book is the outcome of a collaboration among talented, dedicated people. First to mind are my wonderful editors Pamela Cannon and Clio Seraphim. Pamela trusted me to bake whatever I wanted in my Southold kitchen, and her confidence freed me to push myself in untried directions. Clio led me through the design process and helped me produce the book I imagined. The entire team at Penguin Random House has been terrific. Sydney Shiffman deserves special thanks for keeping me on track when I returned to work and life began pulling me. I also want to express my appreciation to Elizabeth Rendfleisch, the gifted designer who brought my vision to life, and Kathy Brock, the copy editor who carefully poured over each and every word.

Thinking of the people who made this book happen, I owe my friend and agent David Black a special toast. David encouraged me to put this collection together and continues to offer me his invaluable assistance whenever I call, just as he has since we first began working together over twenty years ago. Thank you, David, and everyone at DBA!

The beautiful photographs in this book were taken by the incredibly talented Johnny Miller. Johnny deserves massive thanks for letting the natural beauty of the food shine and keeping the atmosphere at my North Fork cottage cheerful as we worked. Johnny was supported by the remarkable Sarah Smart, a stylish and elegant prop stylist who always chose just the right plate and setting for every dish. Laurie Ellen Pellicano is a brilliant and lovely food stylist. She helped me cook and style the food pictured in this book. The week of photography simply couldn't have happened without Laurie Ellen's mad baking skill and organizational intelligence. My heartfelt thanks also go to my friend Paula DiDonato for supplying us with her delicious juices during the long, scorching days. And, remembering that week shooting at my house, I must give special recognition to my dearest friend and former business partner Mary Mraz; she assisted us however we needed her to. Mary, you fed us all week, keeping us energized and sane. You kept me going—as you always do. Thank you.

My life in food began at home. I found my way back there with these recipes. My sister, Lauren Regan, knows that better than anyone. I am the luckiest little sister to have her by my side and blessed to know I will always have her unconditional love.

I am very grateful to my friends who supported me through this process. I want to thank Susan Spungen, Francesca Abbracciamento, and Melissa Clark. Special thanks to you, Melissa, for leading me to Agatha Khishchenko, who worked diligently to make sure all my measurements are in line. Thank you also to my North Fork neighbors, particularly AJ Hanley and Jim Radosevic, for tasting my pies, cakes, and cookies and offering their input.

Many remarkable people in the restaurant

community have had a silent hand in this project. Specific thanks go to Danny Meyer and Tom Colicchio—bosses, mentors, and friends—for all they have taught me. Looking further, I am eternally grateful to all the women and men who bake brilliantly and inspire me and make me better. Nancy Silverton, Dorie Greenspan, Sherry Yard, Emily Luchetti, Elizabeth Faulkner, Shuna Lydon, Zoë François, Kim Boyce, Dahlia Navarro, Claire Saffitz, Kelly Fields, Stella Parks, Natasha Pickowicz, Francisco Migoya, Miro Uskovic, and Daniel Skurnick, to name just a few, I thank you, and I thank each person on every pastry team I've ever had the honor to be a part of.

Finally, greatest thanks to Cathy Young, my dear friend, collaborator, coach, therapist, and all-around wonderful person, without whom this book would not exist. Your dedication and discipline kept us going each and every day and got us over the finish line. I am so grateful for your excellence; you have made me better.

INDEX

Note: Page numbers in *italics* indicate/include photos.

ABOUT THE AUTHORS

CLAUDIA FLEMING is a pastry chef, restaurateur, and author. She has worked in a number of New York restaurants, including Union Square Cafe, Montrachet, TriBeCa Grill, and Gramercy Tavern, and Fauchon in Paris. Fleming and her husband, chef Gerry Hayden, opened The North Fork Table and Inn in Southold, New York. She is currently executive pastry director at Union Square Hospitality Group. Fleming has been named Outstanding Pastry Chef by the James Beard Foundation, and her recipes have been featured in publications such as *Town & Country*, *Martha Stewart Living*, *O: The Oprah Magazine*, *InStyle*, and *Vogue*. Fleming has appeared on *Barefoot Contessa* and *Beat Bobby Flay* and served as a judge on *Chopped* and *Top Chef: Just Desserts*. She lives in New York City and Long Island's North Fork.

CATHERINE YOUNG is a writer and cook who has collaborated on a number of critically acclaimed and James Beard award-winning cookbooks including *The Beetlebung Farm Cookbook* with Chris Fisher; *Salt to Taste: Keys to Confident Delicious Cooking* with Marco Canora; *Anatomy of a Dish* with Diane Forley; and *Think Like a Chef* and *The Craft of Cooking*, both with Tom Colicchio. Young was an editor at *Saveur* magazine and she began her culinary career (after leaving the practice of law) cooking at leading restaurants including Gramercy Tavern, Lespinasse, Union Square Café, and Tribeca Grill (which is where she first met Claudia Fleming).

ABOUT THE TYPE

This book was set in Garamond, a typeface originally designed by the Parisian type cutter Claude Garamond (c. 1500–61). This version of Garamond was modeled on a 1592 specimen sheet from the Egenolff-Berner foundry, which was produced from types assumed to have been brought to Frankfurt by the punch cutter Jacques Sabon (c. 1520–80).

Claude Garamond's distinguished romans and italics first appeared in *Opera Ciceronis* in 1543–44. The Garamond types are clear, open, and elegant.